"*Purpose & Impact* powerfully brings to
It is a foundation for great careers and c
Purpose isn't a luxury – it is an imperative
            *Aaron Hurst, CEO & (*

"Why retire when you can build a better world? Anita Hoffmann provides a roadmap for business leaders to harness their global experience
to forge a new career solving global problems. Never a timelier book for
leaders and for the world!"
            *Nigel Topping, CEO, We Mean Business coalition, UK*

"We are living longer and technological change is transforming the
future of work. How we think about careers and jobs is an existential
question. This book is a must read for all ages."
            *Frannie Léautier, Founder and Managing Partner,*
            *the Fezembat Group, former SVP African*
            *Development Bank, Tanzania, France and USA*

"Old models of retirement are fading faster than those who they were
meant to benefit. Happily, Anita Hoffmann offers excellent advice for
those who, through choice or necessity, are keen to develop new careers
and roles in later life."
            *John Elkington, Chairman, Volans Ventures, UK*

"Having a passion is key not only to success but also to happiness.
Based on her extensive experience and research, Anita Hoffmann offers
an invaluable roadmap to discover the purpose that will allow you to
make a real impact in society, with passion!"
            *Jean-Claude Larréché, A.H. Heineken Professor,*
            *INSEAD, France*

"Industry 4.0 technology enables unprecedented opportunities for creating valuable products and services for society; and meaningful careers.
This means exploring topics and building relationships far beyond executives' current comfort-zone. Purpose & Impact shows us how to do
this confidently."
            *Peter Lacy, Global Managing Director – Growth,*
            *Strategy & Sustainability, Accenture, UK*

"Anita Hoffmann powerfully shows how tri-sector skills will enable more of us to have impactful and fulfilling later careers – all the more important in an era of increased life expectancy."

*Nick Lovegrove, Professor of the Practice,*
*Georgetown University, USA*

"An insightful and compelling articulation of defining Purpose as the foundation and catalyst for mid and late career development. The need for purpose-driven leadership is essential for making a positive social impact and enhancing human dignity."

*Peter Cowan, Strategic Advisor, former EVP and*
*Country Chairman Unilever South Africa, Australia*

"True leadership starts with putting yourself to the service of others. The SDG's can be a great guide. As Anita explains, it's a life time journey that can span different careers."

*Paul Polman, CEO, Unilever plc, UK*

"The world of work is being disrupted at all organisational levels. This requires a greater focus on corporate purpose and managing later retirement. Leaders need to manage this transition for their entire workforce – including themselves. This book shows them how."

*Sharan Burrow, General Secretary, International Trade*
*Union Confederation, Belgium*

"Living longer, combined with a rapid change in the nature of work, implies several career changes in our lifetimes. This book shows senior leaders how to channel their experience into meaningful work - personally, societally and financially."

*Lynda Gratton, Professor, London Business School, UK*

"Valuable to organisations seeking to make the most of late career managers and to older leaders seeking challenge and fulfilment. It makes an important contribution to wider thinking about future work in the context of population ageing and accelerating change."

*Matthew Taylor, Chief Executive, The RSA (Royal Society for*
*the encouragement of Arts, Manufactures and Commerce), UK*

# Purpose & Impact

*Purpose & Impact* is the first book aiming to provide guidance to senior executives and professionals for how to rethink and even relaunch careers that align with wider purpose and societal impact.

With our increasing longevity, the concept of retirement is becoming redundant, as executives need, financially, and want, motivationally, to continue to work well beyond what is currently considered 'retirement age'. Around age 50, when we often leave our mainstream employers, we could be looking forward to around 30 healthy years, equivalent to a whole second career. This book, therefore, sets out a topic that is becoming increasingly important and urgent for governments, companies and executives alike.

This book is underpinned by research (including interviews with over 90 senior executives) conducted by the author. Many of their stories are interspersed throughout the book to provide the reader with real insight into how very diverse senior executives and professionals created roles that enabled their own personal growth and development and had positive impacts on wider society. In addition, helpful tools and guides are used throughout the book to help the reader in their decision-making processes through the different stages of discovering and developing themselves and their career goals.

**Anita Hoffmann** is Managing Director of Executiva Ltd, London, UK. She holds an MSc Chem Eng from LTH, Sweden, and is Honorary Visiting Fellow at Cranfield University School of Management's Doughty Centre for Corporate Responsibility.

# Purpose & Impact

## How Executives Are Creating Meaningful Second Careers

## Anita Hoffmann

Routledge
Taylor & Francis Group

LONDON AND NEW YORK

First published 2018
by Routledge
2 Park Square, Milton Park, Abingdon, Oxon OX14 4RN

and by Routledge
711 Third Avenue, New York, NY 10017

*Routledge is an imprint of the Taylor & Francis Group, an informa business*

*British Library Cataloguing-in-Publication Data*
A catalogue record for this book is available from the British Library

*Library of Congress Cataloging-in-Publication Data*
Names: Hoffman, Anita, author.
Title: Purpose & impact : how executives are creating meaningful second
    careers / Anita Hoffman. Other titles: Purpose and impact
Description: Abingdon, Oxon ; New York, NY : Routledge, 2018. |
    Includes index.
Identifiers: LCCN 2017054536| ISBN 9780815381310 (hbk) |
    ISBN 9780815381273 (pbk)
Subjects: LCSH: Career changes. | Executives. | Career development.
Classification: LCC HF5384 .H626 2018 | DDC 658.4/09—dc23
LC record available at https://lccn.loc.gov/2017054536


ISBN: 978-0-8153-8131-0 (hbk)
ISBN: 978-0-8153-8127-3 (pbk)
ISBN: 978-1-351-04894-1 (ebk)


Typeset in Sabon
by Swales & Willis Ltd, Exeter, Devon, UK

*For Medlin Spencer and Billy Casey*

In memoriam

Dear friends and wise souls, who devoted their lives
to making life better for others.

# Contents

# Figures, tables, pictures and exercises

## Figures

## Tables

## Pictures

## Exercises

# Foreword

The topic of increasing longevity and our ageing society is of great interest to me personally and business-wise. As CEO for the UK insurance business of Aviva, a division of Aviva plc, a UK-based global insurance, savings and investment firm with total group assets under management £475 billion, helping people plan for their lives and future retirement, these trends have direct and material influence on our business.

During more than 25 years leading companies in the insurance and retirement income industry, I have been deeply involved in thinking about and trying to address the issues and opportunities our ageing society will bring.

Our business – providing long-term income and insurance for people – depends on us being able to generate returns long term. This can only be achieved if the businesses we invest in are sustainable – in every sense – in the long term. Hence, long-term sustainability of business and society is at the core of Aviva's strategy.

One example of this is our investment arm, Aviva Investors, with £351 billion in assets under management, who announced in July 2017 to over 1,000 investee companies that we will vote against the annual reports and accounts that fail to embrace the recommendations set out by the Financial Stability Board on climate risk disclosure.

I am personally engaged in the ageing society topic, particularly how we can get more people over 50 into the workforce, as living longer means we have to support ourselves longer and build bigger pension pots for the future. In addition, new technologies and changing immigration rules around the world mean we need to think about how we enable older workers to stay economically active in what is still an unacceptably ageist job market.

Therefore, I accepted the opportunity to lead the Business in the Community (BITC) programme for Age at Work, where many businesses together are pledging to change this situation. In September 2016, this group was appointed the UK government's Business Champion for Older Workers, with the role to support employers to adapt to the needs of our ageing population through better retention, retraining and recruiting practices for older workers.

We have set a target of an additional 1 million UK workers over age 50 into the workforce by 2022, increasing the number from 9 million to 10 million (out of 15 million in total in this age group).

Reading Anita's book, I realised that I and my fellow executives all over the world are also age 50+ workers, and that many face the same dilemmas as our employees do, looking towards a long time span after our 'big corporate' career, which often ends in our fifties. How will we meaningfully fill it, and if we need income how will we earn it?

I was struck by the fact that although organisations think about recruitment, retraining and retention of older workers, the great majority do not train people in the skills needed to create new careers – 'teaching people to fish, rather than giving them fish'.

Being able to continuously develop new options for ourselves, again and again, if needed, makes us masters of our own destinies and less at risk of being left behind in the employment market.

I had never thought of my leadership of the Age at Work BITC programme as 'job-crafting', but with the definition provided in the book, 'Creating Purpose-driven projects that fit within their companies' business strategies, that help them learn new skills, is good for their business and helps to materially impact issues in society', in a way I am.

What leaders learn by working in coalitions across industries and sectors makes us better, more well-rounded leaders for how business now needs to operate in the world, and I can see how this also would develop knowledge, skills and networks that enable the creation of second and third careers.

The many real-life executive stories from all over the world show that there is a growing understanding around the globe that business needs to be part of the solution, and that executives, with their experience, convening power and organisational resources behind them, have an important role to play, if they learn how to play it.

Anita's book is a thought-provoking, well-researched and practical read for executives looking to do work with material impact on societal issues.

Andy Briggs
CEO Aviva Insurance UK and the UK Government Business
Champion for Older Workers with Business in the Community

# Preface
## It's time to #LoveLikeJo

It is 22 June 2016, one of the few balmy days this grey and cold summer in London. The only thing that is heated is the increasingly acrimonious campaigns for the UK to leave or remain in the EU, the so-called Brexit referendum that is scheduled for the following day.

We are many thousands of people gathered in Trafalgar Square for the memorial event for Jo Cox, who on this day would have turned 42 had she not been brutally murdered six days earlier by a man who shot and stabbed her as she was on her way to meet her local constituents in the library of Birstall, West Yorkshire.

The murder of Jo Cox reverberated around the world. She was one of the youngest UK Members of Parliament (MP), and an activist, humanitarian, wife, and mother of two young children. Before becoming an MP, she worked for Oxfam and in some of the world's most dangerous places, such as Darfur and tribal regions of Pakistan, and was a tireless activist against slavery, hatred, extremism and human injustice in all its forms, at home and abroad. In the 13 months that she had been an MP, she had personally met more of her local constituents than most MPs do in years.

Like most people, I am not a member of any political party, and up to this time I have never been to a public demonstration, but this morning I feel I really need to be there. I cancel my afternoon's meetings with two executives. I explain why and offer them to join me if they wish; one of them does.

Arriving early, I sit down in the gentle sunshine on the benches at the back of Trafalgar Square. Next to me sits Thelma, 92 years of age, who for the first time in her life has travelled alone to London, as her husband of almost 70 years recently died. She lives in a town close to where Jo Cox was killed – she felt she just has to be here, no matter how uncomfortable and scary it seems.

As the event gets underway, faith leaders from all wisdom traditions deposit white roses, the symbol of Yorkshire, in an antique wooden trough on stage. A representative of the White Helmets,[1] the Syrian unarmed and neutral civil defence volunteers, has come out of Syria to lay down a white hard hat, their symbol, with the white roses. There are speeches by artists, politicians and friends of Jo Cox, and by her husband Brendan.[2]

Kids from Jo and Brendan's children's school sing 'If I Had a Hammer', one of Jo's favourite songs, and the event ends with the entire cast of *Les Misérables* singing Jo's all-time favourite, 'Do You Hear the People Sing?'. Most of us are crying.

We hold up placards that we were given, pledging to, from today, #LoveLikeJo, signing with our names next to her favourite saying from her maiden speech in Parliament, 'Far more unites us than divides us', and a drawing of Jo.[3] Our hearts are breaking.

I bring my placard home on the number 24 double-decker bus, and many passengers start to speak with me. From an old alcoholic on his way to the Royal Free Hospital, a builder and a young mother with a baby in a pram, they all speak about how Jo and her death has personally affected them. Extraordinary.

A few days earlier, on 20 June, The UK Parliament held an hour-long exceptional session remembering Jo, which can be seen on YouTube. It is a well-spent 52 minutes where you can learn what it means to be a brave leader in the twenty-first century. It takes love, compassion, passion, understanding, focus, kindness, knowledge, resourcefulness, and a steely commitment to right the things we feel are wrong in the world, near and far. Don't think Jo Cox was a fluffy 'do-gooder'. As her fellow politicians said, she was immensely kind and would collaborate with anybody, but could be 'as tough as old boots' when she wanted to change something, and let nothing stand in her way.[4]

From the moment of Jo Cox's death, the writing of this book took on real urgency. Who knows what happens tomorrow? I could not stop writing, deeply wishing to share my passion and belief that we all need to learn how to cooperate across sectors and communities to create impact on societal issues, and also how to develop second and third careers with Purpose and Impact to make our increasing long lives productive for the world and ourselves.

Despite the current inflamed political language around the world, leaders from all sectors – business, government, not-for-profit, NGOs, academia and communities – realise that problems that are inherently inter-national (hyphenation deliberate) can only be solved by international cooperation, not in national isolation.

Weather disasters do not respect borders, nor do viruses or artificial intelligence. Major floods and earthquakes happen, epidemics happen and cyberattacks happen, no matter who or what is to blame. Issues such as these need global cooperation to solve and mitigate, whether we believe their origin is a hoax or not.

The spotlight has also, justifiably, been turned on income inequality, and the plight of the working and middle class, who have been severely losing out due to many of the trends and events of the past 20 years. This sharp spotlight is a good thing. However, *how* we solve all these issues, will set the tone and trajectory for all our societies for decades to come.

Reading, listening and asking deeply what is asked of us as leaders and human beings at this point, it gradually dawned on me that if there ever was a call to action for business to become Purpose-driven, this is it. We need business, NGOs and government listening to and working with people in their communities to build a society that works for all – a society with compassion and solutions to the changes that are here already, and the ones to come, from climate change to technology, AI, ageing populations and urbanisation.

Every issue is also a business opportunity; most businesses were started once upon a time to solve a particular problem, providing a benefit to society and making reasonable profit in the process. These were the roots of, for example, Unilever (to bring hygiene to homes), Centrica (to provide the electricity to grow the UK's GDP), and Tata (to help poor citizens become participants in the Indian economy).

This is the moment to think this way again: 'What are we here to do, beyond making money for shareholders?'

Or, as Ben & Jerry's CEO Josten Solheim expresses it, 'We are a social-justice organisation that happens to be making ice-cream'.[5]

What an amazing array of innovation – social and technical – we could create if we used this lens to look at our business.

I have come to the conclusion that this really is *the* moment to create Purpose-driven business, and we are seeing a real groundswell develop with major corporations joining this trend.

To do this successfully, leaders need to develop the skills to work in this ultra-collaborative way in broad-based coalitions across all boundaries. By doing this, we also learn to create Purpose-driven careers for ourselves, to the benefit of our society, our businesses and ourselves.

Seeing incredibly capable leaders putting off Purpose in their careers until 'retirement', and then ending up joining a few boards for a decade and then fading away from mainstream societal influence, makes my heart break.

Why are we allowing this enormous amount of capability, experience and convening power to be lost to society, just at the point when their maturity and wisdom could help make major progress on world issues?

In view of the fact that at the age leaders normally leave their mainstream careers, they can today look forward to 20 to 30 years of good health, what will we do with all these years?

Learning to work across sectors and how to develop our own careers will be vital skills going forward – for individuals, organisations and society.

This book was born from the realisation – and my professional experience as a senior executive coach and search consultant – that few executives who have worked for 20 to 30 years in one industry know how to work truly cross-sector (tri-sector), or how to develop their careers beyond their traditional industries or career paths.

The three-year study for this book – and its organisationally oriented companion paper for Cranfield University School of Management's Doughty Centre for Corporate Responsibility[6] – showed that executives who successfully made an impactful transition generally learned how to be effective tri-sector leaders while at their long-term employers.

This has the benefit of maintained earnings and the ability to change the organisation we work in from the inside, while we are learning the leadership skills and competencies needed to be effective working cross-sector and affecting societal issues – and how to create new careers with Purpose.

As you will see through the examples of executives who have developed Purpose-driven careers, Purpose is a direction, gradually emerging and evolving over time – as we Discover and learn. It rarely arrives like a bolt of lightning; it is more like a fog slowly clearing.

At the end of the Jo Cox memorial, Thelma hugged me and walked off alone to explore London, where she had never been. The next day, she was to return to Yorkshire to see what she could do to help in her local community. Thelma had never been politically active, nor done community work, as she had taken care of her husband and family for many years. Thelma was starting a new career, with Purpose. If Thelma can do this at age 92, we all can, at any age.

Jo Cox lived a Purpose-driven life and career, full out, trying to make this world a better place for all, which is what most of us have a deep wish to do. Her sudden death showed, in stark relief, just how unknown our fate is. We could die tomorrow or in the next hour. Why are we putting off what, deep in our hearts, we want to do and we know needs doing?

I realise that it's time to #LoveLikeJo and passionately pursue what we believe we can help solve, whether it is issues in our communities at home or where our business touches communities in the world.

So, today I pledge again to #LoveLikeJo, and I hope this book will inspire you to do the same, in your own unique way.

Anita Hoffmann
London, 6 September 2017

**Today I pledge to #LoveLikeJo. I will**

ANITA

*Far more unites us than divides us*
Jo Cox
1974-2016

@DrueKataoka

*Picture 00.1  I commit to #LoveLikeJo[7,8]*

## Notes

1 White Helmets website: www.whitehelmets.org.
2 Addley, E., Elgot, J. and Perraudin, F. (22 June 2016). *Jo Cox: Thousands Pay Tribute on What Should Have Been MP's Birthday*. Retrieved from: www.theguardian.com.
3 Kataoka, D. (14 July 2016). *#LoveLikeJo: Why We Must Create a Legacy Worthy of Jo Cox*. World Economic Forum blog. Retrieved from: www.weforum.org/agenda/2016/07/the-jo-cox-generation-let-s-lovelikejo.
4 Parliament extraordinary session for Jo Cox MP: www.youtube.com/watch?v=qBxBs3160RE.
5 Hurst, A. (27 January 2017). *Why Ben & Jerry's Founder Pushes His Company to Merge Ice Cream and Social Justice*. Fastcoexist. Retrieved from: www.fastcoexist.com.
6 Hoffmann, A. (2016). *Purpose Driven Leader – Purpose Driven Career*. Cranfield University's School of Management Doughty Centre for Corporate Responsibility. Retrieved from: www.cranfield.ac.uk.
7 Reproduced with the kind permission of the Jo Cox Foundation.
8 Portrait of Jo Cox by Drue Kataoka: www.drue.net.

# Acknowledgements

This three-year research period has been an incredible period of learning and Discovery, in the true sense of this book. As I now close the book and send it on its journey into the world, I will start on my own Fruition process for this particular later career stage of my life.

This could never have happened without the belief and support of a number of people who helped me gain insight, where before I had only anecdotal evidence of what was going on with later careers with Purpose.

*Special thanks go to:*

Professor David Grayson, Professor Emeritus of Cranfield University School of Management's Doughty Centre for Corporate Responsibility, for his unstinting support and courage in agreeing research in the unconventional cross-disciplinary sustainability topic of later carers with Purpose.

Rebecca Marsh at Greenleaf, who believed in my idea, and Judith Lorton at Taylor & Francis, who 'midwifed' the book into reality.

Mehmet Öğütçü, Founder and CEO of the Global Resources Partnership, who took a gamble on me speaking about the emerging 'values gap' in executive ranks at his 2014 Eastern Mediterranean Energy Ministers and CEO meeting, where the later careers with Purpose idea got its first form.

Lindsay Levin, Managing Partner of Leaders Quest – and all the other LQ'ers who helped, Laura Asiala, Senior Fellow at PYXERA Global, Laura Gitman, VP at BSR, Dani Matthews, co-founder LaunchPad Media AU, Catherine van der Meulen, Director ThiNK Business Services, Guido Schmidt-Traub, CEO of UN-SDSN, Sandrine Dixson-Declève, Senior Advisor & Facilitator, Corporate Purpose, Sustainability, & Low Carbon Solutions and Senior Associate at Cambridge Institute for Sustainability Leadership, Steven Tallman, Partner and VP of Global Operations Bain & Co., and Adam Grant, Professor of Management and Psychology at the Wharton School, University of Pennsylvania, for your kind introductions to pertinent experts, executives and organisations.

A big thank you to Actis – the growth markets responsible investment private equity firm and my patient client Sachin Korantak, Global Head of the Industrial practice, who has given me the space and time to research and write, and Paul Fletcher, the previous Chairman & CEO – now pursuing his own later career with Purpose as Chairman of Leaders Quest and in many other ventures.

*I am deeply grateful to the executives who have given their time and agreed to share their experiences in the book:*

Ibrahim Al'Zubi, Laura Asiala, Nick Brooks, Anna Catalano, Courtney della Cava, Paul Dickinson, Katarina Elner-Haglund, Pablo Fetter, Paul Fletcher, Rolf Fouchier, Richard Gillies, David Grayson, Oliver Harrison, Virginie Helias, Eva Holmberg-Tedert, Steven Howard, Naoko Ishii, Nick Jepson, Nihal Kaviratne, Dr Israel Klabin, Jay Koh, Jean-Claude Larréché, Geoff Macdonald, Kenneth McKellar, Yanos Michopolous, Luis Miranda, Laurence Mulliez, Nick O'Donohoe, Sola Oyinlola, Babette Pettersen, Magnus Pousette, Anne Quinn, Kevin Reynolds, Max Robinson, Varun Sahni, Jan-Willem Scheijgrond, Guido Schmidt-Traub, Pallav Sinha, Nina Skorupska, Mark Spelman, Nadia Sood, Sheila Surgey, Martin Swain, Luke Swanson, Gina Tesla, James Wambugu and Clare Woodcraft.

*I am equally indebted to all the executives who have given their time for interviews, given introductions and directed me to relevant research, etc.:*

Danny Almagor, Manny Amadi, Bob Audley, Sally Bailey, Mirco Bardella, Claire Beyou, Osvald Bjelland, Alasdair Blackwell, Lawrence Bloom, Michael Bremans, Marcella Cheung, Mayukh Chouhudry, Denise Collis, Stuart Cook, Ann Cormack, Manisha Dahad, Noeleen Doherty, Gordon D'Silva, Scilla Elworthy, David Erdal, Alison Flemming, Joe Garner, Linda Gerard, Matt Gitsham, Ieda Gomes, Murray Grant, Shaun Gregory, Adam Grodecki, Houchun (Gloria) Guo, Simon Hampel, Emma Hardaker-Jones, Neil Hawkins, Wendy Hawkins, Loughlin Hickey, Polly Higgins, Yetunde Hofmann, Charles Hookey, Carl Hughes, Aaron Hurst, David Hutchison, Manu Janeja, Larissa Joy, Shaun Kingsbury, Frannie Léautier, Katie Levey, David Levin, Adam Liu, Sunil Mathur, Kate Matthews, Rosanda McGrath, Charles Middleton, Alex Milward, Suzanne Nimocks, Alfred Ng, Timothy Ong, Rajan Pandahare, John Pender, Julia Rebholz, Yvette Roozenbeek, Steven Sargent, Sunil Savara, Christine Schmidt, Jonathan Seabrook, Keary Shandler, Mike Smith, Coro Strandberg, Sabine Stanley, Andrew Thornton, Aris Tsikouras, Steven Turpie, Annika Tycer, Devyani Vaishampayan, Maryellen Valaitis, Alexandra van der Ploeg, Miguel Veiga-Pestana, Rosie Warin, Steve Waygood, Peter Wheeler, Kathryn Whightman-Beaven, Neil Whitley, Albert Wong and Brent Wyborn.

*For the kind permission to reproduce their material:*

Brama Kumaris, Marcella Cheung, the Jo Cox Foundation and Richard Barrett.

Without your generosity and openness, this book would not have been possible.

# Why this really is *the* moment to create a Purpose-driven career

# Chapter 1

# Introduction

'One day in my early fifties, I realised that my boss, our CFO and I were approximately the same age and likely would retire at the same time', said Sola Oyinlola, at that time Vice President and Group Treasurer of Schlumberger, and the only African corporate officer of this world-leading French American oilfield services company.

He continued:

> This meant that I was not likely to ever become the company's CFO and I wondered, what do I do now? Should I stay where I am for the next 10 years or I should I try to figure out how I could create a new career somewhere else? I was also passionately interested in African social and economic development issues, including education and women's inclusion in the economy. Should I go and work for charities? Or boards? Where could I have most impact?

Many of us find ourselves in this situation in our late forties, fifties or early sixties, the 'mid/later' career stage. We thought we knew where we were going, but are suddenly forced to stop and take out a new direction. This can be driven by external factors such as downsizing, change of management and strategy, or, as for Sola Oyinlola, a succession planning situation, or it can be personal factors such as our or a family member's health issue, or simply a yearning for 'something else' – work with meaning, Purpose.

The answer to Sola's question above is, surprisingly, that it is not about jumping anywhere in the short term, if you don't have to.

The most effective answer is staying where we are and going on a *learning* journey about ourselves and how we can contribute to solving major issues. A journey to find Purpose, 'a calling, in our business roles', as Professor Andrew Hoffman at Yale describes it.[1]

This book is about how to go on this learning journey, becoming leaders that know how to affect change in society and our organisations *and* creating new career options for ourselves, with Purpose, for as long as we need or wish.

We do this by 'job-crafting' – adding Purpose-driven projects to our roles that fit with the company's strategy. This way, we acquire knowledge while helping our organisations change and impact societal issues. Crucially, we build new cross-sector networks that can affect large-scale impact in our area of interest – these are also the route to our future career opportunities.

In this introductory chapter, we will set out the rationale for why learning to develop our careers is a vital skill that we all need going forward, the general structure of the book, and why *now* really is *the* time to create a Purpose-driven career.

## The 'mid/later' career stage is now age 50–80

This eyebrow-raising statement is due to the fact that what was physiologically considered old a generation ago is now merely considered middle-aged.

The statistical mortality research by John Shoven at MIT shows that men now transition out of middle age at age 60 (versus age 44 in the 1920s) and women at 65. Men and women are considered 'old' at age 70 and 73, and 'elderly' at age 76 and 80, respectively.[2]

There are three vital pieces of insight hidden here. First, we are now 'middle-aged' into our mid-sixties. Second, there is a new, hitherto unnamed, life stage of 10 to 15 years between 'middle-aged' and 'old' – the stage from 60/65 to 70/73 – where we are still healthy and energetic but beyond traditional retirement age. Third, the 'elderly' stage only starts in our late seventies – which means another decade where we normally have good health.

This means we now have 15 to 20 years when we can still be very active from age 60. The question is: How will we use this gift?

Choosing age 50 as the starting point for the new 'mid/later' career span is due to the fact that the job market discriminates – it should not, but it does – from age 50 onwards. It is also the time when we often start contemplating significant career changes.

This means that at this point, *we need to prepare for a whole new 20- to 30-year career*, not merely planning for the next 5 to 10 years of promotions up the corporate ladder, as when we were younger. This mid/later career stage is very different to what we have experienced so far. Making informed decisions for our future at this stage is clearly vital.

### Retirement is a redundant concept

When the retirement age of 65 was set in Germany in the early 1880s by Chancellor Otto von Bismarck, very few people reached this age.[3] Now, at 65 we have just exited 'middle age'.

This means that the old life model of 'study, 35 to 40 years of work, and retire to leisure' clearly will no longer work. Financing 30+ years of retirement from a 35- to 40-year career is difficult, and the thought of spending what is in effect a whole second 'career span' at leisure sends chills up many people's spines.

With the prospect of two-thirds of the extra 2.2 billion people on earth in 2060 being in the 40–79 age group, and the number of 60- to 79-year-olds increasing by 1.1 billion (five times the increase in the number of children and teenagers),[4] there is every reason – from personal economic, physical and mental well-being, to not being a burden on the next generation – as to why we should stay economically active for much longer, and no good reason – apart from ill health – why we might not.

There is an increasing realisation in many countries that job markets need to change, to adapt to these changes, but much more needs to happen, and faster.

### Knowing how to develop our careers will be vital to flourish over the long haul

To be able to continue to work to supplement our pensions or to have a role in society, we need to learn how to create career opportunities for ourselves. This is a vitally important investment for our future well-being.

Yet there is little knowledge among individual executives or organisations about how to develop our careers. Organisations normally train us to be ready for the next promotion in-house, not to own and manage our careers inside and outside our place of employment.

Understanding of how to find Purpose – a direction – to pursue for life and work fulfilment is even more rare. How to combine the two is the 'sweet spot', and the aim of the research for this book and its companion organisationally oriented research paper.[5]

Many organisations have large cadres of senior leaders in the 'baby boomer' generation at the 'classic retirement ages', peaking over the next 10 to 15 years. Helping them learn these career development skills is a good investment, as we will see, as it also helps them become more externally effective leaders in their current organisations and roles. In Chapter 11, we will see how some leading organisations are already benefiting from this way of working.

### Why now really is *the* time to pursue a Purpose-driven career

Speaking to thousands of senior leaders over more than a decade, it is clear that there is a real yearning for having Purpose – impacting societal well-being – in our lives and work.

Yet with the unprecedented upheaval we are seeing in the technology, political, cultural and international landscape, and the lack of trusts in institutions, we could be forgiven for wondering if our best strategy would be to hide under the bed for the foreseeable future.

Luckily, there is a new narrative rapidly developing in society and business. No matter the political rhetoric of the day, there is a growing understanding that we need *inclusive growth and new thinking for how to collaboratively address wider societal issues.*

Businesses, with their knowledge, large-scale reach and resources, are being called on to help. They are increasingly realising the risks to their business models, and the potential opportunities available in addressing them, estimated at more than US$12.2 trillion.[6]

This points to a future where business has a critical role in helping address the inequalities in society, ensuring a good outcome for *all stakeholders.*

Brands are moving from mission-led to activist – declaring and protecting the social values they stand for[7] – as could be seen in the first half of 2017, when mainstream organisations started to step forward on various topics, from the planned US travel restrictions to declaring that 'We Are Still In' when the US government announced their intention to leave the Paris Climate Change Agreement. Increasing activity around the Sustainable Development Goals (SDGs) can be seen around the globe.[8,9]

Ben & Jerry's CEO Josten Solheim pithily states this view of business' future role in society in their mission statement: 'We are a social-justice organisation that happens to be making ice-cream'.[10]

Looking at our businesses through this lens would make for a very different strategy and innovation process, and a radically different way of working, requiring an ability to work collaboratively across sectors and deep community engagement – so-called tri-sector skills.

The rapid advance of technology also means we have de facto solutions to many intractable problems within our grasp – if we can scale them.

With the confluence of these forces, *now* really is *the* time to create a Purpose-driven career.

## Successful careers with Purpose are conceived 'on the job'

In my role as executive search consultant and career coach, I have watched many executives change careers, some with material impact and satisfaction, others less so.

To understand the underlying pattern of how executives successfully created Purpose-driven careers with Impact – and made a living when needed – I spent three years interviewing mid/later career executives all over the world. In this book, they share their experiences and stories.

In summary, the successful career changers usually started the groundwork for this transition while at their long-term employer, long before contemplating leaving.

They did this through 'job-crafting', adding projects to their roles in an area that they deeply cared about that created impact in society, while fitting with the company's strategy. They spent a significant amount of their time and energy on this aspect of their jobs. Only if their topic of choice could in no practical way fit with their current employer's strategy did they create the project extracurricularly.

This way, they learned about their topic of choice, built skills for affecting change in society (tri-sector skills), helped affect change in their own companies, and built knowledge and invaluable external networks through which their future Purpose-driven career opportunities materialised.

That first project often resulted in a new senior position in the same company, incorporating their Purpose in some form, which they pursued until the day their ambition to work on their Purpose 100 per cent of their time created an irresistible momentum for an exit, and the beginning of a new career externally. This exit was executed *when they were personally ready – professionally and financially.*

It is worth noting that this was largely done while working for organisations that we would not normally associate with being particularly Purpose- or sustainability-driven, from banking to industrial waste.

With more mainstream organisations embracing societal Purpose and sustainability as core strategies, the either/or question of income versus Purpose will likely disappear over time.

In the meantime, we can enjoy learning from all these amazing men and women: how they went on a Discovery journey, to find their Big Question – what issues they wanted to help solve, how they converted this to Purpose – a direction to pursue, and how they made it reality in full-time executive or intriguingly diverse portfolio careers.

Another incentive to 'job-craft' over the next few years is to be part of the ongoing digitisation of every aspect of business and society and acquire digital skills. Without these, most of us – including senior executives – risk becoming obsolete in the next few years, whether we aim for second careers as executives, non-executive directors, trustees or advisors to for-profit, not-for-profit, NGOs or government organisations – they are all digitising.

## Why this book?

Personally, I have transitioned careers three times, at age 41, 48 and 55, and have experience of what it is like to go exploring, feeling 'lost' and finding the next direction.

Professionally, for more than a decade, I have helped countless executives, formally and informally, through their mid/later career transitions. I have heard what they yearn for, and what they struggle with, when they try to figure out how to give back and create second and third careers with meaning.

This book is my way of sharing what we have learned together over the years.

This book focuses on the growing number of leaders with wide and multicultural experience who are at a stage where they are more interested in 'scaling up' the Impact they can have on major world issues, rather than 'slowing down' – the focus of many later career books.

Having Impact does not mean working 24/7 and being 'always on', unless we wish to. It is about gradually working in a way that suits us while significantly contributing to the major changes in society we know need to happen.

Most of us find it hard to imagine that there are societal issues that we can materially impact, and we can feel vulnerable faced with being a beginner and asking for help – after many years of being the givers of help and advice.

I have learned that the only really hard part is to get going. Once we get past the first wobbly steps, we catch the 'learning bug'. Curiosity, once kindled, is a flame hard to extinguish. Learning becomes a way of life, a very exciting and rewarding way of life!

And thanks to the incredible speed of change and technological progress, there are many exciting things happening in the world. There really is no limit to the opportunities we can create – if we just go out there and Discover!

That is the point: we will not discover our Purpose sitting in our office or talking to the same people we spent the past decade with. We need to go outside our comfort zone, learn new things and meet new people.

## How this book is organised

There are two recurring and linked themes running through this book. The first is 'Purpose–Impact–Career' and the second is 'Individual–Organisation–Society'.

This is to illustrate the link between how we personally can create careers with Purpose – via our organisations – and that our organisations are a vital component in solving some major challenges in society. Having a material Impact on one or more societal issues is what a career with Purpose is about.

The featured organisations are most often businesses, however the ideas and practices are equally applicable to leaders from organisations from other sectors.

This book has four parts. In Part 1, we cover the topics of *Purpose* and *Impact*. Parts 2–4 are dedicated to *career*, and how we personally and organisationally develop them in theory and in practice.

Below is a short description of what each chapter contains.

### Part 1: Why this really is the moment to create a Purpose-driven career

- Chapter 2, 'Purpose', delves into what Purpose is – and what it is not – and why Purpose is such an important driving force for us as *individuals*, and why it has emerged strongly in *business* and *society* over the past few years.
- Chapter 3, 'Impact', discusses how to *individually* use exponential thinking – 10X – to create solutions to solve big problems in *society*, and how we and our *organisations*, working via cross-sector (tri-sector) Impact Coalitions can achieve solutions at scale.

### Part 2: Career development: how does it work?

Chapters 4, 5 and 6 discuss: why career development skills are a core skill going forward; how career changes and transitions work; the leadership skills we need to become effective cross sector (tri-sector) leaders; and how by developing and using our *Career Transformational Assets* – self-knowledge, openness to new experiences, and building strategic and diverse networks – we can develop these leadership and career development skills.

### Part 3: Creating a Purpose-driven career in practice

The brief Chapters 7 and 8 introduce the concepts of 'job-crafting' and the '9 Questions' we work with to find our *Big Question* – the societal issue we want to impact – and turn it into an action-oriented Purpose.

In Chapter 9, we turn very practical, detailing the steps of going on a *Discovery* journey, exploring societal need and our own interests to find our *Big Question* by using our *Career Transformational Assets*.

Chapter 10 covers the *Fruition* process: how we make this Purpose a practical reality: first, by understanding how to 'job-craft' at our current employer; and second, creating our *Career Investment Portfolio* before we exit – for short-, medium- and long-term optionality and returns – we might have a 20- to 30-year second career to plan earnings for.

### Part 4: What leading organisations are doing

Chapter 11 describes what leading organisations are doing to help executives learn Purpose-driven leadership and career development skills.

Finally, we bring the learnings of the book together with an end word, an afterword, and appendices.

## How to use this book

My hope is that you will find the book interesting and intriguing enough to read all the way through. It is an unfolding story with multiple layers; some topics and findings might come as quite a surprise.

Every reader will be at a different starting point, and there might be topics that you personally are familiar with or at first glance are not very interested in. Feel free to skim-read or skip these topics and go to a topic that interests you, and, if needed, go back to earlier sections.

To help with this, and for the time-poor reader, each chapter has a summary of what will be covered at the top, and a key 'takeaways' section at the end.

You will find questions dotted throughout the book. They are there to help you digest what you have read and start to collect topics you want to explore further – to start building your next career.

Particular questions will ring a big bell and are worth spending more time on; others you might skip and later discover that you want to go back to.

There are also some semi-structured exercises, mainly in Chapters 9 and 10, to ensure that all readers, even if they have never looked at career change, can set out with confidence on their Discovery journey.

If you are further along in your career change journey, pick what suits you from the exercises or draw inspiration from what you read and design your own. Do what works for you – be playful and trust your instinct. There is no right or wrong; our curiosity and passion will lead us to where we need to go.

The book draws on executives' experiences and stories, including my own when relevant, the research done for Cranfield University's School of Management Doughty Centre for Corporate Responsibility,[11] mentioned above, relevant academic research on career change, career transitions, how we learn, how motivations change as we age, how to let go of old views of ourselves, and how it is possible to bring forth our new future.

There are many references to the research included, so the curious reader can quickly access topics of interest. Often, this is all the spark we need to start our Discovery journey!

## Purpose can be found everywhere

Throughout, we will hear from 47 executives – of the almost 100 I interviewed and discussed particular aspects of their career changes with – who incredibly generously have agreed to share their stories, illustrating how they went through various parts of the Purpose-driven career change process and where it led them. As you will find, Purpose can be found literally everywhere – and there are multiple ways to create a future expressing it.

If you are curious about what Sola Oyinlola, who opened the book, decided to do, you will hear his full story in Chapter 7. How he, via job-crafting, created an Impactful Purpose-driven career as a 'Technology Investor for the Bottom Billion', through creating amazing initiatives at his employer, Schlumberger, that was good for business, had real impact in society, and allowed him to build new skills and networks for his future career.

## Notes

1 Hoffman, A. (2016). *Finding Purpose: Environmental Stewardship as a Personal Calling*. Shipley, UK: Greenleaf Publishing, review copy.
2 Vernon. S. (29 June 2017). *What Age Is Considered Old Nowadays?* CBS News. Retrieved from: www.cbsnews.com.
3 Otto von Bismarck. Retrieved from: www.ssa.gov/history/ottob.html.
4 Parker, J. (13 November 2014). *The World Reshaped: The End of The Population Pyramid*. The Economist. Retrieved from: www.economist.com.
5 Hoffmann, A. (2016). *Purpose Driven Leader – Purpose Driven Career*. Cranfield University's School of Management Doughty Centre for Corporate Responsibility. Retrieved from: www.cranfield.ac.uk.
6 Rao, S. (16 January 2017). *Business Can Unlock $12 Trillion via Key Development Goals – Davos Study*. Retrieved from: www.reuters.com.
7 Labarre, S. (2 February 2017). *The Radical Future of Branding*. Fastcodesign. Retrieved from: www.fastcodesign.com.
8 SDG Business Forum (SDGBizForum) (16 July 2017). *With over 1000 business leaders attending, the #SDGBizForum is set to be the biggest private sector event in United Nations #HLPF history* [Tweet]. Retrieved from: https://twitter.com/sdgbizforum/status/886440467474337792?refsrc=email&s=11.
9 Globescan/BSR (17 July 2017). *The State of Sustainable Business 2017*. Retrieved from: www.globescan.com.
10 Hurst, A. (27 January 2017). *Why Ben & Jerry's Founder Pushes His Company to Merge Ice Cream and Social Justice*. Fastcoexist. Retrieved from: www.fastcoexist.com.
11 Hoffmann, A. (2016). *Purpose Driven Leader – Purpose Driven Career*. Cranfield University's School of Management Doughty Centre for Corporate Responsibility. Retrieved from: www.cranfield.ac.uk.

# Chapter 2

# Purpose

*In this chapter, we will explore why Purpose – working for the greater good – has come to the fore in society as well as business, and the role it plays in our personal lives and work.*

*If you are well versed in the Purpose topic, I hope you will still read this section and hopefully find some new insights, as it is becoming increasingly clear that there is a major shift going on in our society.*

*Purpose suddenly seems to be everywhere, and companies large and small are looking at incorporating 'Purpose' into their businesses. This is due to several trends converging to create this unique situation:*

- *Humanity is at a unique point in history in terms of our **collective ability to understand and act** on the issues that face us.*
- *Society is expecting business to be **involved** in solving societal issues.*
- *Employees want to be **engaged** in their work and feel it has **meaning**.*
- *As we age, we wish to '**give back**' and make the world a better place for coming generations.*

*We will cover each of these aspects in turn, starting with the human need for meaning beyond ourselves, and building the picture through business to the ongoing shift in society.*

*We will see how this point in time is pivotal, and that our actions over the next decade are crucial for where society and civilisation is heading. More of the same thinking and acting will not solve our world's issues.*

*We need to create a new point of view, a new consciousness, from where to create new solutions and fresh approaches.*

## Purpose is a verb – not a noun – and it is not a cause

Before we delve into what is going on with our society, business and us as individuals, let's agree on a definition of Purpose. One of the most common confusions for both organisations and individuals is that Purpose is often equated with a particular cause or being a 'do-gooder'. Purpose does *not* equal a cause.

Purpose in this context means answering the question, '*Why* are we here?' or more specifically, '*What* are we here *to do*, and *for whom*?'

As Aaron Hurst in *The Purpose Economy* puts it:

> seeking our Purpose is about finding a direction, not a destination. That is, Purpose is a verb, not a noun. We may never find one true calling, but we can understand the color of our Purpose, which can help us have much more meaningful careers and lives. **TRUTH: Purpose isn't a cause; it is an approach to work and serving others. Purpose is a verb, not a noun.**[1]

An example of what Aaron Hurst means is how James Wambugu, Group Managing Director, General Insurance at UAP Old Mutual Group in Kenya, articulated his Purpose that then helped him transform UAP from a less-known insurance provider in Kenya to the most well-known and respected insurance provider in the country, attracting outside investors and finally the acquisition by the massive Old Mutual group of South Africa: 'I wanted to transform people's lives and my country through access to affordable and relevant insurance'.

We will learn more about how James and other executives figured out their Purpose, how to discover our personal Big Question, and how to convert this to our direction (i.e. our Purpose) in Chapter 9.

## The human desire for Purpose beyond ourselves

'We find Purpose when we are doing things we love, attempt new challenges, and express our voice to the world'. These are the words of Aaron Hurst in his book *The Purpose Economy*.[2]

The desire by human beings to contribute to something larger than themselves and their own needs is as old as humanity. The philosopher Aristotle wrote in 300 BC about 'the good life' being eudaemonia – a good life, a flourishing life, a fulfilled and worthwhile life.

A plethora of books have been published about happiness and well-being over the past decades, and unsurprisingly the common denominator in the more serious of them is our need to have Purpose or meaning in our existence.

Daniel Kahneman, the Nobel Memorial Prize laureate, also discovered that once our basic needs are met, extrinsic rewards – money, recognition etc. – become much less important to us, and actually don't work as motivators for higher performance at work, while intrinsic rewards – internal, emotional satisfactions – become far more critical.[3]

Daniel Pink is one of the most quoted thinkers on this topic, and Peter Diamandis, in his book *Bold*, neatly summarises Daniel Pink's findings for our intrinsic motivators as: 'Autonomy – the desire to steer our own ship, Mastery – the desire to steer it well and Purpose – the need for the journey to mean something'.[4]

Sr. Helen Alford, Vice Dean at the Faculty of Social Sciences at Angelicum, the Vatican University, has spent a lifetime studying the intersection of psychology, philosophy, wisdom traditions and neuroscience. She has drawn the conclusion that human beings are literally hardwired for cooperation – it increased our chance of survival as a species, i.e. cooperative individuals thrived and progenated more successfully than the non-cooperative individuals – and our greatest sense of joy and satisfaction comes from doing things for other people, for the greater good.[5] Other recent studies on life satisfaction confirm these findings.[6,7,8]

That this is a topic on people's minds all around the world is clear from the poignant statistics that Marcella Cheung, when Head of Global Engagement Programmes at LinkedIn, shared in her May 2015 TED Talk on finding Purpose.

When Marcella Googled the question 'What to do with my life?', Google returned *3 billion results*, only surpassed by searching for the word 'man'. As you can see from Figure 2.1, searches for similar questions yielded results in their billions as well. I think we can state with some confidence that Purpose, in life and work, is very much on the minds of the citizens of our societies all over the world.

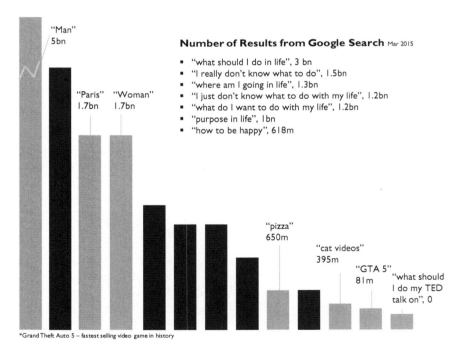

*Figure 2.1* Results when Googling 'What to do with my life'[9]

### Our motivations change as we age

As we age and face our mortality – 'time becomes finite' – our desire for Purpose in our life and work increases. We want to give back, leave a legacy and wonder how the world will see our contributions when we are gone. We have an urge to help others, mentor younger people, and share our experience and knowledge in different forms than the classic 24/7 full-time leadership roles. We discover a wish to 'live our lives' in addition to just working, and we start to want to 'work to live rather than live to work'.

We start to ask ourselves why we are here on earth, what we are supposed to accomplish before we wander into the mist of history. We start to seek answers to questions such as 'there must be more than this?', 'this' normally referring to our material lives.

We are entering the time of life that the Hindu tradition calls our 'forest dweller' time, withdrawing from our humdrum existence, at least mentally, to contemplate life's mysteries. We are seeking our soul, wisdom, and deeper understanding of how we relate to 'the whole', and share this acquired understanding through service to our society.

Many of us might not go on a full-blown spiritual seekers trail, but rather seek more philosophical or action-oriented answers, and there is no contradiction in this. We will find the path that is right for us and will gradually deepen in understanding in our own way.

This seeking and need for giving back is as old as humanity, and has been described in every wisdom tradition since ancient times, by philosophers over millennia and in recent decades by psychologists, anthropologists and other scientists.

This is illustrated in the work of Richard Barrett and his Barrett Values Model, with seven levels based on Maslow's hierarchy of human needs and models of higher consciousness (see Table 2.1).[10]

There are seven levels of needs in his model: *survival* – security and physiological needs, *relationship* – love and belonging needs, *self-esteem* – respect and recognition needs, *transformation* – freedom and autonomy needs, *internal cohesion* – the need to find meaning and Purpose, *making a difference* – the need to make a difference, and *service* – the need to do selfless service for society.

We seek to satisfy the needs of each stage before we can move forward to the next. When we have satisfied that need, we first become happy, a fleeting feeling, and then content, a lasting feeling where we feel in harmony with our situation and context. If our needs cannot be fulfilled, we become unhappy, discontent, and if we are thwarted for a long time, depressed.[11]

In fact, the lack of Purpose in our lives is, in Richard's view, one of the reasons for the epidemic spread of depression in our society, which is the topic of his 2016 book *A New Psychology of Human Well-Being*.

It is worth noting that as we move up the ladder of needs, remnants of the needs of the previous stages are still with us. How strongly they impact our decisions and behaviours depend on how well they were met, or not, when we were younger. We can be stalled at a level – such as respect and recognition – or we might be pulled back to a previous level when we feel threatened. As we work through our old issues and progress on our new needs, we will gradually operate more and more from the higher levels of the model.

Barrett has also related this progression of needs to our age (see Table 2.1). From around age 40, we start to have needs that are more focused on others, rather than with immediate career progression, our societal status or ourselves.

These needs increase as we age and as we reach our sixties and beyond; as we face our mortality, we increasingly wish to serve society and leave the world a better place for coming generations, 'generativity', as Laura Carstensen names this phenomenon in her research on socioemotional selectivity theory.[12]

*Question 2.1:*   Which of these developmental tasks, values, motivations and needs in Table 2.1 ring true for you at this point in time?

*Question 2.2:*   Do you recognise some previous stages when you were fulfilling needs that today are not so important to you anymore?

One example of how giving back and leaving a legacy is playing out in the Middle East is recounted by Ibrahim Al Zu'bi, Senior Advisor – Sustainability, Government of Dubai – Dubai Land Department, Advisory Board Member, Dubai Real Estate Institute (DREI) and Head of Sustainability – Majid Al Futtaim, in the UAE. He expressed what he sees happening with executive committee members around him in the UAE as:

> In the GCC, many companies are family-owned. Most of the first generation decided to have their CSR legacy via creating well-endowed foundations separate from the business. Now the second-generation family firm leaders are now at the age where they want to take business to the second level and start implementing global best practices in the business and having a transparent sustainable business. They are looking to incorporate the legacy leaving into the business. They are starting to see this as an additional way for 'good business', which leads to a good life and balance in society.

Or, as the India CEO of a major European corporation expressed it in our Cranfield later career study, 'Even in young industrial countries like India,

Table 2.1 Motivations, needs and value priorities at each stage of psychological development[13]

| Stages of psychological development | Age range | Developmental task | Motivations and needs | Value priorities | |
|---|---|---|---|---|---|
| | | | | Internal | External |
| Serving | 60+ years | Alleviating suffering and caring for the well-being of humanity | Satisfying your need for selfless service | Compassion, humility, wisdom | Future generations, social justice |
| Integrating | 50–59 years | Aligning with others who share the same values and purpose | Satisfying your need to make a difference | Collaboration, empathy, cooperation | Sustainability, shared purpose |
| Self-actualising | 40–49 years | Becoming more fully yourself by leading a purpose-driven life | Satisfying your need to find meaning and purpose | Fairness, openness, trust, transparency | Authenticity, shared values |
| Individuating | 20–39 years | Becoming more fully yourself by embracing your own values | Satisfying your need for freedom and autonomy | Accountability, continuous learning | Independence, equality, autonomy |
| Differentiating | 8–19 years | Proving yourself by displaying your skills and talents | Satisfying your need for respect and recognition | Self-esteem continuous improvement | Achievement, status. authority, power |
| Conforming | 2–8 years | Feeling safe and protected by staying close to kin and community | Satisfying your need for love and belonging | Safety, protection, loyalty | Harmony, friendship, traditions |
| Surviving | Birth to 2 years | Staying alive and physically healthy in the best possible conditions | Satisfying your security and physiological needs | Security | Survival |

executives in quite senior positions are now starting to look at 'retirement' in their mid to late 40s, wanting to step back and do something for society'.[14]

This need to give back to society as we enter our forties, fifties and sixties is playing out with executives everywhere in the world, but organisationally we rarely seem to take notice.

The way careers are handled in most organisations are still highly linear, in perpetual ascendancy, inflexible, and taking little or no account of changing priorities for the senior leaders.

An example of this linearity and inflexibility is the experience of one Fortune 100 senior executive I spoke to:

> After building the second largest geographical business for my company outside the USA, literally from scratch, working 24/7 and flying to the US each month for global management meetings for 15 to 20 years, I asked the company if I could just do my regional role and stop doing my global role for just a couple of years.
>
> I had almost totally missed my kids growing up and I wanted to be around for them the last two years before they went off to college and on to their own lives. I was quite happy to take a big reduction in my compensation for the period I would do this.
>
> The company was completely inflexible and gave me a flat no – after more than 25 years of outstanding performance for them! So, I said no too . . . and quit.

## Purpose is an important aspect of engagement and well-being for employees

Employee engagement is seen as one of the top factors for company success, which has been shown by many studies. One such study, by Achievers and Harvard Business Review Analytics Services, cites 71 per cent of management and executives agreeing that employee engagement improves company performance.[15]

Yet each year, surveys show that a large part of the workforce is not engaged. As Gallup's *State of the Global Workplace* survey 2014 says:

> 13% of employees across 142 countries worldwide are engaged in their jobs – that is, they are emotionally invested in and focused on creating value for their organisations every day . . . Actively disengaged workers – i.e., those who are negative and potentially hostile to their organisations – continue to outnumber engaged employees at a rate of nearly 2–1.

This implies that 63 per cent of employees just do their jobs without much enthusiasm, and over 25 per cent are negative and potentially hostile. The study also states that executives overestimate how engaged workforces are, whereas managers working for them are more pessimistic regarding their subordinates' engagement levels.

The situation is slightly better for managers, with 35 per cent of them engaged at work, according to Gallup's 2015 survey in the USA. However, 51 per cent of managers are not engaged and 14 per cent are actively disengaged, and disengaged managers create disengaged employees.[16]

Purpose has for a long time been associated with the 'millennial generation', but in fact leaders of all ages now believe that the top responsibility of a company is to provide goods and services that positively impact society, and they want to work for these types of companies.

In fact, 88 per cent of current leaders (baby boomers and Gen X) and 90 per cent of future leaders (millennials) agreed with the statement that 'Business should have a social Purpose' in a study by the Doughty Centre for Corporate Responsibility at Cranfield University's School of Management and FT Remark. They significantly differed, though, in their view on how far advanced they felt their companies were on the road to implementing Purpose – 86 per cent of current leaders but only 19 per cent of future leaders believed business is demonstrating societal Purpose.[17]

The global *2016 Purpose at Work* study surveying over 26,000 LinkedIn members showed clearly how employees who are Purpose-driven are more satisfied, productive and successful in their work. Interestingly, it also shows that older generations (baby boomers age 51+) are more Purpose-'oriented' than Gen X (age 36–50) or millennials (age 18–35), which fits with our changing priorities as we mature, but has not been seen in statistically significant numbers in studies before.[18]

That more should be done in the area of Purpose by companies is also evidenced in the *Core Values Study* by Deloitte, where both employees (68 per cent) and executives (66 per cent) agree that businesses do not do enough to instil a sense of Purpose aimed at making a meaningful societal impact in their culture, although this was deemed to be essential going forward.[19]

In view of this evidence, investing in unleashing this latent potential in executive, managerial and employee ranks should be one of the most important topics a company can engage in going forward.

## Purpose-driven companies deliver better financial returns

Many of you will be familiar with the financial benefits of being a Purpose-driven company, but I wanted to include a short summary here for the sake of completeness, and potentially as a useful armoury of information for developing your own business case to propose adding Purpose to your job or business.

The iconic book *Firms of Endearment* by Raj Sisoda, Jag Sheth and David Wolfe was first published in 2007, 18 months before the financial crisis. They showed us why brands such as Patagonia, Interface, IKEA,

Google and Whole Foods, with their unique focus on delivering Purpose (or shared value) for employees, society and business, engendered extraordinary customer and employee trust and loyalty *and* superior financial returns to investors.[20]

Despite the turbulence caused by the 2008 financial crisis, in their updated book in 2014 they show us that in the 15-year period finishing 30 September 2013, their 28 chosen US public firms and international firms of endearment vastly outperformed the S&P 500; in fact, they dwarf them in both their cumulative and annual returns. This period (1998–2013) includes the many major upheavals in the business world: the dot-com bust, the Enron fallout, the financial crisis and 'the Great Recession', etc. These firms aiming to deliver value to all stakeholders were clearly more resilient than the average firm.[21]

The 2016 study by EY and Harvard Business Review Analytic Services, *The Business Case for Purpose*, reports an interesting link between Purpose and growth. Of the 474 global executives surveyed, of those reporting that their organisation was actively pursuing Purpose, 58 per cent reported growth in the previous three years to over 10 per cent, versus 51 per cent for companies that were developing a Purpose-driven direction and 42 per cent for 'laggards' – companies who are not actively pursuing Purpose.[22]

A budding relationship, or even correlation, between social and environmental performance and company performance seems to be developing with the Global Compact 100 Index time series 2010 to 2014, where these 100 companies' financial performance are compared with the S&P large- and mid-cap in terms of market value. In three of the four years, the Global Compact outperformed the S&P.[23] It holds true also in emerging markets, where MNCI Inc. reports that their Emerging Markets ESG Index has consistently outperformed their general emerging markets index since 2007/2008, and Q2 2017 saw a record gap, to date, of 51.84 per cent versus the general index.[24]

## Delivering Purpose is the next stage of economic development

Aaron Hurst, in his book *The Purpose Economy*, argues eloquently that we can see the emergence of the next era of economic development in the world: after the agrarian, industrial and information economy, we are now seeing the emerging shift to the Purpose economy.

Other terminology for the Purpose economy is, for example, shared value, just capital, inclusive capitalism, capitalism for the long term, and compassionate capitalism. They all make the same point: it is time for business to play a different role in society, providing value for all stakeholders.

A number of books have been written on the topic (e.g. *Confronting Capitalism* by Philip Kotler, *Connect* by Lord Browne and *Conscious Capitalism* by John Mackey and Raj Sisoda), and there are numerous initiatives and organisations developing and promoting new approaches. Cranfield University's School of Management Doughty Centre has mapped more than 130 such new approaches.[25]

I have chosen to use the Purpose-driven definition as it makes the link clear between *societal*, *business* and *individual* motivations and the organisational changes needed.

### Purpose entering the mainstream corporate sphere

In January 2009, in the depth of the financial crisis, Paul Polman took over as CEO of Unilever. Over the past nine years, the world has seen him take a lead in declaring that business has a social Purpose as well as a financial Purpose; that business has a responsibility in using its knowledge, scope and resources to help solve major societal issues. He has even declared that he sees Unilever as 'the world largest NGO'.[26,27,28]

After a more than 25 per cent initial drop in Unilever's share price between 1 January and 1 May 2009, the company's share price has steadily increased from £11.19 per share to £45.20 per share at close of play 31 August 2017.[29] Unilever's sustainable brands – which include Hellmann's, Dove and Ben & Jerry's – grew 50 per cent faster than the rest of the business and delivered more than 60 per cent of the company's growth in 2016.[30] Research from Unilever shows that a third of consumers want to buy sustainable products and would purchase more if their benefits were made clearer, and that brands are missing out on an £820 billion opportunity by not pushing sustainability in their businesses.[31]

In the beginning of Unilever's journey, the rest of the consumer goods industry looked on with suspicion, wondering if this could work with authenticity in such a large company (Unilever turned over €52.7billion in 2016),[32] as hitherto only smaller companies had been successful at taking such a strategy to heart.

Most of the rest of the business world were not yet taking note, as the first wave of 'firms of endearment' were largely consumer-facing. At this stage, industrial B2B companies did not feel this was really meaningful to them.

They got on board, somewhat counter-intuitively, from the time of the financial crisis of 2008 when a few insightful CEOs beyond the FMCG sector saw this as an opportunity to engage their employees and customers in a different way. While business as usual was literally suspended, these CEOs took the opportunity to invite their executives, managers, employees and sometimes customers (often in their thousands) to participate in brainstorms around what the company's strategy should be going forward.

The response was overwhelmingly for 'sustainability', 'solving issues in society', 'contributing to society', 'contributing to something bigger than the company and its products', etc.

Out of this insight, a whole new company vision for their role in society emerged: *they want to help solve major world issues in areas where they can have the most impact with their resources and skills.* They wish to have a Purpose in society, deliver value to *all* stakeholders, including making profit, which is the natural outcome of good business, not the only ultimate goal.

Tata and Mahindra & Mahindra in India are well-known examples of this philosophy. However, diverse companies around the world were embracing stakeholder responsibility as a core principle. These included European and US companies such as DuPont, Dow, IBM, Philips and SAP, South African companies such as Nedbank and Hollard Insurance, as well as other Asian companies such as Scentre Group in Australia and OLAM Group in Singapore.

Most of these strategies were developed and executed quietly, but with big impact. For example, IBM, who were in the doldrums in 2007/2008 after their sale of the PC division – 'isolated in their data centres' doing B2B business – have emerged as a highly financially successful company. Through their 'Smart' strategy (Smart Cities, Smart Health, Smart Energy, etc.) and community engagement, IBM have in fact become a 'firm of endearment'.[33]

Other companies and sectors are following suit. In August 2015, *Fortune* magazine published their first 'Change the World 50', based on research by the think tank FSG and the Shared Value Initiative, and this was updated in 2016.[34]

In the 2015 list of companies, we found 'the usual suspects': Unilever, Patagonia, Whole Foods, Google, etc., but also an Italian utility company (Enel), a cement producer (Cemex), telecoms (Vodafone/Safaricom), technology (IBM and Cisco), and a shipping and oil and gas company (Maersk)! Purpose is slowly but surely entering on the agenda of leading companies in a variety of industries.

By 2016, the list had completely changed shape as more companies with more agile business models had invested effort and seen tangible results from focusing on delivering value for all stakeholders. This does not mean that the previous companies have stopped their efforts; with their asset-heavy business models, they need longer time and more investment to radically shift their businesses.

There is still a long way to go, but this is an intriguing sign that mainstream businesses are shifting their view of their role in society.

Business is also starting to engage with the wider SDGs, beyond Goal 13 (climate action). According to the Ethical Corporation's *Responsible Business Trends* report 2017, 60 per cent of the corporate respondents reported that they were incorporating SDGs into their strategy in 2016, up from 46 per cent in 2015. The most popular goals beyond Goal 13 were Goal 3 (good health and well-being) and Goal 8 (decent work and economic growth).[35]

### CSR is dead – long live CSR

In the above developments, you could say 'CSR is dead – long live CSR'. The traditional CSR role as an expert function on the fringe of business, delivering scientific results, reporting, communications and philanthropy, is declining. This is also the conclusion of previous BP CEO Lord Browne and McKinsey Partner Robert Nuttall in their book *Connect*. They say:

> CSR is dead . . . CSR has failed both companies and society because the initiatives are almost always detached from the core commercial activities . . . The connection between business and the world can only thrive if companies integrate societal and environmental issues deeply into their core business strategy and operations.[36]

This is also supported, from my own executive search experience. In the past seven to eight years, chief sustainability officer (CSO) appointments have mainly been through internal promotion of business leaders, and fewer sustainability subject matter experts have been hired externally or promoted internally into the most senior roles.

If the CSO is recruited from the outside they normally have serious business background in addition to their sustainability credentials, such as Steve Howard – the co-founder of the Climate Group – who joined IKEA as CSO in 2011. Steve's six-year stint with IKEA saw sales for the group's 'sustainable life at home' product line reach €1.8 billion in 2016, compared with €641 million in 2013, and take the company 70 per cent of the way to its target of achieving a fourfold increase in sales by 2020.[37]

In a Purpose-driven business, *the whole company 'becomes the CSR department'*, delivering the true meaning of *corporate* social responsibility, taking responsibility for the organisation's social, environmental and economic impacts. CSR literally *is* the strategy, and CSR has become the core of the corporation, not a fringe function; it *is* the business.

The CEO of Unilever, Paul Polman, expresses his view of Unilever's role: 'We're the world's biggest NGO'.[38]

### Calls to action across sectors

Further proof of Purpose entering the mainstream consciousness in wider society is the enthusiastic sign-up by countries to the UN 2030 Sustainable Development Goals in September 2015 and the historic Paris Climate Change Agreement in December 2015 – signed by 180 countries in 2016, including China and the USA, the world biggest emitters.

How the US government's role in this agreement will play out remains to be discovered over the next years. However, as we will see in Chapter 3, it is clear that many businesses, cities and states intend to continue down the path they have found is good for them, their business and their people.

Organisations quickly realise that they need partnerships to affect this type of systemic change, and we now see the formation of coalitions across business, government agencies and the not-for-profit/NGO sector. We will discuss in depth the arrival of these wide-ranging coalitions in Chapter 3, as they are key to achieve impact at scale on major societal issues. We personally need to learn the skills to work in this cross-sectorial way if we wish to contribute to significant change.

Another interesting sign that change is afoot was when Bank of England's Governor Mark Carney spoke starkly – on climate change and the risk to the world, business and its finances – at a Lloyds of London dinner in September 2015, in the heart of the city, which caused quite a stir.[39]

This speech was followed up in December 2015 by the formation of a new global taskforce to be led by former New York Mayor Michael Bloomberg, under the auspices of the Financial Stability Board (FSB), the G20 body that monitors and makes recommendations about the financial system. This taskforce is aimed at highlighting the financial exposure of companies and developing a voluntary code for disclosure of the vulnerability of their businesses to the risk of climate change in order that investors, insurers, banks and consumers will be provided with more information to make decisions.[40]

In August 2016, insurance company Aviva's CEO Mark Wilson and a coalition of insurers managing US$1.3 trillion in assets warned the G20 ahead of their September meeting that 'Climate change is the "mother of all risks"', and called on them to 'establish a deadline for the phase out of fossil fuel subsidies and public finance for fossil fuels'.[41]

In July 2017, both Schroeders and Aviva Investors (each with US$0.4–0.5 trillion of assets under management) took a shot across the bow of businesses on the climate topic, Schroeders by launching a 'Climate Progress Dashboard', where progress on 12 indicators can be tracked, and Aviva Investors by declaring that they will vote against the annual reports and accounts of companies that fail to embrace the climate risk disclosure guidelines set out by the FSB in June 2017.[42,43]

This shows a growing understanding of the universality of these risk and opportunities in parts of mainstream business and society hitherto not much involved in this debate.

It also suggests that in the future, the skills of board members will need to change, and climate expertise will become a necessity as we are starting to see new demand in this area from investors.

In March 2016, CalPERS, the largest pension fund in the USA, updated its Global Governance Principles, which drive its efforts on corporate engagements, proxy voting and investment decision-making. The principles now state that board members of companies that CalPERS owns should have expertise and experience in climate change risk management strategies.

They also call on companies to assign oversight responsibility on climate change to a board member, board committee or to the full board.[44]

Larry Fink, the CEO of Blackrock – the world's largest asset manager of pension funds, with US$5.1 trillion under management – publicly promoted this demand in his open letter to investee companies in March 2017. If other investors do like Blackrock and create a 30-person outreach team to speak on this topic with the companies who they hold large stakes in, they will need climate-competent board members to speak to.[45]

Although much of the above relates to climate change issues, an increasing engagement with the SDGs signals organisations waking up to their wider role in society. I think we can declare with some confidence that Purpose (working to have Impact on societal issues) has started to enter the consciousness of major institutions, and is giving strong cues to business regarding what society wants and needs from them.

A panel member from a major oil- and gas-producing nation stated this change of consciousness poignantly at an oil and gas conference in early December 2015, when an 'old school' oil and gas executive expressed the view that in light of the persistently low oil price, renewables would become irrelevant going forward. The response was, 'If you think so, you have truly missed the point. There is a complete change of the tide of sentiment in society'.[46]

## Why is this happening now in society – and where are we heading?

Over the past decades, significant research has been published by a number of academics and thinkers around how our society, and we as individuals, have evolved, from when human beings arrived on earth up to today. This research describes how at each stage, when the old model no longer serves us, we develop new models to serve our survival and flourishing. Their conclusion is that *we are at one of these inflection points when our old model no longer works and we are ready to make a leap to a new model.*

Below follows a (very) short summary of the main principles that thinkers such as Otto Scharmer, Peter Senge, Frederic Laloux, John Elkington and Richard Barrett have put forward around the development of human consciousness – our understanding of the world and our place in it – individually and societally, and why Purpose is showing up at this particular point in time. It is well worth reading the full works to get a deeper insight into what is happening in our society.

### *We never stop developing: constant evolution of human consciousness*

At the beginning of this chapter, we explored Richard Barrett's seven-level model of development over our personal life spans, from personal achievement towards Purpose and service to society.

Over time, society develops a collective understanding, as individuals do, of the needs we want our societal system to satisfy. From when the modern human, *Homo sapiens sapiens*, emerged in the world around 200,000 years ago, we have learned to adapt and change, to survive and thrive, through changing societal models when the need arose. These changes happened – *in leaps* – when our context changed and the old models of operating no longer worked for the new situation we found ourselves in.

As Frederic Laloux, in his book *Reinventing Organizations*, says: 'We made a leap in our abilities – cognitively, morally and psychologically . . . every time humanity has shifted to a new stage, it has invented a new way to collaborate, a new organizational model'.[47]

If this sounds somewhat complicated or cryptic, the following summary of the evolution of our societal consciousness and how we have leapt to new levels of understanding based on the stages described in Frederic Laloux's book might help. Other authors have similar groupings, but I found these particularly useful for understanding how society and we are changing right now, and how we got here.

Colours are used to describe the different levels of development, instead of Richard Barrett's numbered levels, and you will quickly see that these two models can be conveniently mapped on to each other.

1  *Infrared*: To maximise our chances of *survival*, human beings organised themselves in small groups or family units that hunted and gathered together, with little role or status differentiation. We were mainly *reactive* to what happened to us. This stage lasted from about 100,000 BC to 50,000 BC.

2  *Magenta*: As we became more numerous, competition for resources started to occur, and a new way of organising was needed. Small tribes were formed – we learned cooperation inside the group and external competition with other tribes to keep safe. To be successful, tribes needed leaders and hierarchy, and differentiated roles emerged (warrior, shaman, chieftain, etc.). We still *did not understand cause and effect* in our environment, and therefore *believed in magic* and spirits that made things happen in our lives. This stage started about 15,000 years ago.

3  *Red*: Next, we realised that we were separate entities from each other, and vis-à-vis our environment; our egos had been fully hatched, but we were not really aware of other people's feelings. *We lived in the here and now, and thus were impulsive*: 'I want it and I want it now'. This type of organisational structure, like 'wolf packs', still exists in some tribal societies or in street gangs, for example. This stage started about 10,000 years ago.

4  *Amber*: In the next stage, we leapt from a tribal world to *realise we could impose our will (our ego) on the world*, and created agriculture,

states and civilisations, institutions, bureaucracies, and organised religions. *To thrive, we needed to conform* to these new norms (morals) and learn self-control and self-discipline. The top of the organisation decides, and the bottom does the work, like in the army. Although this stage in principle started around 4,000 years ago, according to developmental psychologists large parts of the population in developed societies still operate from this paradigm.

5   *Orange*: At this stage, from making decisions on moral grounds, *we moved to making them on grounds of achievement (for the individual ego)*, the thinking being that if we understand the world, we can achieve more. Our global corporations are obviously this type of organisation. They brought progress in terms of innovation, accountability and meritocracy.

From success being measured as being socially accepted and seen as good, and following the rules, success became measured in achievement, particularly in material terms.

We can all see the effect of this type of thinking taking over in the greed and the pursuit of relentless growth. This constant planning ahead to achieve has meant that, as Frederic Laloux expresses it: 'We effectively live in the future, consumed by mental chatter about the things that we need to do as to achieve the goals we have set for ourselves'.[48] This stage has lasted from the Renaissance around 700 years ago, and is still prevalent today in business and politics.

6   *Green*: A new view of the world emerged, *sensitive to all people's feelings and views, and it brought empowerment*, stakeholder perspective and values-driven cultures in organisations. In this world view, *leaders should be in service to those they lead*, and many such organisations have an aspirational Purpose at the heart of what they do. The view is that our personal ego's needs should be curbed and channelled towards achieving well-being for all stakeholders, not just ourselves. This stage started about 50 years ago.

7   *Teal: The emerging world view is that we should all be in service to society and the world, i.e. to each other, for the 'common good' of all stakeholders* – humans, other species and nature – as we are all part of this interconnected world. This includes everyone and all types of organisations, including business. This stage is bringing self-management, wholeness and evolutionary Purpose. *We are here to create the best possible conditions to flourish – for everyone.* This thinking emerged around 15 years ago.

Otto Scharmer, professor at MIT and another famous thinker on this topic, has come to similar conclusions to Frederic Laloux, and names the 'teal stage' (Purpose-driven society) as 'Society 4.0', and describes this transition as:

A shift that requires us to expand our thinking from the head to the heart. It is a shift *from an ego-system awareness* that cares about the well-being of oneself *to an eco-system awareness* that care for the well-being of all, including oneself.[49]

Finding a new model that serves us is a vitally important and a necessary evolution for the survival of the human species, society and the world.

Just like with human beings, when societies leap to the next level of consciousness and organising principle, remnants of the previous stage are still present in the new stage. We add the new beneficial beliefs and principles to the old understanding and try to abolish the beliefs and principles that are no longer perceived as beneficial.

This will happen at different speeds in different cultures and organisations around the world. We can all probably identify countries and organisations whose cultures and predominant belief systems are at various levels of the stages above.

In times of crisis, societal and organisational behaviour can also revert to less conscious behavioural levels.

The conclusion to why Purpose is emerging with such force in society and business right now is that we have reached a stage of development where the previous model no longer enables us to flourish, and a large enough swathe of society 'gets it' – we are approaching a societal consciousness tipping point.

### The cycle time between developmental stages is getting shorter

Scanning across the time spans above, you will find that the timescale for change are is not linear, but exponential.

We can see that the first four stages took about 100,000 years, and the last three have started about 700, 50 and 15 years ago. This continuous evolution with leaps to the next level of consciousness is not going to stop.

We might thus see several shifts in our lifetime, which is worth contemplating in view of 100+ year lifespans for human beings going forward.

We have an extraordinary opportunity in the history of human society – and in organisations – to make a leap to a world view where service to all and the greater good is what matters most. How we choose to act over the next decade will set the trajectory for our world for a long time to come.

### The shift starts with us as individuals

For change to happen in wider society, we personally need to change how we perceive the world around us, and our place in it.

If we don't change how we think about the world and our personal responsibilities for what is happening, only seeing everything as a 'given' and unchangeable, we will not be able to see that it *can* be changed, and will keep creating the same answers and solutions that we all know are no longer working.

We humans have created everything in our society, hence we can also uncreate (abolish), recreate (improve or redesign), or create something entirely new that has not yet been seen or thought of.

Big changes in how society thinks start with a few people thinking differently and believing they *can* change how others see the world. It follows that to change something in society, we first have to start with changing ourselves and our world-view. We need to go from an 'ego-centred view' to an 'eco-centred view', as Otto Scharmer says above.

This thought, that we need to understand ourselves and how we think, to change the trajectory of the future, is not new – it has been around since ancient times. Notably, the sign over the door to the Temple of the Oracle at Delphi declared, 'Know thyself'.

Self-knowledge and new experiences help us change how we see the world, and from here springs all the renewal in our personal lives and the impetus for change in society. As we will see in later chapters, this is also at the heart of developing the leadership skills needed for this new world 'operating model', as well as successful career transitions.

It seems appropriate to end this section with two quotes:

> *As human beings, our greatness lies not so much in being able to remake the world – that is the myth of the atomic age – as in being able to remake ourselves.*
>
> —Mahatma Gandhi[50]

> *Yesterday I was clever, so I wanted to change the world. Today I am wise, so I am changing myself.*
>
> —Jalaluddin Rumi[51]

*Question 2.3:*   What surprised you about Purpose in each section above?

## Takeaways

The need for Purpose – working towards something greater than ourselves – is as old as humanity, and the need to 'give back' grows with age.

Seeking Purpose is about finding a direction for affecting change in society – not a cause.

Humanity creates new societal models that are more suited to deliver their needs at that point in time. This happens in leaps, and is confusing and destabilising, before a new equilibrium is found. Remnants of old models linger with us for a long time.

The time between our changes of societal models is getting shorter; we might see several in our lifetime.

All change starts with us as individuals, learning to see the world from a new perspective. We need to shift, as Otto Sharmer says, 'from an ego-system awareness that cares about the well-being of oneself to an eco-system awareness that care for the well-being of all, including oneself'.[52]

## Notes

1   Hurst, A. (2014). *The Purpose Economy: How Your Desire for Impact, Personal Growth and Community Is Changing the World*. Boise, ID: Elevate, Kindle edition, locations 1160, 1174, original emphasis.
2   Hurst, A. (2014). *The Purpose Economy: How Your Desire for Impact, Personal Growth and Community Is Changing the World*. Boise, ID: Elevate, Kindle edition, location 330.
3   Kahneman, D. et al. (2016). *Would You Be Happier If You Were Richer? A Focusing Illusion*. CEPS Working Paper No. 125.
4   Diamandis, P. (2015). *Bold: How to Go Big, Create Wealth and Impact the World*. New York: Simon & Schuster, reprint edition, Kindle edition, location 1287.
5   Alford, H. (15 April 2015). *On the Human Person and the Common Good. A Blueprint for Better Business*. Podcast. Retrieved from: www.blueprintfor business.org.
6   Buchanan, K.E. and Bardi, A. (2010). Acts of Kindness and Acts of Novelty Affect Life Satisfaction. *Journal of Social Psychology*, 150(3).
7   Aknin, L.B., Dunn, E.W. and Norton, M.I. (6 September 2011) *Happiness Runs in a Circular Motion: Evidence for a Positive Feedback Loop Between Prosocial Spending and Happiness*. Reviewed by A. Dixon. Retrieved from: http://greatergood.berkeley.edu.
8   Tomasello, M. (30 November 2009). *Why We Cooperate*. Cambridge, MA: MIT Press. Reviewed by N. Wade, *New York Times*. Retrieved from: www.nytimes.com.
9   Reproduced with the permission of: Cheung, M. (2015). *Using Memories to Find What to Do in Life*. TEDxRiverNorth. Retrieved from: www.youtube.com.
10   The Barrett Model. Retrieved from: www.valuescentre.com/mapping-values/barrett-model.
11   Barrett, R. (2015). *Delivering the UN Global Goals: The Consciousness Perspective*. Barrett Values Centre. Retrieved from: www.valuescentre.com.
12   Carstensen, L.L. (2007). Growing Old or Living Long: Take Your Pick. *Issues in Science and Technology*, 23(2). Retrieved from: http://issues.org.
13   Reproduced with the kind permission of: Barrett, R. (2016). *A New Psychology of Human Well-Being: An Exploration of the Influence Ego-Soul Dynamics on Mental and Physical Health*. Raleigh, NC: Lulu Publishing Services, Table 5.1.
14   Hoffmann, A. (2016). *Purpose Driven Leader – Purpose Driven Career*. Cranfield University's School of Management Doughty Centre for Corporate Responsibility, p. 12. Retrieved from: www.cranfield.ac.uk.
15   Harvard Business Review Analytic Services and Achievers (2013). *The Impact of Employee Engagement on Performance*. Harvard Business Review Publication Services, p. 1. Retrieved from: http://go.achievers.com.
16   Adkins, A. (2 April 2015). *Only 35% of U.S. Managers Are Engaged in Their Jobs*. Gallup. Retrieved from: www.gallup.com.
17   Grayson, D., McLaren, M., Exter, N. and Turner, C. (2014). *Combining Profit and Purpose: A New Dialogue on the Role of Business in Society*. Cranfield

University's School of Management Doughty Centre for Corporate Responsibility & FT Remark.

18 Hurst, A. et al. (2016). *2016 Workforce Purpose Index*. LinkedIn & Imperative. Retrieved from: https://cdn.imperative.com.

19 Deloitte (2013). *Culture of Purpose: A Business Imperative – 2013 Core Beliefs & Culture Survey*. Retrieved from: www2.deloitte.com.

20 Sisodia, R., Sheth, J. and Wolfe, D. (2014). *Firms of Endearment: How World-Class Companies Profit from Passion and Purpose*. London, UK: Pearson FT Press, 2nd edition.

21 Sisodia, R., Sheth, J. and Wolfe, D. (2014). *Firms of Endearment: How World-Class Companies Profit from Passion and Purpose*. London, UK: Pearson FT Press, 2nd edition, pp. 113–117.

22 EY Beacon Institute (2015). *The Business Case for Purpose*. EY & HBR Analytic Services, p. 4. Retrieved from: www.ey.com.

23 Murray, S. (1 June 2015). *Sustainability Measurement: Index Looks to Connect Investor*. Financial Times. Retrieved from: www.ft.com.

24 Kynge, J. (21 July 2017). *Investors in Companies That Do Good Do Better*. Financial Times. Retrieved from: www.ft.com.

25 Doughty Centre (2015). *Renewing Capitalism Doctoral Project*. Retrieved from: www.som.cranfield.ac.uk/som/p20852/Research/Research-Centres/Doughty-Centre-Home/Research/Renewing-Capitalism.

26 SustainAbility/Globescan (2015). *The 2015 Sustainability Leaders*. Retrieved from: www.globescan.com.

27 Schumpeter (9 August 2014). *In Search of the Good Business*. The Economist print edition. Retrieved from: www.economist.com.

28 Macdonald, L. (18 February 2014). *The Surprising and Sensible Remarks of Unilever CEO Paul Polman*. Centre for Global Development. Interview. Retrieved from: www.cgdev.org.

29 London Stock Exchange (2017). *Ulvr Unilever Plc*. Retrieved from: www.london stockexchange.com.

30 Roderock, L. (18 May 2017). *Unilever's Sustainable Brands Grow 50% Faster Than the Rest of the Business*. Marketing Week. Retrieved from: www.marketing week.com.

31 Vizard, S. (3 January 2017). *Brands Missing out on £820bn Opportunity by Not Pushing Sustainability*. Marketing Week. Retrieved from: www.marketingweek.com.

32 2016 Unilever Factsheet. Retrieved from: www.unilever.com.

33 Hoffmann, A. (2016). *Purpose Driven Leader – Purpose Driven Career*. Cranfield University's School of Management Doughty Centre for Corporate Responsibility, pp. 68–69. Retrieved from: www.cranfield.ac.uk.

34 Murray, A. (20 August 2015). *Introducing Fortune's Change the World List: Companies That Are Doing Well by Doing Good*. Retrieved from: http://fortune.com.

35 Dowd, L. (30 May 2017). *60% of Companies Are Integrating the SDGs into Business Strategy*. Retrieved from: www.ethicalcorp.com.

36 Browne, J., Nutall, R. and Stadien, T. (2015). *Connect: How Companies Succeed by Engaging Radically with Society*. London, UK: WH Allen/Virgin Digital, Kindle edition, locations 134, 302.

37 Edie.net (12 December 2016). *Ikea Nears Three-Fold Increase in Sustainable Product Sales*. Retrieved from: www.edie.net.

38 Macdonald, L. (18 February 2014). *The Surprising and Sensible Remarks of Unilever CEO Paul Polman*. Centre for Global Development. Interview. Retrieved from: www.cgdev.org.

39  Clark, P. (29 September 2015). *Mark Carney Warns Investors Face 'Huge' Climate Change Losses*. Retrieved from: https://next.ft.com.
40  Elliott, L. (4 December 2015). *Michael Bloomberg to Head Global Taskforce on Climate Change*. Retrieved from: www.theguardian.com.
41  Frangoul, A. (30 August 2016). *Climate Change 'Mother of All Risks' Says Aviva CEO Amid Calls to End Fossil Fuel Subsidies*. Retrieved from: www.cnbc.com.
42  Mooney, A. (15 July 2017). *Schroeders Issues Climate Change Warning*. Financial Times. Retrieved from: www.ft.com.
43  Mooney, A. (20 July 2017). *Aviva Investors Demand Greater Climate Change Disclosure*. Financial Times. Retrieved from: www.ft.com.
44  Ramani, V. (6 April 2016). *CalPERS Raises Bar on Corporate Directors' Role in Tackling Climate Change*. Retrieved from: www.ceres.org.
45  Kerber, R. (13 March 2017). *Exclusive: Blackrock Vows New Pressure on Climate, Board Diversity*. Retrieved from: http://uk.reuters.com.
46  Bosphorus Energy Club (10 December 2015). *4th Convention of the Bosphorus Energy Club*. Retrieved from: www.bosphorusenergyclub.org.
47  Laloux, F. (2014). *Reinventing Organizations: A Guide to Creating Organizations Inspired by the Next Stage of Human Consciousness*. Brussels, Belgium: Nelson Parker, Kindle edition, location 369.
48  Laloux, F. (2014). *Reinventing Organizations: A Guide to Creating Organizations Inspired by the Next Stage of Human Consciousness*. Brussels, Belgium: Nelson Parker, Kindle edition, location 728.
49  Scharmer, O. (2013). *Leading from the Emerging Future: From Ego-System to Eco-System Economies*. Oakland, CA: Berrett-Koehler, Kindle edition, location 52, original emphasis.
50  Edberg, H. (n.d.). *Gandhi's Top 10 Fundamentals for Changing the World*. Retrieved from: www.positivityblog.com.
51  Goodreads (n.d.). *Jalahuddin Rumi Author Biography*. Retrieved from: www.goodreads.com/author/show/875661.Jalaluddin_Rumi.
52  Scharmer, O. (2013). *Leading from the Emerging Future: From Ego-System to Eco-System Economies*. Oakland, CA: Berrett-Koehler, Kindle edition, location 52.

# Chapter 3

# Impact

*'Impact' is a word constantly mentioned when solutions to challenges in society are discussed. Facing large-scale challenges, we can wonder if it is possible that we, as individuals, can affect these issues, never mind have any material impact on them. We can, in our own unique way, as we will see.*

*Despite what we read, we have made significant progress in the past decades in addressing a number of major societal issues – by mobilising resources together.*

*The incredible pace of technological advancement in every sphere means we have solutions to many previously intractable problems within our grasp – if we mobilise ourselves.*

*We are now witnessing the rise of Impact Coalitions – large numbers of organisations teaming up across sectors (business, governments and NGOs/ not-for-profits) – to focus on creating and delivering solutions at scale on a particular issue.*

*With business awakening to their role (and profitable business opportunity) and solutions becoming available, this really is **the** right moment to create a Purpose-driven career.*

## Impact: material effect on solving an issue in society

Impact originally means 'to have marked effect or influence'.[1] But as with the term 'Purpose', the term 'Impact' is becoming blurred, and is used interchangeably with several meanings.

The most confusing alternative definition is due to the use, particularly in business, of 'Impact' as meaning: '*Measure* of the tangible and intangible effects (consequences) of one thing's or entity's action or influence upon another'.[2]

Measuring impact is important, but not Impact as we mean it here.

We will use the following definition of Impact in our Purpose context:

*Impact – having material effect on solving an issue in society.*

As we will see in later chapters, Impact is a vital link for strategising and realising our Purpose – where we personally want to focus our own experience, expertise and passion to best effect.

## Impact: for individuals, business and society

As with Purpose, it is useful to see the link between personal, organisational and societal Impact. As we will see in Chapter 9, to Discover our Purpose in practice, we want to find the fulcrum of where our skills, personal interests and passion meet a significant need in society. This way, we can work our way back from the Impact of solving a societal need, via what our organisation could do, to what we can do.

### Society: '10X Impact' needed

We are all aware that our world faces major challenges and that major societal shifts are under way: increasing inequality; ageing societies; urbanisation; the rise of AI with the potential displacement of millions of workers; and climate change. Climate change alone could have cataclysmic consequences, from the collapse of our financial systems,[3] mass famine due to simultaneous crop failures,[4] to the spectre of 2 billion climate change refugees.[5]

John Elkington, a world authority on corporate responsibility and sustainable development, as well as author, advisor and serial entrepreneur – who coined such terms as environmental excellence, green growth, green consumer, the triple bottom line, and people, planet and profit – argues that the exponential problems facing us cannot be solved with incremental thinking; they need exponential solutions:

> As leaders learn to 'Think Sustainably', they will also need to learn to 'Think X', shorthand for 'Think Exponential'. In the same way that they once looked to activists and social entrepreneurs for evidence of where markets were headed, they must now engage a very different set of players. These new players are not happy with 1% or even 10% year-on-year improvements, instead pushing towards 10X – or 10-fold – improvements over time.[6]

### Business: the US$12+ trillion opportunity[7]

Project Breakthrough – John Elkington's project together with the UN Global Compact[8] – calls for business models to become exponentially more social, lean, integrated and circular. It discusses how meeting the goals for just four out of 60 sectors (food and agriculture, cities, energy and materials, and health and well-being) could open up market opportunities worth up to US$12 trillion per year in less than 15 years.[9]

This is a prize well worth having. The price for an established organisation not engaging – as disruptors adopting new business models move in – is loss of customers and revenue, reputation, talent, and potentially extinction of their business.

Before the Great Recession, a limited but growing number of companies had embraced Purpose at the heart of their business. Many were small to medium-size enterprises, with the exception of the well-known Patagonia, Interflora, Whole Foods Market, Marks & Spencer, etc. They were profitable and admired, but at this point had mainly impact on their own organisation, their immediate supply chains and surrounding communities.

In the aftermath of the Great Recession, a number of larger corporations emerged, realising that with their resources they could make real dents in societal issues – have Impact – and gain profitable business from this strategy. Examples are Unilever, with their Sustainable Living Plan (to, by 2020, significantly improve the well-being of more than 1 billion people and enhance the livelihoods for millions, while growing their sales and halving their environmental footprint),[10] and IBM, with their 'Smart' strategy (Smart Cities, Smart Healthcare, etc.). These corporations realised they could have substantial Impact by using their size, expertise, resources and reach to affect change in their supply chain and the communities they touch, but also much wider in society.

In the period 2010–2015, we saw many public–private partnerships form, as companies implementing their Purpose- or sustainability-driven strategies naturally started to work in cross-sector partnerships with local governments and NGOs, or other not-for-profits, often on a national or regional basis.

These were named *Corporate Responsibility Coalitions* by Professor David Grayson and Jane Nelson in their 2013 book of the same name. The book describes the role played by business-led coalitions in generating and disseminating socially responsible business practices, and the results of this work.[11]

## The rise of global Impact Coalitions to achieve scale

From the period leading up to the Paris Climate Change Agreement in late 2015, we have been seeing the emergence of what I call *Impact Coalitions* – coalitions, often global, of organisations aiming at creating and delivering solutions at scale, action-oriented, going beyond sharing best practices, and with very senior leaders involved and committed.

This has come about as businesses and other organisations realise that if we 'club' together our resources in a focused way, we can multiply the Impact instead of risking spreading our resources thin and fragmenting the effort working more on our own.

There is an ever-increasing wave of businesses committing to goals and targets with these new global Impact collaboration platforms. It is something we have never seen before in history.

Many coalitions are (as of 2017) working on climate change and renewable energy topics, but businesses are increasingly engaging with the wider SDGs (Ethical Corporation reports that 60 per cent of their members are incorporating the SDGs into strategy in 2016, versus 46 per cent in 2015),[12] and many of the companies that lead on climate change are often the leading players in other areas.

Some examples of Impact Coalitions are given below.

*The Sustainable Development Solutions Network (SDSN)* was created in 2012 under the leadership of Jeffrey Sachs and launched by UN Secretary-General Ban Ki-moon. It mobilises scientific and technical expertise from academia, civil society and the private sector in support of sustainable development problem-solving at local, national and global scales. The SDSN works closely with United Nations agencies, multilateral financing institutions, the private sector and civil society.[13]

We will hear in Chapter 5 Guido Schmidt-Traub's story of how he became the CEO of SDSN.

*We Mean Business* is a coalition engaging with thousands of the world's most influential businesses to transition to a low-carbon economy, securing sustainable economic growth and prosperity for all. Their role is to be a platform to amplify the business voice, catalyse bold climate action by all, and promote smart policy frameworks. It consists (in July 2017) of 585 companies representing over US$8.1 trillion in revenue, and 183 investors representing over US$20.7 trillion in assets under management. They have made 1,235 commitments towards a low-carbon future.[14]

Nigel Topping, the CEO, spent almost eight years working with the CDP (see below) before starting the We Mean Business coalition.[15]

*RE100* is organised by the Climate Group in partnership with the CDP, as part of the We Mean Business coalition. Members commit to procuring 100 per cent renewable electricity by a certain year. It reached a membership of 100 companies in July 2017, three years ahead of schedule. This represented 146 terawatt hours (TWh) per year of renewable electricity demand – the equivalent of the electricity required to power Poland or New York State – a remarkable progress from 2014, when 13 companies representing 19 TWh set out on this journey. As many members are global organisations, including 30 Fortune Global 500 companies representing US$2.5 trillion in revenue, this activity will have global Impact.[16,17]

In Chapter 10, we will hear how Paul Dickinson created his Purpose-driven career through creating the CDP.

The companies involved with RE100 realise that moving to renewable energy is contributing to their company profits, by lowering energy costs and increasing energy security, as well as lowering greenhouse gas emissions. This is exemplified by IKEA, the Nordic furniture maker and retailer who have deployed €1.5 billion worldwide in renewable energy projects. They are already energy-independent in the Nordic area, producing more energy than they consume. The same will be true for IKEA in the US shortly. Around €1.5 billion has been deployed worldwide into renewable generation projects. Savings from energy-efficiency measures between 2010 and 2015 were €133 million, achieved before the renewable energy investments took effect.[18]

*Science Based Targets* is a collaboration between the CDP, the World Resources Institute (WRI), the World Wide Fund for Nature (WWF) and the United Nations Global Compact (UNGC). Science Based Targets provide We Mean Business Coalition member companies with clearly defined pathways to future-proof growth by specifying how much and how quickly they need to reduce their greenhouse gas emissions to meet their part to fulfilling the Paris Climate Change Agreement, as well as staying competitive in their industries.[19]

An average of two companies per week are signing up to Science Based Targets, and in February 2018 the total number of companies signed up, according to their website, was over 340.

*Circular Fibres Initiative*, for the clothes manufacturing and retail industry, was launched in May 2017 by the Ellen MacArthur foundation (the think tank founded to promote the circular economy) with partners H&M, Nike, C&A Foundation, the Danish Fashion Institute, Fashion for Good, Cradle to Cradle, and Mistra Future Fashion.

Reusing fibre will be vital going forward as clothing production has doubled between 2000 and 2014, due to consumers' purchases of garments increasing by 60 per cent annually, yet keeping their clothing for half the time they did 15 years ago. Up to 85 per cent of those discarded textiles go to landfill, a total of 15 million tons annually across Europe and North America. As apparel consumption is projected to rise by a further 63 per cent in 2030, the need to address the apparel environmental footprint is essential.

*Partnership on AI* was formed in 2016 'to study and formulate best practice on AI technologies, to advance the public's understanding of AI, and to serve as an open platform for discussion and engagement about AI and it's influences on people and society', as their website says. The founding members include Amazon, DeepMind, Google, Facebook, Microsoft and IBM, and they have (as of July 2017) 25 members from different spheres of society and business.[20]

*The Natural Capital Coalition* is a unique global multi-stakeholder collaboration that brings together around 250 leading initiatives and organisations to harmonise approaches to natural capital. This includes some of the world's largest engineering and construction companies, FMCG companies, ACCA (the global body for certified accountants), investors, sustainability associations, consultants and universities.[21]

Looking inside the SDGs, we can find many further coalitions working on delivering solutions for a goal or sub-segments of a goal.

The *Coalition for Epidemic Preparedness Innovations (CEPI)* in health (Goal 3), between the pharma sector and the WHO, to research and make 'just in case' vaccines for potential epidemic outbreaks, announced at the January 2017 WEF meeting in Davos.[22]

*The Global Coalition for Education* for Goal 4 was formed in 2012, with 15 founding member companies, and now consists of around 30 companies, including Accenture, BHP Billiton, Chevron, Dangote, Discovery Communications, Econet Wireless Group, Gucci, Hess Corporation, HP, Intel Corporation, Lenovo Group Limited, McKinsey, Microsoft, Pearson, Reed Smith, Tata Sons and Western Union.[23]

The list goes on and on, with one theme in common – global *partnerships across sectors for Impact* focusing on a particular area to achieve Impact.

### The unexpected Impact Coalitions

There is a new willingness to reach out across boundaries that previously seemed impossible. Organisations large and small, as well as individuals, from professions not often linked with business or government, are starting to cooperate in creative ways to achieve Impact.

Even countries are getting innovative, as the novel bilateral climate cooperation agreements between California and China,[24] and the EU and China,[25] show.

Some examples of unusual Impact Coalitions of various scale are detailed below.

*We Are Still In* is the ultra-fast mobilisation – orchestrated by Michael Bloomberg, founder of Bloomberg and previous New York Mayor – of more than 2,200 leaders from America's city halls, state houses, boardrooms and college campuses, representing more than 127 million Americans and US$6.2 trillion of the US economy, declaring that 'We Are Still In' the Paris Climate Change Agreement, just before the US federal government declared their intent to withdraw from the agreement. This includes businesses and investors accounting for a total annual revenue of US$1.4 trillion and over 20 Fortune 500 companies, including Apple, eBay, Gap Inc., Google, Intel, Microsoft and Nike, and it keeps on growing.[26]

*The B-Team* is a group of very high-profile business and societal leaders (Richard Branson, Jochen Zeitz, Paul Polman, Mark Benioff, Christiana Figures, Shannan Burrow, Gro Harlem Bruntland, etc.), formed in 2014, who are using their positions to 'work in partnership with businesses, governments, thought-leaders and civil society advocates to identify solutions and drive bold action to transform the global economy, for the benefit of people and the planet'.

They have 10 different initiative areas; many of them are *people-focused*, which is distinctive for this Impact coalition. They promote the B Corps concept, for benefit corporation certification and registration, meaning that these companies are legally accountable to all stakeholders, not just shareholders.[27]

*The TPG Rise* Fund,[28] announced at the end of 2016, is a US$2 billion private equity Impact investing fund with future plans to reach US$5 billion. It was created by Texas Pacific Group (TPG), with US$74 billion under management, a firm previously not much seen in the sustainable investing space.

This move signals the arrival of big mainstream firms into the Impact investing space, with the aim to Impact invest at scale.

The singer Bono and many of the 'famous billionaire club' are founding investors and board members, including Jeff Skoll, Pierre Omidyar, Richard Branson, Lynne Benioff, Reid Hoffman, Melody Hobson, Mo Ibrahim and Laurene Powell Jobs. A few pension funds and sovereign wealth funds (SWFs) are said to have invested 'nine-figure sums'.[29]

Investments are to be spread between US and emerging markets over seven sectors: education, energy, food and agriculture, financial services, growth infrastructure, healthcare, and technology, media and telecommunications. The first investments have borne this out, first being lead investor for a US$190 million financing of EverFi (an educational technology start-up in Washington, DC), and second investing US$50 million in the Indian dairy producer Dodla.[30,31]

The case of Dodla is poignant as it shows that Impact can be achieved in many ways.

Due to the high perishability of dairy products, nearly all of Dodla's milk is procured locally from smallholder farmers. Dodla's partnership with farmers and local distribution networks drive the company's business strategy and social impact. Dodla sources milk from 250,000 farmers across 7,000 villages every day of the year. They work with more than 3,000 distributors across nine states, and Dodla's products are sold by more than 50,000 retail outlets across the country.

A serious investor putting such sums and expertise at the company's disposal will undoubtedly help them serve many more farmers and customers safely and efficiently. That will have tremendous Impact for the local communities, with increased earnings and food hygiene throughout the supply chain, from farmer to consumer – but maybe not in the way we have been used to think about Impact.

*Unreasonable Group*, at the other end of the financial spectrum, is an accelerator founded in 2012 by Daniel Epstein. The aim is to scale for-profit socially minded start-ups, spun out from the Unreasonable Institute, a not-for-profit organisation also founded by Daniel.[32]

*Unreasonable Goals*, his latest project, looks to help 16 start-ups per year grow, one around each of the SDGs. To illustrate Goal 17, which calls for Partnerships for the Goals, the plan is to run the SDG-themed programme each year until 2030, working with different government and corporate partners around the world each time. For this first round, the government host is the US State Department, and includes representatives from organisations such as Johnson & Johnson and Lowe's.[33]

Daniel expresses his vision: 'We believe desperately in entrepreneurs as the beacons for the most promising solutions. But if we are going to take those to scale faster, we need to drive relationships between these start-ups and the largest institutions of our time'.

Their inaugural start-ups include Liberty & Justice, a Liberia-based apparel maker with a record of empowering its largely female workforce, as well as giving away free school uniforms (SDG 5: gender equality).[34]

## The ultimate goal is to address inequalities for people in local communities

The last two examples of organisations being financed and helped to scale for Impact are important. They draw our attention to the fact that although we might work in big global coalitions for Impact, the ultimate goal is to materially improve the conditions in communities around the world, whether it concerns income, food, health, or access to clean energy, etc.

Major organisations are realising that they touch people in communities along their global supply chains, and are starting to address this. But it is easy to forget that there might be communities who need our help right on our local office doorstep.

An example of how entangled this issue can be is the case of a struggling worker employed by suppliers to Facebook's headquarter cafeteria in California. Despite being paid well above the US$10.50 per hour California minimum wage and well above the Facebook minimum wage of US$15 per hour for suppliers, the family has ended up living in a garage due to the area being so high-cost.[35,36]

The statistics from the UK show the scale of this issue. Despite the fact that UK employment in 2016 stood at an all-time high and unemployment at an 11-year low, a staggering 2.25 million people out of the 8.8 million inhabitants of London – just over 25 per cent of the population(!) – experience poverty, and in-work poverty is increasing.[37,38,39]

That these issues can literally be hiding on our doorstep was expressed by a partner at a major professional services firm:

> I have been visiting our office near Euston station weekly for several years. Only last week did I learn from a taxi driver that only one block away is one of the most deprived communities in the UK and financially in the bottom 5% of London Boroughs.[40]

These kinds of insights led Sacha Romanovitch, the CEO of the UK accounting and consulting firm Grant Thornton, to set a completely new direction for the firm, making it a shared enterprise with a profit-sharing policy, capping her salary, and leading the company's initiative to make the UK economy vibrant from the front.[41,42]

It is becoming clear that whether looking at financial, environmental or social issues, globally or locally, leading businesses are realising that being part of Impact Coalitions affecting change is a great way of staying at the forefront of innovation, generating profit, mitigating business risk, influencing future policy, *and* creating material Impact through pooling knowledge, resources and reach.

If these businesses did not believe that addressing societal issues was vital for their business today and tomorrow, they would not so wholeheartedly commit their people, time, resources, and personal and organisational reputations.

This does not mean that all these companies have truly embedded Purpose at the heart of their strategy, but they can increasingly see that addressing societal issues, whether climate change or other societal issues, means they can have Impact *and* make profit.

As we will see, from executives' stories later in the book, the journey towards more large-scale organisational engagement often starts with experimental projects on the edges of the business, which over time becomes mainstream strategy.

This is where we as individual leaders come in – we are the instigators of these projects.

*Question 3.1:*    What ideas come to mind when you read the above? Are there any organisations and topics you'd like to research further? From whom could you find out if your organisation is or thinks of being involved in any of these coalitions or ways of working?

## Personal: how can I make material Impact?

'Never doubt that a small group of thoughtful, committed, citizens can change the world. Indeed, it is the only thing that ever has', says the quote generally attributed to the late Margaret Mead, an American cultural anthropologist.

If we think about it, every innovation, societal movement and other major change starts with one person's idea that grows by involving others and creating scalable concepts and solutions.

To illustrate this principle, think of the abolition of slavery. This did not happen by a sudden global collective flash of insight and immediate agreement. A few people started to think that this state of affairs was unacceptable. They gradually convinced others who started to think the same way. When a large enough proportion of the population and decision-makers thought the same – a tipping point was reached and the societal point of view had changed – the legislation was changed.

One of the things holding many of us back from personally trying to achieve impactful change is that we mainly remember people who left organisations to pursue large-scale change on the outside – 'heroic stories by lone warriors'. This is not a practical route for most of us, but up until the financial crisis it was often necessary to leave our mainstream employer to pursue Purpose – it was an either/or choice. This is no longer the case, as we will discover.

With businesses gearing up for their new roles and committing to targets via the Impact Coalitions, we now have an increasingly viable (and lower-risk) option to stay where we are, find a way to help create and deliver strategies with Impact in our organisations, and deliver towards these goals – via 'job-crafting'. This way, we also learn and prepare for the day when we might want to, or need to, pursue a new career elsewhere.

### 10X as a personal strategy tool

When we want to try to figure out what our Purpose could be, it is useful to think 'at scale' and use Impact as a strategy tool. Peter Diamandis, the author and founder of the X-Prize and co-founder of the Singularity University expresses this as: 'If you want to be a billionaire – find a billion-people problem to solve'.[43]

This is a different way of expressing John Elkington's 10X principle, adding in a personal wealth creation dimension. Not all of us wish to become billionaires, but most of us need to earn an income, so it is a useful and 'uncomplicated' way of experimenting with thinking about achieving significant Impact.

### Triggering maximum Impact without trying to solve the whole puzzle on our own

This becomes the next question, because if we feel that it is down to us, individually, to shoulder the whole weight of solving a major societal issue, we have a recipe for disillusionment and burnout.

Some of us might feel that large-scale work is intimidating or that at this career stage we would rather work at a smaller scale. Luckily, one does not preclude the other: creating and piloting a 10X solution or 10X business model, and then handing the baton to the next team for scaling, can also be the perfect Purpose-driven second career. We will see examples of executives deliberately setting out to do exactly this later in the book.

The point of 10X is: think 10X, then design and test a pilot of a size that suits you to prove the concept, instead of creating something that you later find out achieves only incremental change. Thinking 10X helps creative thinking – trying to solve 'impossible' problems means we have to think up completely new, 'not yet possible' solutions.

## We *can* effect change on major world issues – working together

In media, it seems like the world is spiralling inexorably into crisis in every area, from nutrition, health and security to climate change. One nasty scandal after another is revealed in business, government or charities. We could be forgiven for thinking it is hopeless for us as individuals to do anything about the 'big issues' and feel paralysed.

This is exacerbated as media reports mainly 'negative' news, as it gets the attention of our 'security-conscious' minds. How often do you see or hear 'a good news story'? The ratio is said to be 17:1 of 'bad news' to 'good news'.[44]

This bias towards reporting disasters hides the fact that together we have made massive progress on a number of important fronts.

### Progress on some major world issues from 1988 to 2015

Launched by world leaders and the UN in 2000, the Millennium Development Goals provided eight concrete and measurable goals to alleviate poverty and improve lives around the world by the end of 2015. Although a lot of work had been done previously in these and other areas, in 2000 businesses, civil society groups and individuals mobilised at local, regional, national and global levels in a way that had previously not been seen. Here are some of the achievements, as reported by the World Health Organization, the UN Foundation, and Liu et al. in *The Lancet*.

Since 1988, the following progress has been made:

- Polio was once a disease feared worldwide, striking suddenly and paralysing mainly children for life; it is now reduced by 99 per cent.[45]

Since 1990:

- More than 1 billion people moved out of extreme poverty, and the share of people in the developing world living in extreme poverty dropped from 47 per cent to a projected 14 per cent.
- Some 2.6 billion people have gained access to an improved source of drinking water.
- Child deaths have been reduced by more than half. In 1990, 12.7 million children under age 5 died, and in 2013 that number dropped to 6.3 million.[46]
- Maternal deaths have declined by 45 per cent.
- The projected share of undernourished people in developing regions is expected to drop by almost half, from 23.3 per cent in 1990–1992 to 12.9 per cent in 2014–2016.

Since 2000:

- The number of out-of-school children of primary school age has almost been cut in half, from 100 million children in 2000 to an estimated 57 million children in 2015.
- Between 2000 and 2013, new HIV infections decreased by approximately 40 per cent.
- From 2000 to 2015, more than 6.2 million malaria deaths were prevented, mostly of children under age 5.
- An estimated 37 million lives were saved through tuberculosis prevention, treatment and diagnosis solutions from 2000 to 2013.
- About two-thirds of countries in developing regions have closed the gender gap in primary education.[47]

Most surprisingly, even counting the current conflict in Syria, the number of armed conflicts, battle deaths, genocides and other mass killings are showing steep declines compared to a few decades ago. If you want to check for yourself, just follow the link in the reference; the article leads to further links to several institutions who track conflicts where the data can be verified.[48]

This does not mean that all problems are solved, far from, but it proves that when we act together we can make huge inroads into any area we choose to address.

*Question 3.2:*   What of the progress on major issues surprised you?

## Scandals and outrage: food for momentous change

Apart from world health, poverty, food, security and environmental issues, we are on almost a daily basis bombarded with other 'bad news' on a wide range of topics that we find outrageous: LIBOR (interbank interest lending rates) manipulation, rogue trading, tax evasion, corruption, increasing income inequality, diesel engine emissions cheating, security leaks, data system breaches, etc. These are also urgent, big and tough challenges.

Without minimising the severity of any of these issues, or denying the outrage of them, I ask you to experiment with applying a different viewpoint when you contemplate these issues: 'What could be done, and what could I do (with my knowledge, experience and contacts), to help change this?'

To practise another point of view is a useful technique for learning to see strategic opportunities for where we can help affect change.

To illustrate: think about the 'Panama Papers' scandal and the scale of tax evasion it revealed. Think of just how much important and purposeful work there will be in sorting all this out globally at every level of business and society. In governments, tax authorities, consulting, accounting and audit firms, businesses, financial services institutions, software companies, etc.

Affecting change around this topic, at scale, would be a huge benefit to society, law-abiding business and individuals. There will be worthwhile work in many areas, from policy and systems to governance.

A concrete example is the anti-corruption project by the B-Team, Transparency International, Global Witness and OpenCorporates, to create a Global Beneficial Ownership Register (GBOR) to end anonymous company ownership around the world – which got a huge boost in momentum due to the Panama Papers scandal.[49]

Our personal outrage is a great driving force for change. Where one person sees only a problem, someone else with other skills can see an opportunity for change. It all depends on our point of view. As the old story goes of the two shoe salesmen visiting a developing country for the first time. Telegraphing back to headquarters, one salesman writes, 'No future business potential. No one wears shoes here'. The other one writes, 'Huge business opportunity! No one wears shoes here!'.

Many of us are outraged at the inequalities we see in society, and we are seeing a change in the political stance around this topic. The message is clear: there are huge swathes of our populations that feel excluded, hard done by, left behind, and most importantly *not listened to*.

Whatever area we work in, we have a unique window of opportunity to create inclusive solutions. *To do this, we need to listen deeply and work open-mindedly with community leaders, develop solutions with them – not for them or to them – seeing them as equal partners and part of our teams.*

People are not 'the problem', they are the solution to unjust systems developed over time, as Dorian Burton and Brian Barnes, both affiliates of the Charles Hamilton Houston Institute for Race and Justice at Harvard Law School, point out in their article 'Shifting Philanthropy from Charity to Justice'.[50]

*Question 3.3:*   What issues outrage you? What could solutions to these issues be? How could you contribute to these solutions?

## Why this really is *the* time to start a Purpose-driven career

As mentioned, a few years ago, executives in a mainstream organisation wishing to pursue projects that had Impact in society had mainly two options: leave the organisation to pursue Purpose, or leave their position in the power structure through a sideways move into CSR or another functional area.

With citizens demanding change and major corporations waking up to their role in helping deliver this, we will likely see increasing numbers of organisations sign up to tri-sectorial Impact Coalitions. Society is becoming an important stakeholder for business and societal impact is gradually moving into the operational mainstream.

Helping your organisation understand how they can contribute to solving world issues, in tri-sectorial Impact Coalitions, shows strategic foresight and initiative, whether we work in a corporate – learning to work with government and NGOs/not-for-profits – or in one of the other sectors – learning to work with business.

We realise that we are at a pivotal point as a human family. What we do in the next few years will determine the trajectory of the world. We have a historic convergence of forces pushing and enabling us to affect real change – including the explosion of digital technology. We can create twenty-first-century solutions for twenty-first-century problems, instead of extrapolating old business models.

It is up to each one of us to seize this unique moment and create this new future we all want – together.

Let's end this chapter with the inspirational story of Nihal Kaviratne. It shows how we really can affect change in society from inside the organisation we work for, create profitable business for the company and real progress for the local community – and have a rewarding life. It shows how learning these skills in our executive positions sets the stage for impactful career transitioning when the time is right for us.

Nihal Kaviratne is a thoughtful, insightful and incredibly active executive now in his early seventies. Until 2005, he held several CEO and senior regional roles around the world with Unilever, a company he worked in for 40 years.

Nihal has always had a social conscience, and thanks to his long career with Unilever he was trusted to work on social issues as part of the business, when he saw them as key to Unilever's success. This was long before Paul Polman arrived at Unilever and made this approach a core part of the Unilever strategy going forward, articulated as the 'Sustainable Living Plan'.

Nihal reminisces:

> I learned the critical importance of this way of working when I was heading up Unilever Indonesia. When I arrived, it was a difficult business and environment. The country was literally 'on fire' with crises erupting everywhere. To understand what was going on, I went to see the territorial commander (who was to later become the country's president), explaining that it was important for Unilever's operations to not be interrupted as basic civil supplies of soap, toothpaste and so on were vital to the people.
>
> The territorial commander explained to me the concept of 'circles of interest' that is now embedded globally in Unilever's operations; the inner circle – the immediate vicinity of the plant, next to it the circle of influence, and thirdly the circle of interest. The key is to understand what the local community [on your doorstep] needs, and do you have a resource that matches that need? When their situation changes, it becomes in the community's interest to keep your operations going.

Unilever was originally founded on the Purpose of 'bringing hygiene to homes', and as unhygienic conditions are rife in many developing countries, Nihal decided to take on the project of cleaning up the Brantas River in East Java (Surabaya).

The local tradition was to have latrines at the back of houses, emptying into the river. It was very polluted, and local residents and industries used it as a dump for all kinds of rubbish. It was a real health hazard.

Nihal's philosophy is 'think big, start small, move fast' (pretty much like Silicon Valley VCs). Starting with five pilot villages, they 'turned people's houses back to front', moving the fronts of the houses to face the river, and the latrines from where they were emptying into the river to the street side of the houses, and building latrine blocks.

Once this was successful, he convinced other businesses to adopt five villages each, and over the next few years cleaned up the entire length of the river. It changed the behaviour of the residents, who now don't want to throw anything into the river. A physical change created a behavioural change.

And while he was at it, he created work for 600,000 farmers. Unilever had acquired a soya sauce company with a very small market share. This low market share was due to the low availability of the type of black soya beans needed, as they could not be productively grown in Indonesia.

Nihal thus set up an R&D project with an Indonesian university for developing high-yielding black soya beans that could be grown in Indonesia. They tested them out first with 600 farmers, then with 6,000, and growing these soya beans is now the livelihood of 600,000 Indonesian farmers. Unilever are now the market leader, and growing these black soya beans in other Asian countries such as Myanmar. Unilever and the university hold joint patent rights, and the patent is called Mallika (named after Nihal's daughter). This development project has benefited the country and the region hugely, as well as Unilever.

To successfully implement such strategies, according to Nihal:

> A company needs to focus on selected themes, where they have resources for change, and the company needs to 'own' that theme. It needs to relate to the community you are addressing, and serious resources need to be put behind it. If you don't, the investment will be dissipated.

After his successes in Indonesia, Nihal was asked to move to various locations and illustrious positions, but instead he asked Unilever for a 'fade-out' period where he could prepare his transition to 'post-Unilever' life and work. This was very important according to Nihal, in order to explore and plan for the next stage.

In his usual understated way, when asked how he orchestrated a transition to such a purposeful and impactful second career, he said: 'I guess I am just following the Hindu philosophy, that life is a series of stages and you just plan and prepare for the next one'.

Nihal is currently Chairman AkzoNobel in India as well as on the Board of GSK Pharma, on the board of OLAM, StarHub and DBS bank in Singapore (and their foundation for social enterprise), advises the UK's DFID on development project lending in India, is involved in the NFP sector in the cancer area, and founded St Judes, the charity he started to provide housing and holistic care for poor children and their families when the children receive cancer treatment, as otherwise they often live on the street.

When you meet Nihal, you meet a man living truly in line with his values, with huge Impact, who also enjoys and honours his life and family to the fullest.

*Question 3.4:*    What strikes you in Nihal's story?

## Takeaways

'Impact' in the context of this book means having a material effect on solving an issue in society.

We need 10X Impact solutions (exponential solutions) to solve exponential problems. The business opportunity to deliver just four of the 17 SDGs is a US$12 trillion opportunity for business.

Impact Coalitions – global, cross-sectorial coalitions – are rapidly emerging, with large numbers of major businesses and other organisations signing up to deliver SDGs and other societal goals.

We can make amazing progress on major issues – if we work together – as can be seen from the progress on the Millennium Development Goals, for example.

With the confluence of businesses realising their need to be increasingly engaged in solving societal issues, the rapid technology development putting solutions within our grasp to many problems and the rise of Impact Coalitions, this really is *the* moment to start a Purpose-driven career.

## Notes

1  *Oxford Living English Dictionaries.* Retrieved at: https://en.oxforddictionaries.com/definition/impact.
2  *Business Dictionary.* Retrieved at: www.businessdictionary.com/definition/impact.html.
3  Carney, M. (29 September 2015). *Breaking the Tragedy of the Horizon: Climate Change and Financial Stability.* Speech. Retrieved from: www.bankofengland.co.uk.
4  McKie, R. (15 July 2017). *Maize, Rice, Wheat: Alarm at Rising Climate Risk to Vital Crops.* The Guardian. Retrieved from: www.theguardian.com.
5  Friedlander, B. (26 June 2017). *Rising Sea Levels Could Make One Fifth of the World's Population Refugees by 2100.* World Economic Forum. Retrieved from: www.weforum.org.

6  Elkington, J. (27 September 2016). *Tomorrow's Business Models Will Be X-Rated*. Medium Corporation. Retrieved from: https://medium.com.

7  System.IQ. (17 January 2017). *Better Business Better World*. BSDC. Retrieved from: http://report.businesscommission.org.

8  Project Breakthrough website: http://breakthrough.unglobalcompact.org.

9  Elkington, J. (4 May 2017). *Saving the Planet from Ecological Disaster Is a $12 Trillion Opportunity*. Harvard Business Review. Retrieved from: www.hbr.com.

10 Unilever (n.d.) *Sustainable Living Plan*. Retrieved from: www.unilever.com/sustainable-living/.

11 Grayson, D. and Nelson, J. (2013). *Corporate Responsibility Coalitions*. Shipley, UK: Greenleaf Publishing.

12 Dowd, L. (30 May 2017). *60% of Companies Are Integrating the SDGs into Business Strategy*. Ethical Corporation. Retrieved from: www.ethicalcorp.com.

13 SDSN website: www.unsdsn.org.

14 We Mean Business website: www.wemeanbusinesscoalition.org.

15 Nigel Topping LinkedIn profile: www.linkedin.com/in/nigel-topping-14633b6/.

16 Sustainable Brands (11 July 2017). *RE100 Reaches 100 Companies Committed TO 100% Renewable Energy*. Retrieved from: www.sustainablebrands.com.

17 RE100 News (10 July 2017). *World First as 100 Multi Nationals Target 100% Renewable Electricity*. Retrieved from: http://re100.org.

18 E.ON (8 March 2017). *The Business Benefits of Using Renewable Electricity*. The Telegraph. Retrieved from: www.telegraph.co.uk.

19 Science Based Targets website: http://sciencebasedtargets.org.

20 Partnership on AI website: www.partnershiponai.org/partners/.

21 Natural Capital Coalition website: http://naturalcapitalcoalition.org.

22 Rathu, A. (18 January 2017). *A Global Alliance Is Investing $500 Million to Stop the Spread of Deadly Outbreaks We Are Utterly Unprepared For*. Quartz. Retrieved from: https://qz.com.

23 Global Business Coalition for Education website: http://gbc-education.org.

24 Busch, C. (14 June 2017). *China–California Climate Cooperation: A New Model for States, Nations in the Trump Era*. Forbes. Retrieved from: www.forbes.com.

25 Boffey, D. and Neslen, A. (1 June 2017). *China and EU Strengthen Promise to Paris Deal with US Poised to Step Away*. The Guardian. Retrieved from: www.theguardian.com.

26 We Are Still In website: http://wearestillin.com.

27 B-Team website: http://bteam.org/team/.

28 The Rise Fund website: http://therisefund.com.

29 Bank, D. (21 December 2016). *Billionaires' Ball: A Look at TPG's $2 Billion Rise Fund*. Impact Alpha. Retrieved from: https://news.impactalpha.com.

30 TPG Announcement (26 April 2017). *The Rise Fund Invests in Education Technology Platform EverFi*. BusinessWire. Retrieved from: www.businesswire.com.

31 Dorbion, I. (4 May 2017). *TPG's The Rise Fund to Provide $50 Mln to Dodla*. PE Hub. Retrieved from: www.pehub.com.

32 Wikipedia (n.d.) *Daniel A. Epstein Biography*. Retrieved from: https://en.wikipedia.org/wiki/Daniel_A._Epstein.

33 Unreasonable Goals website: https://unreasonable-goals.com.

34 Schiller, B. (14 July 2017). *This Accelerator Is Helping a Social Purpose for Each of the Sustainable Development Goals*. Fast Company. Retrieved from: www.fastcompany.com.

35 Wong, J.C. (24 July 2017). *Facebook Worker Living in Garage to Zuckerberg: Challenges Are Right Outside Your Door*. The Guardian. Retrieved from: www. theguardian.com.

36 Isidore, C. and Wattles, J. (29 March 2016). *California Hikes Minimum Wage to $15*. CNN Money. Retrieved from: http://money.cnn.com.

37 Department of Work and Pensions (15 February 2017). *The Employment Rate Is at a Record 74.6% – the Highest Employment Rate Since Records Began in 1971*. Retrieved from: www.gov.uk.

38 Office of National Statistics (21 July 2017). *Overview of the UK population: July 2017*. Retrieved from: www.ons.gov.uk.

39 International Centre for Social Franchising (25 July 2017). *Franchising: The Potential to Create High Quality Jobs in London*. Retrieved from: https://tsip.co.uk.

40 Somerstown Profile. UK Police. Retrieved from: www. http://crimeinlondon.com/camden/st-pancras-and-somers-town/profile/.

41 Medland, D. (2 May 2017). *The Secret to Grant Thornton's New-Found Strength*. CMI. Retrieved from: www.managers.org.uk.

42 Scott, N. (4 April 2016). *Sacha Romanovitch: The Grant Thornton CEO on Making the UK Economy Vibrant*. IoD. Retrieved from: www.director.co.uk.

43 Winfrey, G. (13 June 2014). *Peter Diamandis: Want to Be a Billionaire? Solve a Billion-Person Problem*. Inc.com. Retrieved from: www.inc.com.

44 Williams, R. (1 November 2014). *Why We Love Bad News*. Psychology Today Blog. Retrieved from: www.psychologytoday.com.

45 World Health Organization (2015). *10 Facts About Polio*. Retrieved from: www.who.int.

46 Liu, L., Oza, S., Hogan, D., Perin, J., Rudan, I., Lawn, J., et al. (31 January 2015). Analysis. *The Lancet*, 385(9966): 430–440.

47 Myers, S. (6 July 2015). *Yes We Can Solve Global Problems*. UN Foundation Blog. Retrieved from: http://unfoundationblog.org.

48 Pinker, S. (20 March 2015). *Guess What? More People Are Living in Peace Now. Just Look at the Numbers*. The Guardian Opinion. Retrieved from: www.theguardian.com.

49 Global Witness (4 April 2016). *New Global Register to Shine Light on Anonymous Companies, a Root Cause of Corrupt, Illegal Activities*. Retrieved from: www.globalwitness.org.

50 Burton, D. and Barnes, B. (3 January 2017). *Shifting Philanthropy from Charity to Justice*. Stanford Social Innovation Review. Retrieved from: www.ssir.org.

# Part II

# Career development

## How does it work?

In Chapter 4, we will cover why learning career development skills and continuously developing ourselves and generating new career options is crucial.

In Chapter 5, we move on to how a career change process works, both practically (career change) and psychologically (career transition). We often put a lot of effort into understanding how to execute the practical career change process, but not the psychological process we go through when we try to create new identities for ourselves.

As any executive who has done a career change will tell you, this second aspect is the tough part. Understanding what is happening to us is useful – we realise that this is all part of the natural process, and that it is in fact essential to go through this period of uncertainty and questioning.

In Chapter 6, we will discover the skills and competencies we need to be effective tri-sector leaders and develop our careers.

As we progress through these chapters, we will get increasingly practical in approach, and you will see many executives' personal stories appear.

# Chapter 4

# Career development skills a high priority for all

*We will live longer, and to finance our later years many of us will need to work well into our seventies or even eighties. At the same time, employment security is more and more unpredictable.*

*Learning how to develop career options is one of the most important things we can invest in for our future well-being. This strategic skill will become literally survival-critical, and should be taught by our employers as part of every person's basic development curriculum.*

## Why career development skills will be a vital skill going forward

With the combination of increased longevity and the ever-increasing unpredictability of our medium- and longer-term employment situations, one would think that learning how to generate options for reshaping our careers would be a high-priority activity for executives and their organisations.

This is rarely the case. Very few organisations have this as a part of their leadership development curriculum, and most executives don't allocate time to this until they are faced with redundancy or looming retirement.

As we will live longer and want or need to work well beyond age 70 or even 80, learning how to develop career options is one of the most important things we can invest in for our future well-being. This strategic skill will become literally survival-critical.

In my view, we should all be taught career development skills as part of the mandatory leadership development curriculum in the organisations we work in, just like time management, team management and all the other '-ments'.

This would be a practical option for organisations and society, as all pension systems – state, company and private – will not cope with the financial burden of all of us living longer and drawing pensions for 30 to 40 years.

While the organisations we work for are not teaching us these skills, learning them ourselves is a very good investment for the future.

## 'No one works for McKinsey forever' – or for any other organisation

Few of us think seriously or act proactively about the reality that one day we *will* all leave our employer. We (and our employers) behave as if this is not a fact and stick our heads in the sand until forced to act.

Anyone who has been around in business the past few decades knows that we might end up leaving well before the time we would have chosen ourselves, due to changes outside our control, or we might ourselves one day decide that we want a change in how we work. Ultimately, we will all 'retire'.

Currently, in a majority of organisations, the career development processes are mainly 'promotion readiness' processes, and career development skills training is largely non-existent, and mainly served via 'outplacement' services during redundancy programmes.

Martin Swain, previously Vice President for Global Employee Relations, Inclusion and Diversity at GSK, expresses this succinctly: 'I have always wondered why we wait until redundancy to give the best possible career advice to our people'.[1]

One of the reasons for this underinvestment is that although most organisations claim that people are their greatest asset, they still frequently see them as an 'asset', not a human being.

If people in our organisations are seen as 'divestible assets', little wonder that fear of being divested is high in employees. When employees leave such organisations, it is as if they never existed. Who thinks of a divested machine? Why would you invest in the 'future life' of an asset as long as it is well maintained enough to work here and now?

If you find this a harsh statement, contemplate the following: when people leave your organisation, do you, your colleagues or your company speak about them, keep in touch with them, invite them to training events or allow them to work with you on a consulting basis?

If you answered no to most of the above, you are with the majority of how organisations work today. Briefly below, and in more detail in Chapter 11, we will see that some leading organisations are answering yes to all of the above; they see employees as lifetime employees, inside or outside the organisation.

Organisations might also fear that executives they wish to keep will leave if they know how to generate new career options for themselves. Hence, investing in preparing employees for the day they might or might not leave can seem as neither urgent nor important in the short term.

In terms of the fear that executives might leave if they become well prepared to find options for themselves, I have personally observed the opposite effect.

Executives who learn how to develop their own careers and know that they will have other options, if needed, are more confident in themselves.

They don't feel that reorganisations are life-or-death situations, and become calmer leaders, able to keep their heads cool in a situation that might threaten their employment. Often, they become quite sanguine about their own positions, and might choose very objectively to eliminate their own jobs in a merger. Likewise, they will not hang on by the skin of their teeth to jobs or organisations that don't treat them with respect or are draining their energy out of them.

Richard Branson summarises this thought perfectly on Virgin's website: 'Train people well enough so they can leave, treat them well enough so they don't want to'.[2]

## Alumni: we are also immensely valuable after leaving an organisation

There are enlightened companies out there who view this question of life-long career development differently. They all have one thing in common – they have discovered the terrific 'lifetime value of past employees' – alumni.

Particularly, tech and strategy consulting firms are ahead of the curve on this. For tech firms, alumni are literally a 'life-or-death' issue, as these networks are their sources of help, market intelligence, business and innovation, and one of the key factors of success in Silicon Valley.[3]

When you leave organisations who do not value alumni, it is like you have never existed. These organisations only view executives currently on their payroll as having 'value', and it follows that they would not see any incentive in investing in their futures beyond the current employment.

In contrast, in *The Alliance*, Reid Hoffman – the founder of LinkedIn – explains that at LinkedIn, although they wish employees to stay, their policy is to develop them for whatever they want to achieve at LinkedIn *or elsewhere*. This means that if LinkedIn can't deliver what the employee aspires to do, they will be excellent candidates to achieve their aspirations elsewhere.[4]

If we all had such honest conversations, with our organisations and ourselves, we would automatically learn to continuously develop ourselves in a way that reflects the changes in the outside world and become more effective leaders in our own organisations – whether we choose to affect change where we are or leave to do this elsewhere.

Another organisation that for many years has had a radically different view on this topic is McKinsey. The expression 'No one works for McKinsey forever' is a saying McKinsey leaders are familiar with, and the firm's 'Executive Talent Network' helps to place Partners in prestigious organisations around the world when they feel that it is time to leave McKinsey.

The firm is known as 'the CEO factory', and it is easy to see why when you look at the list of where current and former McKinsey Partners have ended up. Over 175 current or previous leaders of major corporations, government bodies, NFPs and world-class educational institutions have McKinsey heritage.[5]

What McKinsey realised years ago was that by helping Partners transition into senior executive positions on the client side, they would have a favourably disposed client base. To McKinsey, alumni are deemed critical for their future business success.

Bain & Co. is another organisation who, over the past few years, have developed a sophisticated global Partner service to help them transition to second careers.

Other professional services firms are also starting to develop career transition services. Most are still 'pre-retirement programmes' allowing Partners to think of what they wish to do when the (often more or less mandatory) retirement date is looming. Most such programmes give guidance on financial planning and how to become a non-executive director for businesses or a trustee in charities, and an opportunity to gradually phase out work, time-wise.

These pre-retirement programmes are a start; however, they are not addressing the fact that many senior leaders are not yet ready to go part-time, portfolio or 100 per cent non-executive. And they do not address the wish to pursue Purpose – to contribute in a way that has real and measureable impact on major issues in society.[6]

In Chapter 11, we will explore more about what leading companies are doing to help executives develop second and third careers.

*Question 4.1:*   How does your organisation relate to alumni – people who have left?

## We should have our careers in 'permanent beta'

If our employers are not investing in our career development skills, we need to personally invest in learning how to truly own our lives and careers. This way, we will be able to steer our own ships through the tough spots that will inevitably show up during our careers, being in charge of our own journey.

In his book *The Start-Up of You*, Reid Hoffman makes the case for why we should look at our careers as a 'start-up business' and keep them in continuous 'beta-testing': 'Keeping your career in permanent beta forces you to acknowledge that you have bugs, that there's new development to do on yourself, that you will need to adapt and evolve'.[7]

'Permanent beta' in career development terms means a lifelong commitment to continuous learning and personal growth. Career development is not something done early in a career and then executed as a one-off project, or done once when we are made redundant or plan to retire. As the world around us and our organisations are constantly changing, we have to continue to change and adapt as well.

This is what Reid Hoffman calls continuous *ABZ planning*. Plan A is what you are doing now, and it represents your current competitive advantage. Small continuous iterations are made to Plan A.

Plan B is what you aim to change for and pivot to when you need or want to change. It is not a fixed destination, and keeps on developing as we learn. We develop new skills and competencies to reach our Plan B.[8] Creating Purpose-driven Plan B's is what this book is about.

Plan Z is your fallback plan if things go wrong, your lifeboat. Plan Z is what allows you to take on the risks in Plan A and Plan B. Another way of thinking of Plan Z is: What is your certain, reliable and stable plan if all your career plans fall over? This is a short-term stopgap solution that allows you time to regroup and relaunch a Plan A without going bankrupt, becoming homeless or unemployable.[9]

For most executives, Plan Z is normally about how much financial runway we have before we need to earn new income. A practical benchmark is to have enough financial resources to keep yourself and your family finically afloat for at least two to three, and ideally four to five, years without any additional income. This allows for most career restarts, educational periods and periods of societal service at lower pay.

This means negotiating with the family about what you can agree to save on in order to lower outgoings for this period without severely impacting the standard of living to such a degree that it would cause serious friction.

For a number of us, for if or when the pension 'time bomb' hits, it might be wise to have more radical plans in place for 'if it all goes really pear-shaped' for a significant period of time.

Remember what it was like at the height of the financial crisis, when we were not sure if the banking system – and our savings – would survive? Many of us made contingency plans for if this catastrophe would become reality. We might have a similar feeling of free fall when our pensions won't pay anywhere near what was planned. Having a robust Plan Z in place will be an absolute necessity. This is a topic most people avoid discussing, as it is very uncomfortable; however, in my discussions with many executives, it is clear that this topic is very real.

*Question 4.2:*   How much financial runway, in months or years, do you have if you would lose your job and had to launch a career change – without radically changing your lifestyle – before you have to earn new income?

*Question 4.3:*   If everything went utterly pear-shaped, what is your fallback plan?

## Takeaways

With our increasing longevity and need for providing earnings for probably many years into the future, learning how to develop our careers will be vital.

We need to look at our careers like a constant 'work in progress', so we are ready to move to a new opportunity with reasonable ease, should we need to.

Organisations need to become better at helping employees develop later careers, in-house or externally, and value their alumni, as we will have fewer young workers in the future – especially willing to work in mature industries.

## Notes

1 Hoffmann, A. (2016). *Purpose Driven Leader – Purpose Driven Career*. Cranfield University's School of Management Doughty Centre for Corporate Responsibility, p. 12. Retrieved from: www.cranfield.ac.uk.
2 Virgin Website: www.virgin.com/richard-branson/look-after-your-staff.
3 Hoffman, R., Casnocha, B. and Yeh, C. (2014). *The Alliance: Managing Talent in the Networked Age*. Brighton, MA: Harvard Business Review Press, Kindle edition, location 905.
4 Hoffman, R., Casnocha, B. and Yeh, C. (2014). *The Alliance: Managing Talent in the Networked Age*. Brighton, MA: Harvard Business Review Press, Kindle edition, location 297.
5 Wikipedia (n.d.) *List of Current and Former McKinsey Company Consultants*. Retrieved from: https://en.wikipedia.org/wiki/List_of_current_and_former_McKinsey_%26_Company_consultants.
6 Hoffmann, A. (2016). *Purpose Driven Leader – Purpose Driven Career*. Cranfield University's School of Management Doughty Centre for Corporate Responsibility, pp. 39–42. Retrieved from: www.cranfield.ac.uk.
7 Hoffman, R. (2012). *The Start-Up of You: Adapt to the Future, Invest in Yourself, and Transform Your Career*. London, UK: Cornerstone Digital, Kindle edition, location 339.
8 Hoffman, R. (2012). *The Start-Up of You: Adapt to the Future, Invest in Yourself, and Transform Your Career*. London, UK: Cornerstone Digital, Kindle edition, location 713.
9 Hoffman, R. (2012). *The Start-Up of You: Adapt to the Future, Invest in Yourself, and Transform Your Career*. London, UK: Cornerstone Digital, Kindle edition, location 947.

# Chapter 5

# How career change and career transitions work

*In this chapter, we will discuss how the career change (physical) and career transition (psychological) processes happen, and why going through career change is often such an anxious and agonising time.*

*We will also cover the Career Transformational Assets – self-knowledge, openness to new experiences, and ability to build strategic and dynamic networks – that are vital for developing our leadership skills and careers, enabling us to get a new view of ourselves and what we could contribute to in our organisations and in society.*

## Career Change, Career Transitions and Career Transformational Assets

William Bridges, the American authority on career and life transitions, told us over 25 years ago, '*Change* is situational. *Transition* is psychological'.

He continues:

> It is not those events [the changes], but rather the inner reorientation and self-redefinition that you have to go through in order to incorporate any of those changes into your life. Without a transition, a change is just a rearrangement of the furniture. Unless transition happens, the change won't work, because it doesn't 'take'. Our society talks a lot about change; but it seldom deals with transition. Unfortunately for us, it is the transition that blind-sides us and is often the source of our troubles.[1]

The Career Change process and Career Transition process each have three stages, and we successfully move through them by developing and using our three Career Transformational Assets – the latter named by Lynda Gratton and Andrew Scott in their 2016 seminal book *The 100-Year Life*.[2] We will cover the two career processes in this chapter, and the Career Transformational Assets in detail in Chapters 6 and 9.

*Table 5.1* Summary of stages of the Career Change and Career Transition processes and Career Transformational Assets

| Career Change process | Career Transition process | Career Transformational Assets |
| --- | --- | --- |
| Germination | Ending | Self-knowledge |
| Discovery | Unknown Zone | Dynamic/diverse network building |
| Fruition | New Beginnings | Openness to new experiences |

In reality, these stages are neither sequential nor clearly divided, and the two processes happen at the same time and blur into each other.

This is why changing career is so unsettling and confusing. We have no idea where we are heading, and this consumes a lot of energy and lowers our self-confidence, just as we need this energy and confidence to go out and explore the world outside our comfort zone. Knowing what is going on, and that it is normal, might help to make the process more manageable.

A major career change takes considerable time and is disruptive. Learning how to do this while we are long-term employed is clearly useful. We can learn, expand our knowledge and networks, and practise some of our new leadership skills while earning income. The principles below also apply if we are starting from scratch after leaving an organisation.

Looking back on *career changes*, most executives can recognise these three stages:

- Germination;
- Discovery; and
- Fruition.

In the *Germination* stage, a gradual increase in dissatisfaction with the status quo and increased momentum for a change is building. We are literally germinating the change inside.

Once we realise that we need to do something about our situation, the activity-oriented and quite lengthy *Discovery* stage begins. We are exploring new ideas for what we might do next, building new strategic networks and trying on new identities.

As we start to see where we would like to head, and that this is practically possible, our decision to change ripens, and we start to manifest real opportunities to contribute in our chosen area. We are reaping the concrete fruits of our labours – *Fruition*.

At the same time as we are active with our change activities, the inner *career transition* stages are taking place:

- Ending;
- Unknown Zone; and
- New Beginnings.

For something new to begin, we need to let go of the old – *Ending*. This is necessary as we define ourselves, who we are, and what we can or can't do by the association and attachment to activities, people and places we have been comfortable with for a long time. It becomes the way we define our identity. To build a new identity, a new view of how we see ourselves, we will have to let a considerable part of the old self-definitions go.

I am quite sure that this simple statement has already given an inkling of why it is so hard to career-transition. Who am I if I am not a VP in GE/Unilever/Tata . . . ?

All life transitions are times of confusion, and career transitions are no exception. How well we will be able to go through these confusing times with a minimum of personal stress depends on how well we have developed our *Career Transformational Assets*. These are:

- Self-knowledge;
- Ability to build strategic and diverse networks; and
- Openness to new experiences.

Without some degree of *self-knowledge*, about our values and motivations, we are not able to understand and make decisions regarding what might be right for us for the next stage of our lives.

Without the ability to build *strategic and diverse networks*, we will not be able to connect to people who can help us transition into new sectors and new roles.

Finally, without *openness to new experiences* where we can learn about the world and ourselves, get new ideas and try out new identities, we will not be able to complete our transitions.

We will not cover the theory of these skills in more detail as they are fairly self-explanatory; instead, you will see them play out again and again through the other processes and in executives' stories, which you will now see appearing with increasing frequency.

As we will see in Chapter 6, in addition to being vital for successfully navigating a career change, the Career Transformational Assets are also key for developing the leadership skills now needed to succeed as a leader and ensuring that we can successfully create Purpose-driven careers with Impact.

## The Career Transition process

We will begin by exploring the Career Transition process (Endings – Unknown Zone – New Beginnings) in some depth, as this is the part of the process that we find the hardest to deal with – and it is vital for developing a successful new career.

### Endings

Every transition begins with an ending. We often don't realise that we have made an ending until we have made a lot of changes and realise that we are now 'someone else and somewhere else' psychologically.

We then have to accept and make peace with the ending to make sure we can fully enjoy our new beginnings. If we don't internalise the changes, we will be partly stuck in the past and unlikely to reap the full benefits of the changes we have made.

As a simple illustration for what we mean by this, think about the behaviour of the almost caricature-like individuals who try to pretend they are in their twenties when they are actually in their forties or fifties. They have not internalised the fact that their youth stage has ended.

To make room for the new, we have to let go of the old. When we change careers, we don't just change roles – the external change – we change our internal definitions of who we are, our identity. Who we think we are is defined to a large extent by our current roles and relationships. If we don't let go of some of them, we cannot move forward.

As Helen Rose Ebaugh, Professor Emeritus at the University of Houston, showed in her groundbreaking research on role exits in the late 1980s, the bigger change we make to our roles – especially if this role change is irreversible and is central to our identity – the harder it is for us to work through the changes, and the longer the transition needs to take to work all this through.

If we spend the required time working through the transition, we are normally happy with our new role and identity. It is when we have not been aware of some potential major sequential changes and prepared for them that we struggle with the new role and identity.[3]

We often hang on to our previous roles long after we have left an organisation, and may define ourselves by them for a long time.

As one previous senior Shell executive described it:

> After choosing to leave Shell in my early fifties, I was doing the most incredibly high-profile, important and rewarding work with the government and in my county. Yet it took me seven years to stop saying 'I used to work for Shell' when people asked me what I do.

Part of our job is to shake off this previous identification, to prepare a new identity, accept that we have had an ending, and mourn the loss of what now will be no more.

This acceptance of a new stage is particularly poignant at the mid/later career stage, as at this point many decisions are not really reversible.

When we are younger, we can take a career detour for a couple of years and still go back to our previous career, with maybe only the loss of a couple of years on the promotional ladder as a consequence. This is not the case in the later stages of our careers.

It should be, but current societal and business attitudes make many decisions more or less irreversible from our early/mid-fifties. If we at this point decide to focus on a non-executive director career, the likelihood to be approached for a full-time executive job is quite small. Likewise, once we reach age 70 (at least in the West, where youth and ambition is more prized than age and wisdom) few calls are likely to come for board positions in major listed companies.

This means that when we make career decisions in our fifties, we have a lot of endings we need to acknowledge, mourn and make peace with. We are facing several forks in the road, and once we have decided to take a particular direction we cannot easily – or not at all – turn back.

Women, who often go through 'the change' in their fifties, have additional endings to deal with while creating their new identities. I am no longer a young woman (ending role and identity), neither am I an old woman (far ahead) – who am I now? Men, of course, go through the same questions, but not necessarily at the same time as major career direction decisions crop up.

This is why the mid/later career change and transition process takes time. We need to be finished with our endings and feel happy and excited about our new beginnings.

It takes several years to prepare a new career and explore new future directions and identities. Staying at our current employer, in a well-known environment where we are trusted, contributing to change in our current organisation, is thus a practical route while we figure out what we want to do.

Endings are so hard, says William Bridges, because we all deal with endings differently and new endings bring up our old mindsets to previous endings and expose all kinds of feelings.[4]

In our society, we don't learn how to deal with such strong feelings. Each of us needs to understand how we personally deal with endings so we can work through them to the best of our abilities. Pushing these feelings down does not make them go away; they will just become a psychological ball and chain, holding us back from fully realising the potential of our new direction.

### Unknown Zone

Once we have realised that change has to happen, we enter the Unknown Zone. We know we do not want to stay where we are, but we have no idea where we are heading or 'who we want to be'. Sometimes we don't even know 'who we are' as we might not recognise our own behaviour, thoughts or dreams.

This can feel like being in a small anchorless and rudderless dinghy with no sight of the shore we left or any inkling of where there is any land ahead. We might wish ourselves back in our safe well-known situation, and for a while we are mentally vacillating between new possibilities and the old certainties. William Bridges expresses this perfectly: 'One day everything seems to be coming apart; the next day, life goes on as usual, and we wonder whether we have been imagining our difficulties'.[5]

Like nature shedding leaves in autumn, hibernating over winter to make spring possible, the time in the Unknown Zone where we let go of old beliefs and ways of doing things and try out new identities is *crucial*.

This can be very uncomfortable, but without this time we will not find our new destination. We have to go through this crucible, this melting and burning of old ideas and identities, to be able to forge our new direction.

As Herminia Ibarra, the INSEAD professor and doyenne of leadership and career transitions, expresses it in *Working Identity*:

> No matter how common it has become, no one has figured out how to avoid the turmoil of career change. Most people experience the transition to a new working life as a time of confusion, loss, insecurity, and uncertainty. And this uncertain period lasts much longer than anyone imagines at the outset.[6]

When it feels really unsettling, it can be good to remind ourselves of the brilliant quote attributed to John Lennon, immortalised in the 2011 British film *The Best Exotic Marigold Hotel*. The young and idealistic hotel manager Simil Patel says to his exasperated guests, while everything is falling down around his ears in total chaos, 'Everything will be all right in the end . . . if it's not all right, then it's not yet the end'.[7]

The experience of many executives – including my own – is that once we have found our new direction, most of us realise that this time of chaos and uncertainty was in reality one of the greatest gifts of our lives.

### New Beginnings

As we gradually come to clarity of what our next stage will contain and experiment with a new identity, we start to see new possibilities, New Beginnings.

What we are meant to be or do next, 'our Purpose', rarely arrives perfectly defined, complete with bolts of lightning and fanfares by heavenly trumpets. It is more often like the gradual lifting of a fog. Gradually it lightens, and one day sunshine is breaking through.

William Bridges expresses this as: 'Sometimes the beginning results from careful and conscious effort, but for most people important new beginnings have a mysterious and sometimes accidental quality to them'.[8]

Or as Albert Einstein said: 'The intellect has little to do on the road to discovery. There comes a leap in consciousness, call it Intuition or what you will, the solution comes to you and you don't know how or why'.[9]

There are 'aha moments' along the way, where we suddenly gain real insights. We will hear from a number of executives on how their 'moments of insight' arrived, but let me first share a pivotal moment from my own career to illustrate what William Bridges means with 'accidental' new beginnings. At the end of this chapter, I will share the gradual arrival of my Purpose that also illustrates many of the aspects we will have covered.

### Other people see what you don't see: how I found out I was a good coach

'Great news, I have resigned!' said Anna Catalano, then Group Vice President Marketing of BP, as I arrived at our table at Mosimann's private dining club in London's elegant Belgravia in July 2003. 'Great news,' I echoed, 'Deloitte just made me redundant after our failed buyout of the firm!'

A highly celebratory lunch with plenty of champagne followed, where a number of life changing insights were exchanged.

'It is your "fault" that I have resigned,' Anna said. Seeing my surprised face, she continued:

> Do you remember when you came for lunch that first time in my office after we met at that Fortune conference? You asked me some very good questions about my work and my life. I started to question myself as well as the organisation about my future. It became clear that my dreams and ambitions were not going to be fulfilled there, so I decided to resign. I'd rather go now at 42 and do something new and interesting than coast until 50-something and then leave feeling I missed the boat . . .

Her next statement stunned me: 'You are very good at making people think about important questions, you should do this for a living.'

I would never, in a million years, have thought that my ability to coach was something unique, had she not pointed it out. As it came naturally to me, I assumed that everyone could do this.

A life-changing journey had started for us both: for Anna, to become one of the USA's most experienced industrial non-executive directors and proponents of corporate governance also active in the Alzheimer's Association; for me, a second career change (my first career change was from corporate executive to management consulting) to become an executive coach, senior executive 'headhunter' and part-time academic working to help executives find Purpose and help change how we do business.

How this unfolded can be seen at the end of this chapter, and you will recognise many of the things we will have covered.

*Making decisions quickly to stop the uncertainty: emotional foreclosure*

Not knowing where we are heading is sometimes so painful that we try to 'take charge' and make a quick decision to stop the agonising uncertainty.

We end up doing the adult equivalent of what James E. Marcia, an American clinical and developmental psychologist, defined as *identity foreclosure* when studying adolescents: 'The foreclosure status is when a commitment is made without exploring alternatives. Often these commitments are based on parental ideas and beliefs that are accepted without question'.[10]

From what I have observed, the same also holds true for us adults. Either settling for something that other people are comfortable with – spouse, family, peers, friends or business circle – or making a decision, *any decision*, regarding what we'll do next, to just stop the agony of not knowing where we are heading.

I use the term '*emotional foreclosure*' to describe this phenomenon to executives, for which I have no scientific basis; however, it seems to make the point clear when they are desperate to make a decision to just stop the pain of not knowing where they are heading.

'Emotional foreclosure' can lead to disastrous career decisions that stop the uncertainty in the short term, but often result in us quickly leaving our new employer. The unfinished transition process we were in will continue to its conclusion, even if we think we have stopped it by making a decision. In William Bridges' language: we made a change, but not a transition.

What follows, then, in terms of self-recrimination and loss of self-confidence, is much worse than putting up with a longer period of uncertainty while we are already in it. It can be extremely difficult to say no to a new job when we need the income, as the following story illustrates.

Cathy, not her real name, storms in late to our lunch meeting. She is looking tired and stressed, and at speed tells me about the job offer she needs to answer within the next 24 hours.

Cathy has been looking for a job for the past six months after taking time out to recover from a traumatic exit process from a major corporation where she was the only female senior executive. Cathy is still working through the trauma of this unexpected event after two happy decades at the company and expecting her long-term future to be there.

She is in the middle of her Unknown Zone, not sure of what she wants to do next – executive or portfolio work. She has discovered a budding yearning to return to her first love, the academic world, and she is also passionate about sustainability – she had launched the world's first sustainable products in their industry at her previous employer.

Being the sole provider for her two teenage children – in expensive private education – means that there is no financial cushion to draw from for long. The need to find a new position is very real.

For the next 45 minutes, Cathy regales me with all the details of the job, the stressful interview process, the unexpectedly low pay, and the unreasonable demands this company are making. Due to her children's age and stage of education, she can't move country for at least a year. The company demands that she agrees to be available for management calls and work during evening and weekends and to be present in the regional head office if required – in an inconvenient travel location in another country – at least two weekends per month.

They are putting massive pressure on her to accept quickly – she would be an exceptional 'catch' for them. Cathy is getting more and more distressed about the decision, not wanting to agree, but feeling she has to agree in order to earn money for her family.

She finally stops and says, 'What do you think?'

I reply:

> Do you want me to tell you to decline the job offer, or have you noticed that you have actually talked yourself out of the job all by yourself – despite the risk of losing 'a bird in the hand'?

Cathy looked at me in stunned silence and said, 'You are right, but what if I don't find another job?'

My reply was, 'Think yourself six months into this job . . . what do you see and feel?' With agony in her eyes, Cathy said:

> I don't yet have enough stamina to cope with the travel and work schedule this company are demanding of me. Being so much away from my children at this critical year in their lives would put unbearable stress on me. I would quickly get burnout.

I asked, 'And what might happen then?' Cathy's answer was, 'I would have to leave, cope with recovering from burnout and have no income.'

My next question was, 'What would be better with that scenario versus saying no now?' Her answer was:

> Nothing. In fact, everything would be worse! If I get really rundown, I might not be able to earn money for a very long time! And much as I would love to be back in a senior position and run an organisation again, it is not worth my or my family's well-being. Though I am worried about having no money going forward, this is really scary . . .

Our fear of something undefined that 'might happen' is normally worse than the actual event. Looking 'disaster scenarios' fully in the face means that we know what the worst that can happen is. If we have a plan for this, our 'Plan Z', the future does not look quite so frightening.

I asked Cathy a question about her 'worst fear' outcome: 'If you don't find work for the next even two to three years, will you and your children be on the street?' With a laugh, Cathy said, 'No, we won't. If worst comes to worst, we can move back in with my mother. The schools are very good there, and even if it would be embarrassing, we will be able to start again.'

At this point, you could see the tenseness and tiredness leaving Cathy's face and entire body. She said, 'I never thought of it that way. It would not be fun, but we would be all right, and that is all that matters'. Beaming, she added, 'I will make that call and decline the job as soon as we finish our lunch'.

And she did . . . (NB: Cathy did not have to move back to her mother's, and has continued to build a non-executive and advisory portfolio on the topics of sustainability and education.)

Sometimes we are forced to make a decision in the middle of our transition process due to positive or negative externalities. This does not mean that the transition process stops. It continues to its natural conclusion, as Anne Quinn's story shows.

Anne was previously CEO of BP's gas business. Then, in her mid-fifties, she was in the middle of contemplating her longer-term future, like most of us do at this time, when she was asked to join Lord Browne in his new venture at the private equity firm Riverstone to invest several billions of dollars in renewable energy:

> This was a fantastic opportunity and I was thrilled to join the team. However, after a short time, it became clear to me that this wasn't the way I wanted to spend the next 10 or so years of my life. I needed to take time for myself but still stay engaged in the business world. I was fortunate enough to have the opportunity to be a non-executive director of several FTSE 100 companies. And within that role, I have specialised as the chair of the remuneration committees. I still have time for a wonderful personal life. I haven't been happier.

The impetus for change was positive, one of the most amazing opportunities one could imagine, but this was not the right change, and as Anne's transition process progressed, a second career change happened within a couple of years.

### You will know when it is the right time to act

I am not advocating eons of procrastination, simply the courage to be honest with ourselves about what is going on inside. When the time is right to decide, when the decision really is ripe, you will know – with utter and complete clarity – that it is time to act, as Ken McKellar's story shows.

Ken McKellar describes his moment of clarity about leaving his equity Partner position at Deloitte in the Middle East as follows:

> When you told me that I would know 'viscerally and with utter clarity' when it was the right time to leave, I did not believe you. But that is exactly how it happened.

After going through a long time of reflection, figuring out that what I actually loved to do is coaching and developing experience in coaching, both inside and outside Deloitte, I was in a position when my work – largely due to external circumstances – became less and less enjoyable.

'The moment' came as I was driving back to Abu Dhabi after a difficult New Year holiday with the family in Oman. I had missed my family deeply and had looked forward so very much to seeing them, but I was so exhausted and embroiled in my transition that I was almost 'absent'. The fact that we all got food poisoning and were terribly ill did not exactly help how we all felt.

Driving back alone through the desert from Muscat to Abu Dhabi, a six-hour drive, it all became utterly clear. I realised that I never wanted us to have such a time together again, and that I now was emotionally ready to leave – come what may. Complete calm descended over me for the first time in, frankly, years.

During that trip, I worked out the whole strategy for how this needed to be executed with the best possible outcome for me and for my employer. As soon as I arrived back in Abu Dhabi, I booked a meeting with my boss, and a day or so later we met and I informed him of my decision. It all worked out beautifully, with a very amicable parting, and I still do work, as a coach, for Deloitte in the Middle East.

I will never forget that moment of clarity, though; as you said, you 'just know'.

### There is no going back

James E. Marcia, in his research on adolescents, also stressed that once the person has experienced an identity crisis, returning to the foreclosure state is no longer a possibility.[11] Speaking from personal experience, as well as what research implies, this also applies to grown-ups, including mature leaders. Once you have smelled a 'sniff' of what it could be like living your life differently and doing different work, it is impossible to be content with 'what was'.

Kevin Reynolds, who semi-retired as Partner at the private equity firm Bridgepoint in 2013, and is now non-executive director for some of their portfolio companies and mentoring colleagues, expressed this phenomenon of not being able to go back to the old ways once a new insight is gained as: 'The knowledge that I wanted a change bubbled under the surface for a long time. I had a sabbatical with four months off in 2008, and after "tasting the forbidden fruit" it was never the same again'.

After having been through this process once, rare is the executive who goes back to 'work as usual' and shuts the door on all the new external contacts and inputs. Once we discover how energising exploring the outside world is, we don't want to stop.

*Question 5.1:*   Looking at your life right now, do you have any unfinished endings going on?

*Question 5.2:*   Do you feel adrift, like you are in the middle of an Unknown Zone?

*Question 5.3:*   Can you see any New Beginnings emerging?

## The Career Change process

After gaining insight into how career transitions work psychologically, let us now turn to the practical career change process (Germination–Discovery–Fruition). We will spend time particularly on Discovery as it is the centre-piece of finding our new direction, as the name indicates.

### Germination

When I ask executives how far back they first started to feel a new direction was needed, the answer is often two, three or more years before the urgency to change become so strong that they started to pursue a career change in earnest – they were Germinating.

The first inkling of change might be a feeling that something has some-how changed, but we don't know quite what. We might wake up one morn-ing not being quite as excited about going to work as we used to be, or not feeling as motivated by taking on the next major organisational change.

This feeling of 'being slightly off our game' might come and go for some time, and in between we are, or try to be, our usual energetic selves. We might push our feelings of discomfort out of sight and try to make the best of the situation, especially if we need to stay on in our jobs for a length of time for financial reasons.

But no matter how much we try to hide from these signals, we have 'begun an ending', and there comes a day when the internal voice becomes so insistent that it can no longer be ignored. This is when the 'Germination' is over and we enter into the 'Discovery' period.

Ken McKellar, who shared his 'you just know' moment earlier, describes his Germination period as follows:

> My career journey started years before I knew that this what was hap-pening to me. I was just not enjoying my work as much as I used to, for various reasons, many outside my own control.
>
> I had to hang in there as I have three daughters who were either already studying at Cambridge or on their way there. There was no way I could have risked a drop in income at this critical point. I had been liv-ing in the Middle East, with my family far away in the UK, for six years due to this schooling situation. This took its toll on all of us.

A couple of years earlier, I had discovered a passion for and real success in coaching, and junior members of staff as well as senior Partners sought out my counsel. I was a member of the Partner selection committee in the Middle East and trusted on people matters. I asked if I could do coaching and Partner development full-time in the firm. This turned out to not be possible for a number of reasons.

Gradually, this dissonance between what I had to do and what my heart told me I should be doing created health problems, including constant colds and chest infections, and other symptoms that could have become serious had they not been addressed. My body was giving me a very strong signal to change my situation.

It also dawned on me that I was 55 years old, a watershed age for most people. I wondered if I should stay on and do something I *quite* enjoy or go and do something I *really* enjoy for the next 10 years?

This gave me a real sense of urgency as various things were 'coming at me' from different directions, creating an unstoppable momentum . . . it was like a 'perfect storm'.

Luis Miranda, who was one of the first infrastructure investors in India, expresses his Germination phase as follows:

I was investing in infrastructure, being Partner in a business we started in 2002, when no one else was doing this. Few people thought at that time that you could make money in infrastructure investing in India. We proved them wrong and were very successful.

Our fund grew significantly, and an unintended consequence of our success was that far too much money flowed into the sector; people started making stupid deals and made it difficult for everyone. It stopped being fun. Our now much larger firm became less entrepreneurial; again, this was less fun than before.

In addition, my kids were 13 and 15 years old, and I said to myself that I should spend more time at home before they were going on to college. I knew I wanted to leave but I had no idea what to do next . . .

This is the time we often start to talk with friends and family about feeling dissatisfied. This is natural, but they might not always be the best advisors at this time in our lives, or should at least not be our only advisors.

The reason is that they can have a vested interest in retaining the status quo or find our need to change frightening. They don't know who is going to emerge from this process, and if it might upend a lifestyle cherished by them. If so, they are not likely to be highly supportive of our change, and might try to persuade us to stay as we are.

As the vast majority of our initial ideas will be discarded – they are 'thought experiments' – it is often better that they get their first airing with a neutral party. Hearing our ideas going in a myriad of directions of possible futures can be very threatening to spouses, old friends and business partners.

I am not saying don't speak to them, I am saying that their reactions might not be what you had hoped for, and we need to be compassionate and acknowledge their fears.

### Discovery

The Discovery process is where we explore, learn new things in the world, meet new people, internalise these learnings, and try on new identities until we are ready to move forward and make our new roles and identities reality.

This is *the* crucial phase for a career change, and should not be hurried, or we can end up making premature decisions that will not serve us in the long run.

For many executives, setting out on what might be our first major career change exploration can feel challenging. This is not surprising, especially if we have been working in one company, one type of business or one type of work for 20, 30 or more years.

We are highly knowledgeable in our fields and are used to others seeking our advice and help. Being a beginner – learning completely new things and asking for help from new people – is uncomfortable, and the part many executives find hard to start. This is the part of the process that I – as a coach – am most often asked to help with.

Whether we seek to change what we do in our current organisation or change career and employer, we need to understand how to go about our Discovery process. After describing the principles, we will spend considerable time exploring how to do this in practice in Chapter 9, illustrated by many executives' experiences.

### Discovery is an outside-in process

The Discovery stage is defined by exploration of what Herminia Ibarra calls 'our possible selves':

> First, our working identity is not a hidden treasure waiting to be discovered at the very core of our inner being. Rather, it is made up of many possibilities: some tangible and concrete, defined by the things we do, the company we keep, and the stories we tell about our work and lives; others existing only in the realm of future potential and private dreams. Second, changing careers means changing our selves. Since we are many selves, changing is not a process of swapping one identity for another but rather a transition process in which we reconfigure the full set of possibilities.

She continues:

> We learn who we are – in practice, not in theory – by testing reality, not by looking inside. We discover the true possibilities by doing – trying out new activities, reaching out to new groups, finding new role models, and reworking our story as we tell it to those around us. What we want clarifies with experience and validation from others along the way.[12]

This is seconded by management guru Richard Pascale, who says, 'Adults are more likely to act their way into a new way of thinking than to think their way into a new way of acting'.[13] Reid Hoffman's description about continuous small iterations to develop ourselves and Plan A and B is the same process Herminia Ibarra and Richard Pascale speak about – we need to explore and test, step by step, in small iterations, before we can comfortably present ourselves as credible candidates for new roles or have impact in a new field.

We need a certain amount of *introspection* to become aware of our own internal environment, our changing needs, and internalise new learning. However, in her 2015 book *Act Like a Leader, Think Like a Leader*, Herminia Ibarra states without new external input (what she calls out-sight) to digest and incorporate into our view of the world and our place in it, all we do is process old and often self-limiting information and beliefs.[14]

Consequently, the Discovery process is the most important part of the entire career change process. Investing time and effort in collecting out-sight to gain in-sight will pay handsome dividends.

### Discovery is not a process you can force

When we start out on a career change project, we rarely have a clear idea of what we really want to do. How can we? We only know what we have experience of to date. This is the time to open our horizons and not to be too result-focused, no matter how much we would like to know where we are going to end up.

If we try to force the process in a direction we have predetermined, we are setting ourselves up for a lot of disappointment if we don't get what we had decided we wanted, or if it ends in a short-lived or unsuccessful job change.

As we go through the Discovery process, we often learn that what we thought we wanted is not what we personally deeply wanted, or we discover something entirely new we didn't know existed.

By trying to speed up the Discovery process, you could be missing out on what is the true joy of this time: discovering just how big the world out there is; how many exciting things are going on; how many amazing and interesting people there are doing such interesting work; how capable and extraordinary they think you are; and *the things only you can contribute* – that you had no idea existed or realised you could contribute to.

Forcing your career change is like trying to force torrential rainfall down an established riverbed and insisting it keeps to its old run, no matter how much water is accumulating. This could create the same kind of havoc in your life as a flood does in nature.

Instead, let your river gently overflow out on the floodplain, slowing the speed and covering a bigger area for a while. When the time is right, the water naturally finds a new riverbed and peacefully but energetically continues in a new route towards the sea, now carrying new seeds, plants and nutrients with it downstream – and so will your Discovery process.

### The truth is out there ... with people you don't yet know

In career terms, 'the truth' is not found in the office or with what Herminia Ibarra calls our 'lazy or narcissistic' networks.[15] The issue with these lazy networks is that they are facing backwards in our history, not towards the future, and they are quickly antiquated in terms of usefulness for our development.

Instead, we need to extend our networks to gain new information. As Mark Granovetter, an American sociologist and professor at Stanford University, known for his work in social network theory and economic sociology and *The Strength of Weak Ties*, said:[16]

> In short; more novel information flows to individuals through weak rather than strong ties. Because our close friends tend to move in the same circles that we do, the information they receive overlaps to a large extent with what we already know. Acquaintances, by contrast, know people that we do not, and thus receive more novel information.[17]

In my experience, close friends might give you some contacts, but are not likely to be the ones offering you job opportunities. They know your great attributes and they also know your flaws, intimately. They might also associate you with weaknesses that you remedied years ago, or worry that they might lose out in the career race if you join their employer.

Introducing you to their organisation thus carries a high perceived risk for them if they have recommended you, as their own position might be compromised whether you succeed or fail.

Does this sound unfair? Try the thought experiment of imagining introducing and hiring one of your closest friends into your own organisation.

To change career, it is therefore vital to build new strategic networks in the area where you want to seek your new future, well beyond your current network.

### Acquiring new knowledge

When we start to explore new areas of interest, we need to invest a considerable amount of time and effort in learning about this new field.

This is vital in order to understand what are important issues, trends and technology developments, as well as acquiring enough knowledge to hold an interesting conversation with people from the sector when we get introduced for meetings.

Reading widely, deeply and specifically at this stage is important. Reading widely refers to opening your horizons and deeply to acquiring knew knowledge to be effective in a specific area or acquiring new skills. Reading specifically refers to preparing for meetings with people – something often neglected (we will see more about the importance of this in Chapter 9).

### Reading widely

One of the joys of the Discovery period is giving ourselves permission to read and explore every interesting area that takes our fancy. Especially in the beginning, it is important to not have a goal with our reading list – except variety.

This period is about discovering how the world has changed since the last time we explored outside our organisation or topics of immediate business interest. You will be amazed at how fast things are changing and how many exciting developments are going on.

It is also about discovering what you are interested in now, at this stage of your life, not what other people think you should be interested in or what you used to be interested in, unless you rediscover a passion from a younger age.

### Twitter: brilliant for reading widely, and sometimes deeply (and new positioning)

To date, in my experience, surprisingly few senior executives actively use Twitter, and many feel Twitter is not a serious medium. If that is the case, I wonder why Paul Polman (the CEO of Unilever), the IMF, the UN, the World Bank, the Dalai Lama and the Queen of England feel the need to have Twitter accounts.

Twitter is excellent when you want to find out what is going on in any particular sphere. By following people or organisations, you instantly get fed the latest news, studies and issues in their field. You also get to know about new TED Talks, free online seminars and broadcasts. If you have not tried this yet, you will be amazed at what you get for free, without effort and in real time – all invaluable for your Discovery process.

You can quickly learn about your new areas of interest and later become a useful contributor to the area where you want to make your future, which is how you become a valued member of a new professional community. This is clearly useful for executing a career change – and you can start to publish when you are ready.

*Reading deeply*

Once you start to identify a few focus areas, it is time to start reading deeply. Serious pieces of research and other publications will help you acquire the professional knowledge and insights that makes you a contender for a role in the new field.

If you are, for example, aiming to become a trustee in a charity active in combating malaria, areas you would probably like to bone up on could be roles and responsibilities of trustees, trends and issues in the charity sector, latest trends in malaria medicine, the latest findings in how health programmes in developing countries can be successful, etc.

If we want to have significant impact on issues in society, it is important to learn to take a 'whole-systems' view. Reading serious pieces of work in adjacent and different areas deepens our understanding of where our work might have the most impact. Through this, we learn to find the 'acupressure points' that, if pressed, release a whole set of interconnected issues, and as we will discuss later, this is where we find new exciting opportunities with Impact.

This is also the experience and advice given by Guido Schmidt-Traub, the CEO of the United Nations Sustainable Development Solutions Network (UNSDSN), who we mentioned in Chapter 3:

> Some of the most exciting work requires connecting operational business experience with insights into policies and science. For example, if you want to work on climate change you need to have a very good grasp of the climate science. This does require reading extensively from many different sources. In my own typical day, I read an extended piece on a new topic to maintain and expand my knowledge.
>
> It is also important to develop writing skills and publish blogs or op-eds. These build your voice and help sharpen your own thoughts. In most business settings, one does not write much, so I have found it helpful to cultivate writing skills and practice deliberately.
>
> To work in the intersection of business and policy, you have to apply many different skill sets, so you will always be a rookie in some of them.

Guido has successfully transitioned between public positions and different corporate positions four times (so far) in his career. From working in the intellectual property (IP) investment space, he became the project manager working for Jeffrey Sachs developing the Millennium Development Goals, then a carbon fund investor – including CEO for the French bank CDC's Climate Asset Management's Carbon Fund – before transitioning back into the UNSDSN, leading their efforts to get business, NGOs, governments and academia to collaborate to solve major issues, as identified in the 2030 Sustainable Development Goals.

To illustrate the point that we can successfully learn new areas after many years in one field, Naoko Ishii, CEO of Global Environmental Facility (GEF) went through the decision-making and election process for this position when she was Deputy Vice Minister for Finance for Japan, and describes her learning process as follows:

> When I was recommended to apply for this position, I was not sure originally that this was the right one for me. I spent a year meeting people and understanding what the position meant and what was expected. Gradually, I got comfortable and even excited with the concept, even though one of the three core experience areas – financial, developmental and environmental – was not within my background. I have over 30 years' experience in the financial and development areas, bilateral and multilateral government work, and aspects of public policy work, but at that point had no real experience in the environmental area.
>
> Therefore, I immersed myself in learning about this field at very high speed, while at the same time I learned how to orchestrate a political election campaign as the appointment is by public election. I have now been elected for a second and final term, and when that finishes I am approaching another transition as all government work has a fixed term, so we know our finish date when we start.

*Question 5.4:*   What surprised you in the above section about Discovery and the need to learn and meet new people?

### Asking for advice, help and meetings: being a rookie

I frequently hear from senior leaders that they wonder why the other person would want to take their meeting or call.

As always, I turn it around and ask them, 'If someone asks for an hour of your time for advice, do you answer them and meet with them?'. The answer is invariably, 'Yes, of course I do. I really enjoy helping other people'.

My answer invariably is, 'Why are you then depriving other people of the joy of helping you?'.

By reframing the situation in our own minds from 'my request will be an imposition' to 'like me, they probably like to help others', approaching new people becomes less daunting.

Another fear is that our request might be rejected or not answered. That can of course happen, but is quite rare – especially if you are introduced by a trusted contact.

After a while, we develop resilience to rejections, and we know it is neither the end of the world nor a reflection on us. All of us forget to answer people occasionally, even when we want to.

Turning it around, looking at how we deal with these things ourselves teaches us that people rarely mean anything with not answering; they are simply overrun by circumstances. Gentle and courteous reminders work wonders. If they still don't answer, move on and forgive. The timing is *wrong for them* to be able to be helpful.

### Gap periods: new experiences

Executives are increasingly taking longer times out to explore and refresh, something that used to be the privilege of graduates in their twenties. Taking a break, whether a few months or a full year, can also be a wonderful and life-changing experience for adults.

After working 20 or more years, we can feel really stale and stuck. A complete change of scenery might be what is needed to refresh ourselves. If our working lives will be 50 or 60 years in the future, can you really imagine doing this without a few gap periods? This we could say is the modern version of the Hindu concept of 'forest dwelling' that we mentioned in Chapter 2. It is also a great way to experience new things and get 'out-sight'.

Taking six months or a year out can sound scary; should we not spend every minute job-hunting? What if we can't find a new job coming back? The experience of executives who have taken time out is that when we have done it once, we know it will be fine, and we learn to do this in a way that does not endanger our future employability. What we experience and incorporate into our own life and identity is priceless, and makes us more employable in our chosen fields.

A couple of senior executives who have found a gap period invaluable are Sheila Surgey in South Africa and Rolf Fouchier in the Netherlands.

Sheila Surgey was previously an executive member of the highly respected Purpose-driven South African insurance company Hollard. She was part of the team tasked with blueprinting the change journey to make real the strategy to drive inclusive growth through measuring financial returns alongside social dividend returns. She is now transitioning into working as a consultant helping companies and social enterprises achieve similar journeys to Hollard's. Sheila has taken a number of gap years in her career. In her own words:

> I have given myself gap years, as I find this the best way to rethink and recalibrate my life. This came from, when early in my marriage, I had a cancer scare. The night before the operation, my husband asked me, 'After the operation, whatever the outcome is, what would you not put off doing?' I said, 'TRAVEL!'
>
> As it turned out, I did not have cancer, but we both left our jobs after six months (other people thought we were mad!) and went travelling for a year, to Asia, Australia, Europe and the USA. It was an amazing experience and really kindled the thirst for knowledge and opened my eyes. I realised the value of stepping off the hamster wheel.

In total, I have taken four gap years. For lots of people, this might be a horrific prospect, but each gap year has served me well to refresh and rethink. Sometimes we have changed countries, from the US to the UK, back to Zimbabwe and now South Africa.

I have never regretted the breaks – in fact, they have afforded me the space to discover new horizons and new opportunities . . . opportunities that ensure I wake up excited about what I do every day.

Rolf Fouchier, previously CEO of the energy giant E.ON Vertrieb Deutschland and E.On Netherlands, now the founder of Exceleration, an angel investor in early-stage energy tech companies, took six months out travelling with his family before starting his new firm:

My last change was a big step, from CEO of a €20 billion business with 7,000 employees, to angel investor. I stopped with E.ON due to a personal drive to pursue another direction – without having a job to go to.

Part of my core values is to experience fantastic moments with my family, so we took six months travelling together around the world. I used to work a lot, and not exercise much, so it was great to enjoy life with the family for six months.

Learning about the world and other perspectives was always important to me, as are human rights and environmental issues.

On this trip, I got an extra eye-opener: you don't need money to be happy. We found that the poorer the people, the more hospitable they are and the more help they give. The richer they are, the less helpful they are and they close their doors when you need help.

I wanted something entrepreneurial and in a results-driven area. It led to me setting up my own company with a Partner. We are working on realising growth for equity stakes in early-stage companies. We are now investors in seven or eight companies, and I am really enjoying it, and these last few months I am at my core Purpose.

*Question 5.5:*    What surprised you in this section about Discovery, and the need to have quiet time, support and gap periods?

## Fruition

As we go through the Discovery process, we at some point start to see patterns develop, we start to discard some options and delve deeper into others that attract us. We are on our way to developing a new identity and a new career – we are bringing our project to Fruition.

At this stage, this new idea of ours is very much a work in progress (WIP) and needs refining – through iteration. We need to digest what we learn about a new area, understand how we can contribute, figure out how to present ourselves and our experience in this context, and try out our new identity in our chosen environment. We then digest the feedback, adjust, and start the cycle again. This is how we gradually develop new identities and new careers.

This principle applies whether we decide to change what we do at our current employer or we decide to join a new organisation. If we want to change what we do in our current organisation, people around us will have a firm view of who we are, what we do and how we do it. To change this view takes time and continuous effort, but gradually we establish a new identity – that both our colleagues and we are comfortable with.

If we want to change careers outside, it also takes time to develop an identity that is congruent between the new direction we want to pursue and our own perception of ourselves. To feel fully comfortable in our new identities and roles can take several years if the change of direction is considerable. In Chapter 10, we will cover how the Fruition process works in practice.

We will also realise that some options are not for us. Having explored them, we are richer for the experience, and we don't need to wonder 'what if' we had gone down that route. This way, our decisions become conscious decisions, informed by knowledge.

We can be reasonably confident that the experience we will gain through taking a risk on our new route will be useful, no matter what the outcome is.

This is very important, as there is no guarantee a career change works immediately or forever. By this, I mean that your new organisation or sector might be hit with some structural crisis right after you join . . . no one can guarantee that another 'Enron' or 'banking crisis' does not happen.

## Helpful practices

As we go through our Discovery and Fruition process (and transitioning), we will have questions, feel lost, anxious and sometimes very stressed. We can't expect our spouses, family members or closest friends to be able to handle all the ever-changing thoughts and feelings going on inside us. They are a vital source of support, but we need to find some additional support to enable a free flow of thoughts, feelings and insights. This can take many forms, from a coach to a support network.

### Coaches

A coach is a neutral party and has only your well-being and success in mind. They are non-judgemental and you can confidentially speak about anything that is on your mind. This confidentiality is one of the reasons many senior executives have their own coach, sometimes in addition to the coach their company provides.

A coach has no vested interest in you choosing one direction over another or deciding to earn more or less money, etc. They can help you think through the upsides and risks, and getting 'unstuck' when you feel like you are in a dead end or making little progress. One of the greatest values of a coach is their ability to help you see issues from a different point of view and figure out a new way forward.

The difficulty with finding a coach is that there are no universally accepted professional standards or licences needed for coaches; unlike for accountants or financial advisors, anyone can hang out their shingle and claim they are a coach.

Asking around for referrals and meeting several coaches and seeing whom you click with is the best option. Reputable coaches will also happily give you references of previous clients that you can speak with. From these referees, you can normally infer at what seniority level they do their coaching work.

Coaches, like other service professionals, specialise in different types of coaching, in a myriad of areas, from remedial coaching (helping executives overcome career-derailing behaviour) to performance coaching, presentation skills and business development coaching. It is important that the coach you choose to assist you in your career change journey understands and has experience in coaching executives in career change.

There is a never-ending debate if coaches have to have experience in the industry sector they are coaching in or not. When it comes to Purpose-driven career change, deep industry expertise in one industry is probably less useful, and a wide-ranging understanding of many sectors, trends and systems and lateral thinking ability more important. If your coach cannot think outside your current sector, how will they help you move into a new sector? On the other hand, a coach that has not had experience dealing at the level in business or society that you are used to operating at is probably going to be less useful than one that has.

Good coaches don't come cheap. Likewise, just because they are very expensive does not guarantee high quality or that they will be the right coach for you. Personal trust and chemistry is the key. Be prepared to pay about what you earn yourself per hour, as a senior executive, for your senior coach.

### Circle of support and/or your 'Advisory Board'

We all have support networks, even if we don't always think of them as such. We have family, personal friends, business friends, mentors and trusted advisors.

When we are going through transitions, questioning where we are heading in our lives and careers, we are often in need of a different support network, one where we can air with others what is going on in our hearts and heads, as well as get practical advice from.

Such networks often form naturally, by people in a similar situation who are also thinking of where their lives are heading. With them we can safely explore what is going on inside, share successes and drawbacks, and learn from each other, without scaring our near and dear.

Other executives deliberately create what they sometimes name their 'Advisory Board' – a group of mentors they draw on for counsel and advice in their career change – with a mix of long-trusted mentors and targeted mentors who can help them enter their new chosen area of interest.

I was wondering what example I could use of support networks, and had to smile when I realised that our own Rest of Your Life (ROYL) club was exactly this. I never thought of it as a support network or Advisory Board at the time.

Dominic Houlder, the Adjunct Professor of Strategy and Entrepreneurship at London Business School, started ROYL in 2008. We had been talking for a while about the fact that we were in our late forties and early fifties, and wondered what to do with the rest of our lives that would 'matter to us and to the world'.

Dominic gathered a small group of friends and the odd friend of a friend, and we started out with a serious agenda of learning and reflecting.

We met, twice per year, in a private room in a restaurant of the organiser's choice and took turns paying. The privacy, and the fact that no partners were present, meant that everyone could speak freely about questions and insecurities and hear how other people were handling their transitions, without scaring loved ones with our random explorations.

In May 2015, we held the last ROYL dinner. During the seven years we had met up, several of us figured out new directions and created new paths. For example, Alain de Botton created his now well-known 'School of Life';[18] Lynda Gratton, Professor at London Business School, published *The 100-Year Life* in 2016;[19] Dominic Houlder is still with LBS, and spends more of his time writing on his beloved island Skye; Glen Peters, previously a Partner with PwC, has cemented his reputation as writer of detective stories, and has built an opera house in Wales where cultural festivals are held; and yet others have taken different routes.

Reflecting back on something I took for granted at the time, I am now deeply grateful to these brave fellow explorers for their support on the journey, their insights and ability to challenge my rubbish ideas and self-limiting beliefs about myself and what I am capable of.

This is what your circle of support and Advisory Board does for you.

### Quiet time

Going through the Discovery phase and the Unknown Zone can be confusing, and we use up a lot of our energy reserves. We need to have time for reflection, to make our 'out-sight' into 'in-sight', to rest and regenerate our mental and physical batteries.

One of the ways I have found most useful for finding balance, regenerating and thinking clearly is to spend time alone, in silence. Most of us are not used to spending time alone, observing our thoughts and our own states (mindfulness) as we have become addicted to interacting with other people or our many electronic devices that clamour for our attention. We lead busy lives and it can be hard to find time to be alone.

Not everyone finds the thought of meditating attractive or easy, even if this is increasingly proven to lower stress, promote well-being and alleviate anxiety and depression.[20] There is increasing clinical evidence that meditation actually physically changes our brains, from protecting the ageing brain, helping concentration and focus,[21] to coping better with unemployment by reducing physiological inflammation and stress markers.[22]

If full-blown meditation sounds too challenging, executives often find a practical first step is by going for a walk, alone, during the day. We can normally find time for a 15- to 20-minute walk, even in a busy schedule. This can be a real safety valve, especially if we are going through a stressful time at work while we are trying to figure out where we are heading.

Others spend a quiet hour – with the phone off – each week with a journal, either in a café or on early morning flights while they are fresh, to reflect in silence. Yet other executives take away days, longer gap periods, or attend leadership development programmes or retreats. You will know what is right for you.

## We keep discovering and iterating – there is no 'final' destination

As we progress through our career transitions, most of us realise that we will never reach a 'final' destination. The process of discovery and iterations to develop our new roles and identities is continuous and will go on our entire lives.

What we reach are plateaus of understanding, 'staging posts', where we stay for a while before something triggers the next transition journey. Life is 'constant beta', constant iteration, we just didn't realise until we faced a major life dilemma that this is what we were already doing. This is as it should be, and once we have worked through our first major transitions, we realise that the joy is in the ever-evolving journey, not the destination.

Kenneth McKellar, who we met earlier, expressed this feeling when I asked him how he felt about his transition after 18 months in his new career:

> I thought I fully knew and understood the business I was getting into, but I find that I learn something new every day, that both shapes the future direction of the business and also how I present myself and what we do. It is constantly evolving. When I was leaving a big firm after many years, I needed clarity and security of where I was heading – I thought. Once the scary leap was done, I am fine with this constant evolving of my identity and our work.

### *Gradual insight: Discovering my passion for Purpose-driven careers*

To illustrate how slowly and gradually the shape of where we are going emerges, and how much serendipity is involved, the story of how I discovered my Purpose to help mid/later career executives find Purpose-driven careers might be useful.

It is a bit lengthy, but you will be able to see what was described above in the Career Change, Career Transition and Career Transformational Assets sections, and topics we mentioned in earlier chapters such as job-crafting, permanent beta, etc. You might even recognise some of the patterns in how your own career and life has unfolded.

This realisation happened in July 2014 as I was overlooking the magnificent Ionian Sea, but the beginning of the whole career shift started with the 'aha' moment above in 2003, and progressively evolved over a decade.

Having acquired a Business Coach[23] certification during my 2004/2005 gap year, I joined Heidrick & Struggles, the NASDAQ quoted premier executive search firm, as a Partner, utilising my coaching skills in a different way.

Although I was tasked to build the oil and gas practice, my interest in sustainability led me to founding and co-leading the global renewable energy and sustainability practice – originally against some of my colleagues' wishes (extracurricular job-crafting!). We became well accepted in the organisation when we went from US$0.6 million to over US$10 million global turnover in two years . . .

After leaving Heidrick & Struggles, I spent 2011 recovering from a chest infection I had picked up during travelling. This made me reconsider my life and work, and I decided to set up my own business, originally focusing on executive search in sustainable business in all its forms.

To my surprise, my coaching business started up again, by itself. I have always tried to assist executives looking for a job, whether I am working on something of interest to them or not – just listening to them, sharing some insights and making a few introductions. Having personally been on their side of the table, I know that this makes a real difference. Now these executives referred clients to me, including themselves.

Since the financial crisis, I had felt a shift in what was required of leaders to lead sustainable business, and I published my first major leadership paper in 2012, together with BSR, titled *Sustainability and Leadership Competencies for Business Leaders*.[24]

At the 2013 launch for LeadersQuest CEO Lindsay Levin's book *Invisible Giants*, I bumped into Professor Grayson, Director of Cranfield University's School of Management Doughty Centre for Corporate Responsibility, who I had known for a few years via my previous employer's (Accenture) events.

My leadership study had a fit with Cranfield's new teaching module on Ethics and Sustainability for the International Masters of HR course, and after delivering these lectures for a couple of years I was offered an Honorary

Visiting Fellowship at the Doughty Centre. Now I had added an academic sustainability leadership angle to my work in coaching and executive search.

While researching for the BSR paper, I had the privilege of speaking with Unilever executives who introduced me to the concept of Purpose in business. This really resonated as it articulated what I had been trying to express in my 2012 leadership study: creating profitable business *through* affecting societal change.

It became increasingly clear to me that something was going on with senior executives around the world. There was a change of mood – much less of 'I want another big new job' and much more of 'I want to find a way to give back'. These topics kept percolating in the back of my mind.

In June 2014, I was asked to be part of a panel at an energy conference in Istanbul, discussing the talent gap in the energy industry. I suggested I speak about the increasing 'age and values gap' in the energy industry instead of the 'talent gap'. It just popped out, without any conscious plan. Luckily for me, Mehmet Öğütçü, the Chairman, a great thinker and a prolific writer, had recently left his executive position at the BG Group to develop a portfolio career, so he related personally to the topic and bravely agreed to this unusual approach.

I spoke about this emerging need for new career options for senior executives as their motivations change later in their careers, generating a lot of interest and many nodding heads in the audience, who were mainly in the 45- to 65-year age bracket.[25]

The following weeks were spent preparing to decamp to Corfu, where I spend time each summer working and attending meditation retreats. I put the Purpose topic out of my mind.

In the week between the two meditation retreats, I let my mind 'percolate' with the question: Where is all this leading? Not trying to figure anything out, just putting the question out there and seeing what surfaced.

Sitting quietly looking at the sea, suddenly the fog lifted and the idea was just there: 'it is all about helping executives find Purpose and develop their careers to express this, especially at mid/later career, and thereby helping to change how we do business in the world'.

My Purpose, and the idea for the research paper for Cranfield and this book, was born.

In March 2016, the Doughty Centre published the paper *Purpose Driven Leader – Purpose Driven Career*,[26] aimed at what *organisations* can do to help senior executives develop the leadership and career development skills needed to be effective leaders in the world we now live in, and for their own futures. And work continued on this book for *executives*.

There are three rounds of Endings, Unknown Zones and New Beginnings in my two personal stories in this chapter, occurring about every five years. We will see this pattern of five-year waves of 'refining direction' with other executives as well.

It also shows that serendipity is a huge factor in career change. What if I had not persisted with doing that first research paper? What if I had not gone to the book launch? What if I had not taken the risk to suggest an unusual topic for the speech for the energy conference?

The vital importance of doing new things, meeting new people in new settings and contemplating what they mean – our Career Transformational Assets – cannot be overstated.

## Takeaways

Changing careers means going through a *change* process (practical) and a *transition* process (psychological).

Understanding the transition process – Ending, Unknown Zone and New Beginnings – is vital for successfully navigating a career change and not jumping too quickly into a new job, as career change can be an anxious time.

The change process – Germination, Discovery and Fruition – is an iterative process where we learn, practice and refine our understanding of where we would like to work, and how to create knowledge and a new identity in this field. It is essential to spend significant time in Discovery – learning externally 'out-sight' to reflect and gain 'in-sight'.

We do this through employing our Career Transformational Assets – self-knowledge, openness to new experiences, and building strategic and diverse networks.

Finding Purpose, and understanding how we can create a professional role incorporating this, is a gradual process. It is rarely a bolt of lightning from the sky – and it keeps evolving over time.

## Notes

1 Bridges, W. (2004). *Transitions: Making Sense of Life's Changes*. Cambridge, MA: Da Capo Press, Kindle edition, location 70.
2 Gratton, L. and Scott, A. (2016). *The 100-Year Life: Living and Working in an Age of Longevity*. London, UK: Bloomsbury Information, Kindle edition, locations 1545–1549.
3 Ebaugh, H.R. (1988). *Becoming an Ex*. Chicago, IL: University of Chicago Press, 2nd edition, pp. 181–206.
4 Bridges, W. (2004). *Transitions: Making Sense of Life's Changes*. Cambridge, MA: Da Capo Press, Kindle edition, location 267.
5 Bridges, W. (2004). *Transitions: Making Sense of Life's Changes*. Cambridge, MA: Da Capo Press, Kindle edition, location 326.
6 Ibarra, H. (2003). *Working Identity: Unconventional Strategies for Reinventing Your Career*. Brighton, MA: Harvard Business School Press, Kindle edition, location 55.
7 Clip from *The Best Exotic Marigold Hotel* (2011). Retrieved from: www.youtube.com/watch?v=wg20uxPRp0E.

8  Bridges, W. (2004). *Transitions: Making Sense of Life's Changes*. Cambridge, MA: Da Capo Press, Kindle edition, location 307.

9  *Albert Einstein Quotes*. Retrieved from: www.sfheart.com.

10  Marcia, J.E. (1973). Ego-Identity Status. In M. Argyle (ed.), *Social Encounters*. London, UK: Penguin, p. 353. Retrieved from: https://en.wikipedia.org/wiki/James_Marcia.

11  Marcia, J.E. (1973). Ego-Identity Status. In M. Argyle (ed.), *Social Encounters*. London, UK: Penguin, p. 341. Retrieved from: https://en.wikipedia.org/wiki/James_Marcia.

12  Ibarra, H. (2003). *Working Identity: Unconventional Strategies for Reinventing Your Career*. Brighton, MA: Harvard Business School Press, Kindle edition, location 66.

13  Pascale, R. and Gioja, L. (1997). Changing the Way We Change. *Harvard Business Review*, 75(6): 126–139.

14  Ibarra, H. (2015). *Act Like a Leader, Think Like a Leader*. Brighton, MA: Harvard Business Review Press, Kindle edition, location 117.

15  Ibarra, H. (2015). *Act Like a Leader, Think Like a Leader*. Brighton, MA: Harvard Business Review Press, Kindle edition, location 1537.

16  Granovetter, M. (1978). Threshold Models of Collective Behavior. *American Journal of Sociology*, 83(6): 1420–1443.

17  Granovetter, M. (2005). The Impact of Social Structure on Economic Outcomes. *Journal of Economic Perspectives*, 19(1): 33–50.

18  School of Life website: http://alaindebotton.com/the-school-of-life/.

19  Lynda Gratton website: www.lyndagratton.com.

20  UK National Health Service website, mindfulness: www.nhs.uk/conditions/stress-anxiety-depression/pages/mindfulness.aspx.

21  Walton, A.G. (2016). *7 Ways Meditation Can Actually Change the Brain*. Forbes. Retrieved from: www.forbes.com.

22  Creswell, J.D. et al. (2016). Alterations in Resting-State Functional Connectivity Link Mindfulness Meditation with Reduced Interleukin-6: A Randomized Controlled Trial. *Biological Psychiatry Journal*, 80(1): 53–56. DOI: http://dx.doi.org/10.1016/j.biopsych.2016.01.008.

23  MeylerCampbell website: www.meylercampbell.com.

24  Hoffmann, A. and Farouk, A. (2012). *Sustainability and Leadership Competencies for Business Leaders*. New York: BSR. Retrieved from: www.executiva.co.

25  East Med Energy Ministers and Executive meeting on Next Generation Leadership. Talent: Bridging the age and values gap. Retrieved from: www.executiva.co.

26  Hoffmann, A. (2016). *Purpose Driven Leader – Purpose Driven Career*. Cranfield University School of Management's Doughty Centre for Corporate Responsibility. Retrieved from: www.executiva.co.

# Chapter 6

# Leadership skills for a collaborative world

*Before we go into how to practically affect a career change – Discovery and Fruition – we need to understand what kind of leadership competencies and skills are needed to be successful – as a leader – in affecting societal change, whether at our current employers or in a new career.*

*The aim is not to make you a skills and competencies expert – a whole book could be written about this one topic – it is to provide a reference framework for understanding what you bring to the table today and what you might want to develop.*

*It is perfectly fine to skim-read and return in earnest when you have potential target areas for your activities in mind and want to present yourself and your accomplishments to this new set of stakeholders and collaborators or re-craft your CV.*

*The below might seem like a long list of skills and competencies, but as we will discover, learning how to become good at our Career Transformational Assets – self-knowledge, openness to new experiences, and building strategic and diverse networks – will unlock many of the skills and competencies for being more effective leaders and developing our new careers.*

## Leadership: then, now and going forward

### Competencies and skills: a quick definition

Most executives are familiar with competencies and skills – we normally get assessed on them annually – but in the interest of clarity, as they often are used interchangeably, let us define them as follows:

- Competencies describe *how* we do things – the behaviours and technical attributes that individuals must have, or must acquire, to perform effectively at work.[1]
- Skills describe *what* we do.

### How it used to be: mainly internally focused leaders were needed

Some 20+ years ago, the 'business of business was business'. Business was to a large extent isolated from the rest of society, except for complying with whatever laws and regulations governments imposed on them.

NFPs and NGOs were often seen, if not as outright adversaries, as organisations that 'complicated' the life of businesses. NGOs/NFPs and government felt similarly about business, and each other, and there was little collaboration between the sectors. Each group saw their role as focusing on their own priorities.

Change happened at a manageable pace, new trends took a long time to develop, and risk was something to be 'managed'. We had long-range plans for our industry and company that we could be reasonably confident could be successfully implemented.

The focus was on internal change, to become ever-more efficient. *The leadership skills that were valued were skills that made the organisation run efficiently internally* and with its immediate stakeholders: employees, suppliers and customers. Leaders where recruited, developed and promoted on these criteria.

### What we need going forward: externally focused collaborative leaders

The issues that society faces today affect leaders of all types of organisations – business, government and not-for-profit – as we start to realise just how interdependent the world is, financially, environmentally and socially.

To solve our interconnected problems, we need to take an 'eco-centred' – whole-systems view – and we need exponential progress on these issues.

As John Elkington and Louise Smith, in their September 2016 report *Breakthrough Business Models*, concluded: 'Achieving exponential progress will require a scale of collective effort rarely seen outside wartime conditions'.[2]

The leadership skills needed for wide-ranging collective effort (such as the Impact Coalitions we saw in Chapter 3) in such a transparent, volatile and fast-changing world are very different to what most executives currently in senior positions were recruited, developed and promoted for over the past decades.

Today, the outside world is not 'manageable', nor does it leave organisations in peace to develop at a self-dictated pace. The outside world is constantly influencing our organisations – the speed of change is exponential and we will need to learn leadership skills for an exponentially changing world.

John Elkington continues:

> As leaders learn to Think Sustainably, they will also need to learn
> to Think X, shorthand for Think Exponential. In the same way they
> once looked to activists and social entrepreneurs for evidence of where
> markets were headed, they must now engage a very different set of
> players. These new players are not happy with 1% or even 10% year-
> on-year improvements, instead pushing towards 10X – or 10-fold –
> improvements over time. And in Thinking X, business leaders need
> to think of four key domains where the X agenda is already playing
> out . . . SocialX, LeanX, IntegratedX and CircularX . . .[3]

Thinking X is what we aim to do when we go Discovering, finding our Big
Question, in Chapters 8 and 9.

Leaders need to be effective in interacting with a previously unimagined
range of stakeholders and form unconventional collaborative partnerships
with them. They need to be able to detect trends that are barely showing on the
horizon, be visionary and able to rapidly formulate and reformulate strategy.

They also need to be able to deep-dive in detail when there is a sudden
crisis, as well as deal with totally new and intertwined risks, whereof some
could, if not handled well, potentially cost them the company – such as BP's
Deepwater Horizon or Volkswagen's diesel emissions scandal. Finally, they
need to be able to clearly communicate what they see and ensure that people
can understand and change tack quickly.

These are to a large extent *externally focused competencies* that help
leaders translate what they see externally into their own organisation so
they can act.

### What we have: mainly recruitment, development and promotion of old criteria

When studying organisations' leadership competency frameworks and
recruitment and promotion criteria, they often reflect the old world view
of what a leader needs to be good at; they are oriented towards internal
organisational change rather than external collaboration.

Leaders now need to be able to affect change internally *and* externally.
We still need to run our operations safely and efficiently, and we also need
to deal effectively with and collaborate with the world outside our organisation to make our organisation prosper and solve societal issues.

### There are four sets of additional leadership competencies and skills

From the above follows that leaders *also* need proficiency in the following
areas going forward:

- *Externally oriented leadership competencies* to understand the world and bring it into our own organisation for action.
- *Corporate Diplomacy skills* to be able to affect change.
- *Tri-sector skills* to understand how to collaborate across sectors.
- *Digital skills* to deploy technology for 10X change on societal issues.

## Externally oriented leadership competencies

In our joint study with BSR in 2012, interviewees ranked 23 internally and externally oriented leadership competencies, for what they thought were the most important for a leader to be able to perform well in an organisation going forward.[4]

The top six ranked were:

1 Ethics and integrity
2 External awareness and appreciation of trends
3 Visioning and strategy formulation
4 Risk awareness
5 Stakeholder engagement
6 Flexibility and adaptability to change

As can be seen, most of these competencies are externally oriented, as were the runners-up, partnership building and organisational buy-in, that also have relationship-building and cooperation across silos at their heart. For more detailed definitions of the competencies, see Appendix 2.

Runner up *Organisational buy-in*, while sounding internally oriented, is vitally important for executives wishing to craft a Purpose-driven career while still at their employer. If they can't convince their own organisation about their idea, it will not happen – and if they fail to convince external stakeholders, the idea will have no impact.

Although this might seem obvious, my experience is that most leaders are good at internal buy-in; it is after all what they do every day – they understand how the people they want to convince operate and what they need. Convincing external stakeholders is often a completely new experience as they have very different needs and priorities and work in ways that are very different to our own organisation.

The UN Global Compact July 2017 strategy document for the journey to implement the SDG in 2030 supports this view:

> For companies to navigate the critical developments of the new millennium, it takes a keen sense of emerging trends, a grounding in ethics and values that consumers and other stakeholders are increasingly invested in, and sustainable operations from start to finish. The businesses that understand this challenge and take action will be a step ahead.[5]

In addition, to be successful in the digital networked economy, according to Barry Libert, Megan Beck and Jerry Wind in their eye-opening book *The Network Imperative*, the 10 main differences between network organisations versus traditional 'legacy' organisations are their opposite foci:

- internal versus external;
- growing slowly versus growing fast;
- uses own capabilities versus uses the network's capabilities;
- sells its own products and services versus letting the network make and sell products; and
- has high marginal cost versus has low marginal cost.[6]

Whether we want to make our own business successful or we want to affect change with impact on societal issues, taking advantage of networks' power to multiply is vital. To do that, we need to learn to work effectively externally as well as internally.

## 'Corporate Diplomacy' skills and competencies

Stakeholders that executives now need to engage and create partnerships with are incredibly diverse, with widely different and ever-shifting demands – governments, NGOs, our own workforce, customers, media, communities, academia, etc. – and looking increasingly like a *political* environment, not the cause-and-effect style business most leaders are used to. Consequently, leaders today need to develop what is termed *Corporate Diplomacy* skills.[7]

Business professors Raymond Saner, Lichia Yiu and Mikael Søndergaard[8] have identified over 20 core *competencies of business diplomats*, which include:

1   international business acumen;
2   knowledge of relevant governing bodies and codes;
3   political skills in dealing with diverse interests and the media;
4   comfort with role versatility; and
5   a high tolerance for ambiguity.

We can see the similarity with the externally oriented leadership skills mentioned earlier. 'Political and policy awareness' did not make the top of the list in our 2012 study, and it is interesting that just two years later they moved towards the fore.

## Tri-sector skills

To be effective at impacting major societal issues, leaders need to become what Professor Joseph Nye, at the Harvard Kennedy School of Government, calls 'a "tri-sector athlete" – someone who can "engage and collaborate across the private, public, and social sectors"'.[9]

This is still a fairly new area of leadership research, but the concept and understanding of the need for such leaders has real resonance within all sectors.

Universities and private leadership development organisations are starting to offer tri-sector leadership skills training, so far sadly with almost exclusive focus on the next-generation leaders who will be at the top in 5 to 10 years' time.

In most organisations, little effort has been spent to date to develop these skills in their senior leaders. Arguments for this stance include that it is harder to influence the older leaders to change than younger leaders, and that originally these leadership development programmes were developed to retain younger leaders, not for leadership development purposes per se. Thus, these programmes were for a long time not seen as serious leadership development curricula.

Senior leaders still occupy the decision-making positions and control the organisation's resources, and if they don't see the world the way younger leaders or society do, how can they make decisions that resonate with the whole organisation and the rest of society?

In Chapter 11, we will explore what leading organisations are doing to develop the new leadership skills and competencies for both younger and more experienced leaders.

One of the more concise definitions of tri-sector skills was created by Nicholas Lovegrove and Matthew Thomas, at the time both McKinsey directors and Fellows of the Harvard Kennedy School. Nicholas is now US Managing Partner at Brunswick, and in 2016 Nicholas expanded on this theme. publishing his acclaimed book on how to build tri-sector skills, called *The Mosaic Principle*.[10]

In their prequel HBR article, they share that *regardless of their backgrounds*, tri-sector athletes display these six key skills:[11]

1  *Balanced motivations.* Desires to create public value no matter where they work, combining their motivations to wield influence (often in government), have social impact (often in nonprofits) and generate wealth (often in business).
2  *Transferrable skills.* A set of distinctive skills valued across sectors, such as quantitative analytics, strategic planning and stakeholder management.
3  *Contextual intelligence.* A deep empathy of the differences within and between sectors, especially those of language, culture and key performance indicators.
4  *Integrated networks.* A set of relationships across sectors to draw on when advancing their careers, building top teams, or convening decision-makers on a particular issue.

5   *Prepared mind.* A willingness to pursue an unconventional career that zigzags across sectors, and the financial readiness to take potential pay cuts from time to time.
6   *Intellectual thread.* Holistic subject matter expertise on a particular tri-sector issue by understanding it from the perspective of each sector.

Developing tri-sector skills is of course ideally done by working in all three sectors at some point in our careers. This is not always easy to accomplish, due to the large pay differentials between the sectors, inflexible career routes in organisations, and the fact that not everyone is personally confident enough to take the risk to zigzag their career.

Luckily, their research also finds that it is possible to develop a high degree of tri-sector skill while staying in one sector by developing the mindsets, knowledge and networks that enable us to interact with and collaborate effectively with the other two sectors.

Let us now explore how to acquire these skills and the considerations we need to take into account when we create Purpose-driven careers.

### Transferrable skills

Once we have figured out what is needed by the other sectors in order to create the kind of influence and impact we desire, there will be skills that we have that the other sectors can use.

Above are mentioned quantitative analytics, strategic planning and stakeholder management. There are many other transferrable skills, for example other financial skills – from accounting to investing, lending and loan guarantees – programme management, technology (all forms) to strategy, HR and marketing; it really depends on what the issue at hand requires, as Oliver Harrison and Pablo Fetters' stories illustrate below, and we will see more about this topic in Chapter 9.

Oliver Harrison has been CEO for Teléfonica's Innovation Alpha Health Moonshot since 2016.

Oliver originally studied medicine and neuroscience, but after a few years in medical practice he realised that he wanted to broaden his horizons in business and technology (while keeping a deep interest in healthcare). He joined McKinsey's healthcare practice for a period, and returned there again after a sabbatical to qualify as a specialist in psychiatry.

In 2006, when he had finished a major public–private partnership (PPP) project with a UK healthcare department, he wondered what he wanted to do next.

A call from a former McKinsey colleague in Abu Dhabi, where they were just starting on a strategy and implementation project to transform the Abu Dhabi Health Authority (HAAD), changed his life and career direction.

For the next seven years, he became first Director of Public Health and Policy and then Director of Strategy for Healthcare for the Government of Abu Dhabi.

For Oliver, Abu Dhabi represented an opportunity to implement the best current thinking in healthcare, working with a population with significant health challenges, particularly with diabetes and chronic disease. Their team in the emirate were empowered by and worked closely with the Abu Dhabi government, and in Oliver's words, 'We achieved together 70 years' worth of healthcare reform in 7 years in areas covering universal health insurance, ubiquitous health data collection, managing H1N1 influenza, school health, diabetes, and e-solutions'.

When it finally became time to hand over to the Emiratis, Oliver returned to the UK and spent a couple of years exploring and figuring out what to do next. During this time, he worked as a consultant with the World Health Organization on mobile technology to help tackle chronic disease, and he also worked on a couple of healthcare start-ups.

In late 2015, the call came from Teléfonica's Innovation Alpha programme,[12] a significant future-oriented digital R&D investment, aimed at affecting major social issues through technology innovation, and in the process creating billion-dollar companies, and Oliver was asked to lead the 'Health Moonshot', pivoting some existing health projects into a true game changer.

Oliver's advice to executives trying to find 'what next' is:

> Be open to new things and take calculated risk. Do not expect to be able to articulate your strategy and where you are going from day one. When you step off the well-trodden path, you don't know where you will end up. Given the world is changing so quickly right now, nothing is really certain over the time frame of a typical career. If you follow your 'North Star', your values and your passions, you will find something interesting.

The story of Pablo Fetter, who started as a scientist, became a venture capital (VC) and private equity (PE) investor at sovereign wealth funds (SWFs), and who is now CEO of Kings' Education in Dubai, also shows how transferrable skills are developed:

> In my career, I have always followed my passion and things I felt strongly about, from studying electronics and computer science (having built electronic devices and programmed computers in my spare time at school) to what I do now.
>
> My PhD in Computer Science culminated in a world-first with Mercedes-Benz installing speech recognition in their 1996 S-series cars. Later, as they wanted to consolidate their advantage in speech

recognition technologies, their M&A department contacted me to help them map out the technology landscape. This was in 1998, at the time when Internet, e-commerce, mobile voice and data, and other technologies were booming, and money was flooding into the tech sector. Venture capital fascinated me, and I started reading voraciously about the topic.

After listening to me talking non-stop about how wonderful VC is, a friend advised me to try to work in this area I was so keen on. Even though it seemed like a stretch from the career point of view (I certainly didn't have the usual formal qualifications), I did apply to a few VCs. As expected, I got multiple rejections, but to my surprise also a couple of offers! So, with the tech bubble in full swing, I accepted a job as investment manager at a small tech VC firm that had just raised a second fund. I came in at the bottom of the organisation, and over a couple of years progressed to become a Partner of the fund.

With the second fund successfully invested, we wanted to raise our third fund, including from Middle Eastern investors, given that the region was experiencing a big boom back then. Over time, we got to know a number of Middle Eastern funds and learned how they work and operate.

While fundraising, different companies approached me, and the SWF [sovereign wealth fund] Istithmar World offered me a very attractive role. The division of Istithmar under my responsibility had more money to invest per year than our VC company had managed to raise for the total third fund! The work was more weighted towards Private Equity (PE) versus VC, so I had to learn PE dealmaking on the job. I was also fascinated with the new environment, the exotic culture and Dubai as a fantastically diverse place.

After a few years, another SWF, Mumtalakat in Bahrain, offered me a role as Head of PE and Investments, which gave me a second stage of PE experience. The focus was originally on international investments, but after the Arab Spring events we were asked to focus on domestic investments instead, in order to generate more economic development for the region. This meant that we had to go back to more VC-style investing, as few 'classical' PE size deals were available.

We looked at sectors that had supply/demand gaps, and identified areas where the SWF had competitive advantages and could contribute to developing a company or industry. Among others, we focused on the education sector and evaluated different development and investment approaches. We discussed with the Dubai-based organisation GEMS (the largest private kindergarten-to-grade-12 school operator in the world)[13] to create a partnership, where Mumtalakat would supply the land and building (the fund owned a real estate development company that could build the buildings following the specifications of the operator), and GEMS could run the schools on rented premises. We also wanted a minority stake in the operating company.

Through this experience, I realised that education is where telecoms were 30 years ago, with the sector moving from being predominantly driven by governments to an ever-larger participation of private operators. Similar to telecoms decades ago, the education sector is fragmented and ripe for consolidation, which needs experienced and commercially minded professional management. I could see growth in the sector and for myself for many years to come.

Hence, I joined GEMS as their Global Head of Investments and Business Development, and later became CEO of GEMS Africa to lead the implementation of the investment we had raised to build 35 schools across six countries in Africa, gaining operational experience in the process.

I learned a lot and loved working with people from many cultures. However, constantly flying all across Africa was exhausting, so when I was offered to become CEO of a Dubai-based education company, Kings' Education, I accepted. Kings' have a total capacity for approximately 3,000 children in three premium schools, and around 450 employees. It is considered among the best privately owned school groups in Dubai, with its first school deemed outstanding for eight years in a row.

My advice to other executives is: follow your passion. If you feel passionate about something, you automatically become good at it, and because you're good, you'll be successful, so it becomes a virtuous circle. It does not matter if you don't have the education, skills or experience required for the job today. You can acquire them. It might take a lot of effort, but you will acquire them if you feel passionate about it!

You can see how Oliver and Pablo developed transferrable skills and gradually added tri-sector skills at each career stage.

Oliver moved from the public sector to consulting to the public sector, and now to the corporate sector through his healthcare, policy and technology transferable skills.

Pablo by applying his transferrable skills to enter new sectors in stepwise changes, adding new skills at each stage. R&D to VC investing, VC investing to government investing (SWFs), learning about education thought investing and then transferring to the corporate education sector.

You can also see the how each time they get fascinated by something, they developed new knowledge and new networks, and 'eureka' – new opportunities opened up.

## Deep-T

The consulting industry has a useful concept to describe this development of skills, that they call 'Deep-T': the top of the T represents skills and knowledge everyone needs to have (a little bit of everything the firm does), and the stem is your own specialisation. For example, in a firm such as Accenture that is technology-driven, everyone needs to know a basic amount of technology, strategy, change management, etc., and then specialise in one discipline or area (e.g. sustainability strategy, digital marketing, supply chain performance, etc.).

Question 6.1:   What is your 'Deep-T'? What are your deep skills – that few other people could do as well as you?

Question 6.2:   What are your general skills – top bar of the T – that you know enough of to be a good leader? Are any of these actually a Deep-T skill?

The Deep-T skills do not have to be *immediately* business-related or what you are tasked to do at work right now or before, like my coaching skills; they were not in my job spec either as Marketing Director at Dow Corning, Strategy Manager at Accenture or European Director of Business Development at Deloitte Consulting; neither were Ken McKellar's coaching skills part of his job description as Audit Partner at Deloitte.

Question 6.3:   Are you doing something 'naturally and automatically', which is not in your job spec, that you really enjoy doing?

## Sustainability: a transferrable skill when combined with business skill

Sustainability as an *expert functional skill set* has not seemed as transferable to date as we might first think. This will hopefully change with the increased investor interest and pressure on businesses around sustainability.[14,15,16]

Having worked with a number of executives with great sustainability credentials trying to find executive, non-executive or Advisory Board positions, I am sad to report that there has been little appetite – to date – from most major corporations to engage such deep sustainability expertise in mainstream positions.

What organisations normally want is your operational, financial, business or other core skill, translated into the sustainability issues they are addressing, or vice versa.

Using myself as a simple example: although I am reasonably well versed in Purpose, sustainability and environmental issues, the reason people hire me is because I am a good at my core skills: headhunting and coaching.

If I were not good at this, they would not hire me because of my sustainability or Purpose credentials to work on talent matters.

Another example is Geoff McDonald, previously Global Vice President HR for Marketing, Communications, Sustainability and Talent at Unilever, and one of the key people who helped Paul Polman embed his Purpose-driven journey in Unilever. Geoff is now a consultant in two areas: how to *embed* Purpose in organisations (HR + Purpose) and removing the stigma of mental health issues in the workplace (HR + health and well-being). Clients would not engage him as a consultant, in the areas of Purpose or mental health, were he not an outstanding HR director with a long track record of HR change journeys in a major corporation.

If you are a sustainability or environmental expert reading this, do not get disheartened; instead, aim to add business and strategy skills to create a credible 'horizontal bar of the T in your Deep-T'. Here is an example of someone who has made the transition from a specialist to a business strategist with great Impact.

### Jan-Willem Scheijgrond's story

Jan-Willem is the Global Head of Government Affairs (B2G) and Head of International Partnerships at Royal Philips in the Netherlands.

His responsibility includes, apart from setting up and coordinating a global network of sector and market Government Affairs experts, driving engagements to governmental stakeholders and business growth with and through governmental customers at international, national and local level. Before the spin-off of the lighting business, his responsibility spanned all of Philips' business areas. Now his focus is on Phillips' healthcare business.

Jan-Willem has been instrumental in helping Philips develop and live their mission: 'Improving people's lives through meaningful innovation' with 'the goal to improve the lives of 3 billion people a year by 2025, be the best place to work for people who share our passion, and together deliver superior value for our customers and shareholders'.[17]

He started his career with a degree in Environmental Engineering and was passionate about this topic. This was at the time of the first Rio Summit, and he tried to get Dutch companies or newspapers to send him there. When this did not happen, he decided that he needed to work for the UN – where the 'action' was – and joined UNEP, getting governments, NGOs and companies around the table. This was an entirely new concept in the 1990s. He saw the power of this approach, and it has been his guiding motto throughout his career.

After a few years at the UN, his manager advised him to go to industry and come back to the UN, in 20 years' time, to have real impact. Jan-Willem joined the leather industry, and subsequently the electronics industry, in their HES departments. Both industries were under environmental and consumer fire. He helped them work through their environmental and stakeholder issues and came to the point where he wanted to help a company develop their environmental strategy rather than implementing the strategy other people had developed.

He first joined HP, and subsequently Philips, in headquarter positions in Government Affairs, transferring his environmental and stakeholder strategy and engagement skills.

In 2012, the new Philips CEO held a massive online brainstorm with the top 600 Philips people around what should be the main elements of Philips' mission and vision going forward. The overwhelming result was that sustainability and the environment had to be part of this new strategy.

The result of Jan-Willem and Philips' work on sustainability and the environment is, for example, from being under constant fire from NGOs, now Greenpeace ranks Philips among the most environmentally friendly companies. Philips is now also seen as a valued partner, with impact, in tri-sector work at the highest levels, with the World Bank and the UN.

This new strategy has taught Philips to look at business differently: from the patient's point of view, rather than the doctor's. For example, when looking at the largest gaps in healthcare in developing countries, they found that most systems serve women and children poorly. The age group 10–20, where most of the sexual violence, HIV and illegal and dangerous abortions take place, is even worse off. So Philips has been trying to answer the question: How can we address this issue/create a healthcare system that works for women, children and adolescents?

'As Philips is a consumer business we have consumer insights and can translate this to innovation. Those insights drive our innovation agenda on three fronts: product, price and business model', says Jan-Willem.

> Therefore, Philips set up the Africa Innovation Hub, headquartered in Kenya with satellites across the continent, to meet the needs of the underserved in developing countries. This centre is where Philips develops Innovation for Africa, with Africans, in Africa. The Centre is free from heavy corporate processes and deadlines, as that does not suit their situation. The Centre is linked to innovation centres in India [who have similar issues, and they share innovations] and the Netherlands.

Jan-Willem has taken his original core skills, environmental and sustainability knowledge, first into the UN, where he discovered the power of tri-sector multi-stakeholder engagement and tri-sector strategy, which he has subsequently honed in several companies. This has borne real fruit at Philips, for him, the business and society.

How impactful his work is can be seen from the announcement by Phillips and the Dutch bank ING in 2017 of the world's first revolving

€1 billion loan facility, where the interest rate will vary depending on how well Philips meet their sustainability goals.[18]

### Contextual intelligence

This means understanding differences within and between sectors, what their priorities and KPIs are, how decision-making works, and what their 'language' and culture is.

Many executives have had the experience of working with government officials, where they were 99 per cent ready on both sides to 'sign the deal' on a project after months and years of work, only to come out with a 'no-go' decision an hour later, as the Minister of this department had to change tack 180 degrees due to political reasons. It takes a while for executives from the corporate world to understand and learn to work with this.

As Jay Koh, Founder of The Lightsmith Group and previously Partner at Siguler & Guff, and CFO and Chief Investment Strategist at OPIC, whose story we will hear more in detail shortly, says:

> There are different languages in the public and private sector, and even inside different parts of the public sector. When creating a working group, between the three sectors, normally the government and NGO language is understood by these two sectors, but less well understood by the private sector.

### Our motivations

We saw from Chapter 2 that there is a real change in consciousness of the need for Purpose with individuals, organisations and society. More and more of us realise we cannot continue the way we are going, and that no individual, organisation or sector alone can solve our most pressing needs in society.

The motivations of having influence and social impact as well as generating wealth are no longer as irreconcilable aspirations as they were even four or five years ago, when they could have seemed outlandish in some organisations.

This means that we need to understand three things about ourselves: (1) how much influence we want to wield; (2) how much impact we want to make; and (3) how much money we need to earn.

Without understanding these three aspects of how we look at value creation, there is a risk that we end up doing mainly unpaid work for organisations with small-scale ambitions in the world. That is fine, if that is what we consciously set out to do, but not so fine if we get frustrated because we have so much more to give, if we could paint on a larger canvas or if we need to earn a living. We will explore this topic further in Chapter 9.

### Prepared mind

In the future, we will all have several careers, and learning to plan for a zigzagging career will be required. This requires a prepared mind – psychologically and financially.

For many current senior leaders who have spent their careers in one organisation or sector, the prospect of a zigzagging career is truly frightening – as it is unpredictable both financially and status-wise. Especially in corporate life, this is exactly what most of us have been trained to avoid at almost all cost, as leaving to do 'something else' for a while can in a corporate setting be seen as a failure. You rarely get rehired, and if you do, it will certainly slow your career down – similar to when women take maternity leave. It is as if you suddenly can't be trusted to be 100 per cent committed to the organisation because you wanted to add more skills and different experiences to your armoury. This will make little sense in the future when we will all be zigzagging our careers, but so far HR systems and attitudes in many organisations lag far behind the reality of how the workplace is changing.

The consulting and professional services sectors are better at rehiring people, as is the public sector. Consulting firms are used to demand for their services ebbing and flowing, and public sector positions are often time-limited. This makes it commonplace for people to leave and rejoin somewhere else in the organisation bringing new skills to this team.

The NGO and not-for-profit sectors are a mix of short, medium and sometimes very long tenure of senior leaders so passionate about the cause they are working on that they cannot bear to leave, even when occasionally it would be better for their organisation that they stepped back and let someone new lead.

To be able to zigzag means we need to build up financial resources to draw from for when that interesting call comes to run a world-changing project. We also need to learn to draw from our resources, when all we might ever have done is accumulate money over a long career, when we take pay cuts to work in a different sector or change careers. Many executives I have worked with – including myself – found this quite frightening to start with, before we realise that savings can last a long time if supplemented with enough income to pay for most of our basic running costs.

What most career changers report is that learning to live more frugally – consuming less – is not only OK, but actually absolutely fine, when you are working with something you deeply care about.

Ken McKellar, who we met earlier, expresses his experience and advice on this financial topic to other executives as:

> You need to use a different lens to look at this question of finances – rather than thinking of how big an income you need, think of how small a *cost* you could get away with without major changes to your lifestyle.

For us, when I looked at it, we were debt-free and had made enough savings to go through two to three years with *no* income at all, if needed, when we pared down outgoings. This was a boring exercise but very important.

Be aggressive about the cost – we learned that a lot of 'fat' had crept into our spending over the years, and I have heard the same from many others.

For example, now we hardly ever eat out. Karen is a great cook (she had a career previously in catering), and my part of the deal is that I clear up. We enjoy each other's company even more this way, and this new career stage is a real partnership between us.

Luis Miranda, the ex-infrastructure investor and banker we met earlier, expressed it this way:

Ask yourself, 'How much is enough money?'. At a Booth MBA 25-year class reunion, many people asked me, 'How do you "quit working" – leaving the corporate world to work in the NFP sector – at this young age?'. My answer was: if you want to have a yacht, travel business class and go to fancy restaurants, then you need to work a lot harder, a lot longer. We only spend money on education and travel. This means we can take different decisions.

A prepared mind also means being able to articulate our transferrable skills, knowledge and personal brand so that we can present ourselves as credible cross-sector candidates with confidence.

I have also observed, personally as well as with others, that once the first big job transition has been done – and we 'survived' – zigzagging is no longer scary. It is a practical matter of organising our lives accordingly, having a prepared mind and not taking such wild, or badly thought through, risks that we endanger our future, personally or professionally. Few executives I have met are reckless risk-takers, rather the opposite. Nevertheless, being as well prepared as possible for unforeseen surprises is wise, and having a buffer of two to three years' living costs in the bank is wise. Life is full of surprises, and our plans might take longer to realise than we thought.

*Question 6.4:* How long of a financial runway do you have, if needed?

### Intellectual thread

We already mentioned developing holistic subject matter expertise, and reading widely and deeply, in the section about learning. To be able to affect change across the sectors, we need deep understanding of a particular topic and how this plays out across all three sectors.

This can represent a challenge for many executives, as subject matter expertise is less needed as they rise in their organisations.

Many of the generalist leadership and management skills we learn in our organisations are also valuable in the tri-sector context, but they do not guarantee success unless we have developed *contextual intelligence*, as discussed above.

Guido Schmidt-Traub, the CEO of the United Nations Sustainable Development Solutions Network (UNSDSN) describes the need for a clear intellectual thread as key for success in working across sectors:

> Think of it like in the field of medicine. Doctors are first trained as generalists who understand the whole human body. Then they become specialists, often with a very narrow focus. The trick is to get the balance right between the breadth of a systems-based training and the depth of a specialist.
>
> Senior business leaders can use their sector knowledge as a powerful launch platform for policy-focused work. However, they are often less attuned to other knowledge fields and tend to have less experience in picking up new skill sets. Most business leaders will need to improve their systems-based training.
>
> For example, if you want to work on climate change, you will need to have a good grasp of climate science. Being a good executive is terrific but rarely sufficient.

Let us illustrate with Mark Spelman, previously Global Head of Strategy for Accenture, and how his intellectual thread made it possible for him to transition to becoming the head of the World Economic Forum's Future of the Internet – Shaping the Future of the Digital Economy and Society Initiative, after his transitioning out from Accenture in 2015, around his mid-fifties.

Mark began his career co-founding StratX Consulting with his business school professor at INSEAD Jean-Claude Larréché, the creator of the world's first computerised interactive business game called *Markstrat*. Many of you will have played *Markstrat* as part of leadership development programmes.

Mark then joined Accenture in the Strategy Practice, and over time became the Global Head of Strategy for the Resources Practice, then Global Head of Strategy for all industries and service lines.

A few years back, Mark started to think about what he wanted to do the day when it was time to leave Accenture. Over a few years, he gradually explored what would interest him and took up positions that were non-conflicting with his Accenture work, in sports as a non-executive director for Sport England, and on think tanks, becoming a council member at Chatham House.

Due to his Global Strategy role in Accenture, he was a natural participant and contributor to the World Economic Forum (WEF), and he gradually gravitated to the role of leading Accenture's work with the WEF, creating real value for Accenture and the WEF, and in the process building a formidable network for whatever he wanted to do next.

When he was ready to transition out, the WEF offered him the role to lead one of their key initiatives: Future of the Internet – Shaping the Future of the Digital Economy and Society Initiative.[19]

His new role means acting on this topic, on a tri-sector basis, at the highest level of business and society to help shape where technology takes us in the future. This means real influence and impact on things that matter to the world.

I think it is quite clear what transferrable skills took Mark to where he is: Mark's deep stem of the 'Deep-T' is clearly strategy. He has worked with many aspects of strategy and business (top bar of T), plus he has been at the forefront of the business application of digital technology and its effect on work and society since the 1990s – this is his intellectual thread.

### Integrated – strategic and diverse – networks

As we have seen from every executive story on their career evolution, and with the *Career Transformational Assets*, finding the right people to dialogue with – building your diverse network – is absolutely vital.

When trying to work cross-sectorially, it is doubly important to have strategic and diverse networks, as networks have two pivotal roles:

- They are the conduits for convening and collaborating with decision-makers to solve issues together – how you create influence and Impact.
- They are also *the* most important route for transitioning into another sector, learning new skills and finding new job opportunities.

In a tri-sector context, this is logical, as neither nominations committees nor headhunters in other sectors are likely to know of your existence, or your interest to join them, and would hesitate to recruit you unless someone they trust, in their network, recommends you.

Executives who changed sector often mention that the route to these opportunities was someone who knew and trusted them from the new sector, who either contacted them directly or recommended them for the position.

We will spend a considerable amount of time on the topic of networks in Chapter 9. If there is one thing that can make or break a career change, it is network-building.

## How did executives develop tri-sector skills and competencies?

As you saw from Mark Spelman's story above, he prepared his transition out of his long-time employer, and learned about how to operate at a senior tri-sector level and built his network – while at Accenture.

A different way of learning tri-sector skills and building strategic networks is how Jay Koh, has learned tri-sector skills through zigzagging between sectors and employers throughout his career, and how he is now bringing them together, continuing to impact society – and earning a living.

### Jay Koh: from private equity to civic duty and back

Jay Koh started his career in telecoms and homeland security (aerospace and defence) investing with the private equity firm Carlyle. Most recently, Jay founded the Lightsmith Group, a new sustainable investment firm that plans to launch the world's first fund focused on resilience and adaptation to climate change. This is Jay's enlightening zigzag story – with major impact.

> In 2007, I was headhunted to Lehman Global Principal Strategies (GPS), a US$7 billion internal hedge fund, from Carlyle, to be based in London and help grow the illiquid investment business in EMEA. At GPS, I decided to focus part of our strategy on renewables because Europe had a competitive advantage versus the rest of the world. Although I had no previous experience in renewables, I had studied the development of other emerging sectors like wireless communications and homeland security while at Carlyle – renewables seemed like a sector that was also in transition and ripe for targeted investment, which I knew well how to do.
>
> GPS spun out during the financial crisis and became R3 Capital, which was eventually acquired by Blackrock as the financial sector dislocated. Following the acquisition, I was asked by the Carbon Trust to provide advice on the design of public–private partnerships (PPPs) in the off-shore wind sector – an area that was familiar to me as a result of my experience with investment in regulated industry in telecoms and homeland security sectors. One of the main things I did was to help 'translate' between government policy and private industry in designing PPPs.
>
> How did I end up as CFO, Head of Investment Funds and Chief Investment Strategist at OPIC? Through my interest in public service, my work in Washington, DC at Carlyle, and my early support for the Obama campaign, I was recommended to apply for a position at OPIC, and went through the government selection and appointment process.
>
> OPIC, the Overseas Private Investment Corporation, is a small independent agency that uses private investment to support foreign policy and development. At OPIC, I had the chance to work with US investors and gain experience in emerging markets. As the Head of Investment Funds, I was directly responsible for a US$2.6 billion private equity portfolio investing alongside US investors, pension funds, high net worth individuals, foundations and sovereign wealth funds. As Chief

Investment Strategist, I also oversaw the entire US$17 billion book of deployed assets. At OPIC, I went from being a direct investor to sitting on the limited partner (LP) side of the table and engaging sources of capital and investment. I stayed at OPIC until after President Obama's re-election, and then decided to move to New York and move my family back from the UK, where they had stayed due to my wife's career.

I thus joined Siguler Guff, as Partner and MD. Siguler has over US$10 billion of investments worldwide, and happens to be engaged in all the asset classes where I have been involved, including emerging markets private equity. I am also a Member of the Council for Foreign Relations, the Private Sector Advisory Group for the UN Green Climate Fund, and was appointed by New York Governor Cuomo to the New York State Energy Research and Development Authority (NYSERDA), which is focused on renewable energy in New York State, and on the advisory committee for the New York Green Bank. All these opportunities came through prior relationships in government and the private equity world.

I am currently trying to launch a Global Climate Adaptation & Resilience Fund, investing in companies whose products, services and technologies will help society adapt and build resilience to the physical impact of climate change. These companies will focus on weather analytics and climate resilience data, water efficiency products, drought resistant seeds, climate-resilient healthcare systems, storm-resistant energy systems, and so on. I think this an underinvested area that should generate interesting returns and help society prepare for climate change. It is difficult to raise a first-time fund in this area, and I have been thinking about how to address this problem.

In 2015, I wrote a concept paper on investing in adaptation and climate resilience that was picked up by the insurance industry and the government. We now have the Global Adaptation & Resilience Investment Working Group (GARI), that I lead, which was announced by the UN Secretary-General Ban Ki-moon at the Paris global climate talks in the fall of 2015 in conjunction with his Climate Resilience Initiative.

My idea for a climate resilience and adaptation fund won the Global Innovation Lab on Climate Finance competition in December 2016, and my partner and I are working with Lab members to launch the fund in 2017. At the end of 2016, I left Siguler Guff to found the Lightsmith Group to devote all of my time to the climate resilience fund and other strategies in sustainable investment.

Although I left government, my investment work intersects the public sphere, and I have continued to be engaged at the state, national and international level. I believe that with the right alignment between public policy and private investment, billions of dollars can be directed to address emerging challenges and technology transitions. The fund

I am working on now aims to attack one of the biggest challenges for society – building resilience to climate change – through private equity investment. Making sure the public and private sector speak the same language is critical to success.

My career has not been planned – it has been a series of 'accidents'. There are two themes, though, that run through it – a focus on government and its intersection with investment in the real world.

I have always wanted to do public service as I think it is right to give back when you are given the opportunities that I, the son of Korean immigrants who arrived in the US with US$50 in their pockets, have been given, such as a Harvard, Oxford and Yale education. Through a career that has moved between private equity and government, I have realised that the goals of public service can also be accomplished through the private sector, and an understanding of how the two can work together.

I think you can see the pattern in story after story, how we can acquire leadership skills and opportunities via building new networks and having new experiences, i.e. developing our *Career Transformational Assets*: self-knowledge, openness to new experiences, and building strategic and diverse networks.

Sitting in our office trying to figure it all out and then venturing out to implement our plan does not work. We need to unlearn a lot of old ideas and learn new truths and beliefs about the world and ourselves: what we are able to do, have impact on, and how we can achieve it.

This can only be done by placing ourselves in new environments, meeting new people, learning new knowledge and ways of acting, and then reflecting on what we have learned, again and again, in a continuous virtuous circle.

*Question 6.5:*  Reading the above, what topics surprised you?
*Question 6.6:*  Were there areas where you realise that you already have skills?
*Question 6.7:*  Were there areas you would like to develop?

## Digital skills will be needed everywhere by everyone!

Although hearing ad nauseam about the coming tsunami of disruption by digital, AI or automation, you have probably not yet seen much direct effect on your executive job.

You might consider 'escaping it all' by 'retiring' or changing careers into the not-for-profit sector. This will not be a good strategy. Everyone is going digital – for-profits, government organisations, NGOs and not-for-profits – and the hot strategy and governance topic for board members everywhere is 'Digital'.

This means that instead of trying to skip this topic, we 'digital immigrants' – pretty much everyone born before the millennial generation – need to invest serious time and energy into developing digital skills or we will be close to unemployable in five years' time.

Doing this while 'job-crafting' will ensure that we don't become irrelevant in the job market and can plan for the very long working lives we now need to create.

Let us illustrate with a few examples, from mainstream boards to not-for-profits.

Macy's, the US retailer, pulled way ahead of their competition through their omnichannel strategy – enabled by their board diversity strategy, which included acquiring digital skills.

Macy's board member Craig Weatherup expressed this in an interview with *Fortune*:

> Boards that aren't looking for younger, digitally savvy female and ethnic board members are really going to fall behind. It's a key part of staying relevant in today's market. I agree that if you're just looking for a sitting CEO or a recently retired CEO it is almost impossible. But there is no reason why that stat should be a limiting criteria.[20]

Ouch.

This trend was confirmed by the experience of a previous CEO of a large industrial company, in his early fifties, when commenting on how his NED portfolio-building was going in early 2017: 'Not good! They all want people with finance or digital experience. I am an engineer and a business person'.

Not-for-profits and NGOs of all sizes now frequently seek trustee candidates with digital experience or experience of major change initiatives – building public opinion for a policy change. This is highly social media- and digital network-driven.

A number of high-profile leaders in 'The B-Team'[21] – aiming for societal change – have high social media use, including Paul Polman (Unilever CEO), Marc Benioff (Salesforce.com CEO), Richard Branson (Virgin CEO) and Arianna Huffington (Huffington Post founder and board member of Uber).

In contrast, CEO.com found that in 2016, 60 per cent of Fortune 500 CEOs have no social media presence whatsoever.[22]

Which of these executives will be the most attractive to boards, in your view?

Finally, digital technology and network business models can achieve 10X or more impact for Purpose-driven projects and organisations, as the case study running through Libert, Beck and Wind's book *The Network Imperative* shows.[23]

Enterprise Community Partners, a not-for-profit conceived to improve all aspects of life for low-income families by first providing safe, affordable and adequate housing, during 18 years, invested USD$18 billion and helped build *340,000* affordable homes in the USA, in itself a great result.

By focusing beyond their physical asset business, creating a digital network business model delivering services relevant to their target customers, they could both multiply the life quality outcomes for their current clients plus potentially serve *40 million* families in similar circumstances – as enlarging networks digitally have almost zero marginal cost.

Whether we want to sit on boards, lead, create, contribute to or advise organisations with societal impact, we need to embrace digital business models and skills. (NB: The above examples are already real, without even mentioning how AI and automation might impact society – affecting all of us for a very long time – and that revolution is already under way.)

*Question 6.8:*    What surprised you about the need for digital understanding and skills?

*Question 6.9:*    How can you incorporate digital learning in your day-to-day work and 'job-crafting' project?

## Takeaways

To successfully create a new Purpose-driven career, we need to learn the new skills and competencies enabling work across sectors in this new hyper-collaborative, stakeholder-driven environment. They include:

- *Externally oriented leadership competencies* to understand the world and bring it into our own organisation for action.
- *Corporate Diplomacy skills* to be able to affect change.
- *Tri-sector skills* to understand how to collaborate across sectors.
- *Digital skills* to deploy technology for 10X change on societal issues.

These skills and competencies can be learned in our jobs, or by moving between sectors – zigzagging.

We develop these skills and competencies by using our *Career Transformational Assets* – self-knowledge, openness to new experiences, and building strategic and diverse networks.

*Reading the short section above on digital skills is highly recommended – it might save your second career.*

## Notes

1  CIPD (n.d.). *Competence or Competency?* Retrieved from: www.cipd.co.uk.
2  Elkington, J. and Smith, L. (27 September 2016). *Breakthrough Business Models: How to Drive Sustainable Growth in an Exponential World.* Volans. Retrieved from: www.volans.com.

3  Elkington, J. and Smith, L. (27 September 2016). *Breakthrough Business Models: How to Drive Sustainable Growth in an Exponential World.* Volans. Retrieved from: www.volans.com.

4  Hoffmann, A., Faruk, A. and Gitman, L. (2012). *Sustainability and Leadership Competencies for Business Leaders.* BSR. Retrieved from: www.bsr.org.

5  UN Global Compact (31 July 2017). *Making Global Goals Local Business: A New Era for Responsible Business*, p. 5. Retrieved from: www.unglobalcompact. org.

6  Libert, B., Beck, M. and Wind, J. (2016). *The Network Imperative: How to Survive and Grow in the Age of Digital Business Models.* Boston, MA: Harvard Business Review Press, p. 20.

7  Mirvis, P.H. (2014). Transforming Executives into Corporate Diplomats: The Power of Global Pro Bono Service. *Journal of Organisational Dynamics*, 43(3), July–September: 235–245. DOI: http://dx.doi.org/10.1016/j.orgdyn.2014.08.010.

8  Saner, R., Yiu, L. and Søndergaard, M. (2000). Business Diplomacy Management: A Core Competency for Global Companies. *Academy of Management Perspectives*, 14(1): 80–92. DOI: 10.5465/AME.2000.2909841.

9  Lovegrove, N. and Thomas, M. (2013). Triple-Strength Leadership. *Harvard Business Review*, September. Retrieved from: www.hbr.org.

10  Lovegrove, N. (2017). *The Mosaic Principle: The Six Dimensions of a Successful Life & Career.* London, UK: Profile Books.

11  Lovegrove, N. and Thomas, M. (13 February 2013). *Why the World Needs Tri-Sector Leaders.* HBR blog. Retrieved from: www.hbr.org.

12  El Economista (14 January 2016). *Nace Telefónica Innovación Alpha: La Operadora Quiere Impulsar La Transformación Digital.* Retrieved from: www. eleconomista.es.

13  Rai, S. (2014). Billionaire Education Entrepreneur Varkey Takes His Dubai School Chain Worldwide. *Forbes Asia*, April. Retrieved from: www.forbes.com.

14  Kerber, A. (13 March 2017). *Exclusive: Blackrock Vows New Pressure on Climate, Board Diversity.* Reuters. Retrieved from: www.reuters.com.

15  Mooney, A. (16 July 2017). *Schroeders Warns on Climate Change.* Ftfm. Retrieved from: www.ft.com.

16  Carrington, D. (7 December 2016). *Climate Change Threatens the Ability of Insurers to Manager Risk.* Retrieved from: www.theguardian.com.

17  Philips (2015). *Annual Report 2012: Strategic Focus.* Retrieved from: www. philips.com.

18  Ogleby, G. (20 April 2017). *Philips Agrees €1bn Loan Connecting Sustainability Performance with Finance.* Edie Newsroom. Retrieved from: www.edie.com.

19  World Economic Forum (n.d.). *The Digital Economy and Society.* Retrieved from: www.weforum.org/system-initiatives/the-digital-economy-and-society/.

20  Fairchild, C. (18 February 2015). *How Macy's Quietly Created One of America's Most Diverse Boards.* Fortune. Retrieved from: www.fortune.com.

21  The B-Team website: http://bteam.org.

22  DOMO & CEO.com (2017). *The 2016 Social CEO Report.* CEO.com. Retrieved from: www.ceo.com.

23  Libert, B., Beck, M. and Wind, J. (2016). *The Network Imperative: How to Survive and Grow in the Age of Digital Business Models.* Brighton, MA: Harvard Business Review Press, Kindle edition.

# Part III

# Creating a Purpose-driven career in practice

*In Part 3, we will get into the practical work of developing a Purpose-driven career.*

*Chapters 7 and 8 introduce three key concepts: Purpose as a direction, 'job-crafting', and finally the '9 Questions' we need to find answers for to take out our new Purpose-driven career.*

*Chapter 9 – the key chapter of this book – shows how we figure out our Purpose by going on a Discovery journey.*

*Chapter 10 shows how we make this a reality, in-house by 'job-crafting' or externally when we plan our exit.*

# Chapter 7

# Purpose is a direction – and the power of 'job-crafting'

*We will discuss two central ideas of this book: first, that Purpose is a gradually developed direction; and second, that 'job-crafting' – adding Purpose-driven work to your current job – is an effective way to learn how to be a tri-sector leader now, as well as how to develop a future career.*

## Demystifying 'finding Purpose'

The concept of Purpose has taken on a somewhat mythical quality, and although we crave it in our lives, too many of us worry about not finding 'the right' Purpose or our 'one true' Purpose in life.

There is no 'right' definition of Purpose. My Purpose, which gives me meaning in life, might not engage you at all, and vice versa. Yet we are both affecting change on world issues.

There also seems to be some underlying expectation that unless it arrives like a divine prophecy, complete with a lightning strike, it is not worthy enough.

Mark Zuckerberg eloquently articulated this view of Purpose emerging over time in his Harvard Commencement speech in May 2017 (NB: Facebook's Purpose is to 'to give people the power to share and make the world more open and connected'):[1]

> Ideas don't come out fully formed. They only become clear as you work on them. You just have to get started. If I had to understand everything about connecting people before I began, I never would have started Facebook. Movies and pop culture get this all wrong. The idea of a single eureka moment is a dangerous lie. It makes us feel inadequate since we haven't had ours. It prevents people with seeds of good ideas from getting started.[2]

To get started, then, let's remind ourselves of Aaron Hurst's definition of Purpose from Chapter 2: 'seeking our purpose is about finding a direction, not a destination. That is, purpose is a verb, not a noun'.[3]

In the Discovery process in the next chapter, we will learn about figuring out our 'Big Question' – what major issue we want to focus on solving. What if we could solve X by doing Y or Z? The *action* version of this question becomes our direction – our Purpose: 'I will help solve X by doing Y'.

Imagining potential solutions to pressing issues helps us form a few working ideas. We can then refine them through quick experimentation and small-step iterations, as Mark Zuckerberg says.

This process is different from a classic job change process. There, we know what we are looking for (similar job to today at another firm) and can make a reasonably clear plan from the outset.

In a Purpose-driven career change, we usually we have little idea what the 'job' will look like or in what kind of organisation it will exist – we probably don't know that these organisations even exist – when we start out.

Exploring in the outside world, contemplating our learning, and iterating in small steps over a significant period of time is how we gradually learn about the world and new things we did not even know existed and slowly clarify where we want to contribute.

There are no shortcuts to the personal and experiential understanding we gain when we meet new people and listen to how they see the world. The feedback and ideas we get are what helps us shape our Purpose.

## Job-crafting allows us to build our new career while at our employer

I am often asked if you can have a Purpose-driven career in a company that is not Purpose-driven.

As can be seen from the executive stories so far, very few of them work for or originally worked for organisations with explicitly stated societal Purpose. However, the executives found ways of creating Purpose-driven projects that fit within their companies' business strategies – this is known as 'job-crafting'.[4]

It is the same process most of us use to shape any job position to better suit our background and interests to deliver the organisation's goals by starting new initiatives. Purpose-driven job-crafting is different only in the sense that when we start out, our area of interest might not have an immediate, obvious fit with how our organisation sees itself and its priorities at that moment in time.

The executives' stories show that through their 'job-crafting' projects, they frequently, as a second step, ended up being offered a full-time position where they could express their Purpose and take the entire company on a learning journey that got the organisation closer to working in wider society – becoming more Purpose-driven.

The time when most executives leave their organisations is when they find that they wish to spend 100 per cent of their time on solving issues that are too removed from their organisation's main mission. A better home is now needed for these activities.

If you find that the activities you wish to pursue are so different to your organisation's core activities that your project cannot in any way fit into your current organisation's strategy, you can choose to *job-craft outside* your employer – extracurricularly – to learn, plan and build your new knowledge and networks. We will see versions of both scenarios in the coming chapters.

Executives rarely set out to deliberately change job or career; they just start a project in an area that intrigues them to find a solution to (Purpose), and end up changing career as a happy medium-term consequence.

Richard Gillies' career journey at the British retailer Marks & Spencer (M&S) is an example of this principle.

Richard is now an advisor and board member to many high-profile organisations such as BSR, Business in the Community (BITC) and We Mean Business.[5]

While working as Chief Procurement Officer at M&S, he created a job-crafting project on 10 per cent of his time with the aim to provide 100 per cent renewable energy to M&S – because it intrigued him. This led to him over time becoming Chief Sustainability Officer at M&S, and later being offered the same position at Kingfisher (both British multinational retailers), before transitioning out to affect change across multiple organisations.

Executives who know that they want to leave their employer in a few years' time create second career plans, either with or without their employer's assistance.

Most executives I have spoken to created their exit projects on their own, extracurricularly, without employer assistance, and exited when they were ready.

Others, through an open discussion with their employer, created a part- or full-time role that allowed them to build a position in their chosen sphere externally and launch themselves out with momentum when the agreed departure date arrived.

An example of the latter is Sola Oyinlola, who we met in the opening paragraphs of the book. Below is the insightful story of how Sola engineered his job-crafting, creating a beneficial role for the company and agreeing a timed plan for exit with his employer, and how he transitioned out and created a new Purpose-driven career with impact, scope and creativity.

There is a very brief mention of a critical *extracurricular* job-crafting project Sola took on that enabled his future direction as 'technology investor for the bottom billion'; he created his own small angel fund while at Schlumberger to learn how VC investing works.

As you will see, Sola's story forms a summary of many of the key topics we have discussed around conscious Purpose-driven career change, and illustrates the power of job-crafting.

### Sola Oyinlola, from treasurer in O&G to technology investor for the bottom billion

One day in my early fifties, I realised that my boss, the CFO of our company, and I were approximately the same age and we would likely retire at about the same time. At that time, I was Vice President and Group Treasurer of Schlumberger, and the only black African officer of this highly regarded French-American world-leading oilfield services company.

This similar age issue meant that I was not likely to ever become the company's CFO, and I wondered: What do I do now? Should I stay where I am for the next 10 years, or should I try to figure out how I could create a new career somewhere else?

After some time reading, learning and contemplating, I realised that I really cared about the education and emancipation of women, the ability of technology to change people's lives, and helping to create a more inclusive society that benefits all stakeholders, especially in Africa, where there was a huge income disparity in the society.

I went to the COO with a proposition and business case for how to grow our business in Africa, through harnessing certain trends in inclusiveness and growing national content in the industry, while leveraging the company's leadership in technology, talented local employees and long historic presence. I had previously been Regional CEO for Nigeria and West Africa, so this mission was a logical progression. I was asked later to take on the role as Global Head of Sustainability and CSR.

This meant leading high-level discussions with governments, national oil companies (NOCs), NGOs, etc. to help build our business in the frontier oil and gas provinces and further build the Schlumberger brand across the board.

As this was a new role, I had a white canvas to paint on where I had the opportunity to blend in many things I had learned in my career, as well as my understanding of the impact companies can have on the development of developing countries.

I was looking for a niche where Schlumberger and I could make a unique contribution to our business while also helping the region develop. Colleagues saw my interest and passion for technology, economic and social development, and I became President of the Schlumberger Foundation, where I still sit on the board post-retirement.

The foundation has a programme called Faculty for the Future, a programme that makes grants to women in STEM to pursue advanced degrees abroad in their chosen domain, and agree to go back to their home countries and become role models and catalysts for change and development in their society, leveraging technology and their new global networks in elite academia and research institutions. Today, over 600 women from over 70 countries have been so endowed with these 'Faculty for the Future' fellowships.

Leaving Schlumberger, I wanted to do something transformational. Either via my own investment – I am an angel investor in disruptive technologies – or on boards of companies, bringing existing technologies to solve well-known problems in Africa. With my Schlumberger background, I additionally bring Western standards of governance and accountability that assures investors in these frontier economies.

One of my projects, SpectraLink Wireless, involves using the unused spectrum in the TV broadcast spectrum, the so-called TV white space, for affordable broadband connectivity for underserved communities, or 'the bottom billion'. SpectraLink has pioneered this technology in Africa in 2015.

Broadband connectivity can be leveraged to open huge doors of development in these underserved communities – from telemedicine, to remote education, to expanded access to agricultural markets, and better governance through efficient e-government. Increasing broadband internet penetration by 10 per cent is estimated to lead to 1 per cent point GDP growth. Imagine, if a small investor like myself can help contribute this massively to development!

My Schlumberger technology experience allows me to work on this passion: how to make technology accessible to solve problems for the bottom billion.

*Question 7.1:* Did anything surprise you in Sola's story?

You can see all the things we have spoken about: Germination, Discovery and Fruition, Endings, Unknown Zone, New Beginnings, self-knowledge, strategic and diverse network-building, openness to new experience, learning, immersing himself at the edge, letting a potential new future emerge, acting on it, 'job-crafting', building tri-sector skills, Corporate Diplomacy skills, and a number of the new leadership competencies.

You can also see the tremendous value that Sola helped deliver during his conscious 'transition period', to Schlumberger and the countries in Africa they work in.

Transitions are confusing as we are redefining our identities and our work. This does not mean that they are unproductive; on the contrary, they are often amazing growth spurts in our personal and career development.

It is also important to realise that no one was born a great Purpose-driven tri-sector leader. Like great sportspeople and musicians, great leaders work very hard at constantly learning new capabilities and becoming better and better at what they do.

As a senior leader you have the ability to help create transformational change. You have experience of solving complex problems across cultures and technologies, the convening power the positions and company brands confer to you, and a great ability to learn.

I would encourage you to go on a Discovery journey – and see what issues you could contribute to in the world – before you settle for a classic portfolio of exclusively non-executive director positions.

Watching so many capable executives with all their experience, skill and abilities vanish from the workforce when these abilities could contribute to so much societal change is disheartening.

## Takeaways

Purpose is something we find by exploring and learning; it does not suddenly 'arrive'.

'Job-crafting', creating projects that have societal impact, while at our employer gives us time and space to learn and figure out how we want to pursue our Purpose with Impact.

It is sometimes possible to create a timed exit programme with our employers, where we can pursue our Purpose, deliver value to them and society and create a position for ourselves to have Impact when we leave.

## Notes

1 Zuckerberg, M. (5 February 2012). *Mark Zuckerberg's IPO Letter Describing Facebook's Purpose, Values & Social Mission*. Retrieved from: http://prosperos world.com/.
2 BizNews (27 May 2017). *Mark Zuckerberg's Harvard Address: Why Finding Your Own Purpose Isn't Enough*. Retrieved from: www.biznewspm.com.
3 Hurst, A. (2014). *The Purpose Economy: How Your Desire for Impact, Personal Growth and Community Is Changing the World*. Boise, ID: Elevate, Kindle edition, location 1174.
4 Wrzesniewski, A., LoBuglio, N., Dutton, J. and Berg, J. (2013). Job Crafting and Cultivating Positive Meaning and Identity in Work. *Advances in Positive Organizational Psychology*, 1: 281–302. DOI: 10.1108/S2046-410X(2013) 0000001015.
5 Richard Gillies LinkedIn profile: www.linkedin.com/in/richard-gillies-94b6383/.

# Chapter 8

# The '9 Questions' of Discovery and Fruition

*In this chapter, we will cover the key building blocks of figuring out our Purpose – the '9 Questions' – that we will work with over the following two chapters, and why spending considerable time in Discovery mode is vital.*

## How to affect societal change – and create career change with Purpose

In their 2015 book *Getting Beyond Better*, strategy guru Roger L. Martin and Skoll Foundation President and CEO Sally Osberg, together with Arianna Huffington, say that four stages are needed for successfully creating a significant shift in society:

- *Understanding the world.* The paradox of social transformation is that one has to truly understand the system as it is before any serious attempt can be made to change.
- *Envisioning a new future.* To make a positive difference, every change agent, whether a social entrepreneur or not, needs to set a direction.
- *Building a model for change.* To bring a vision to life, social entrepreneurs must apply creativity and resourcefulness to building a model for change – one that is sustainable in that it reduces costs or increases value in a systemic and permanent way that can be quantified and captured.
- *Scaling the solution.* Scalability is a critical feature of successful social entrepreneurship.[1]

For clarity, social entrepreneurs here is meant as anyone attempting systemic social change, not founders of social enterprises (businesses with a social mission).

Figure 8.1 translates these four areas into the Purpose-driven career change process. The four areas are: us; the outside world; and the finance and organisational models suited to executing our Purpose project. How to find answers to these questions will be the topics of Chapters 9 and 10.

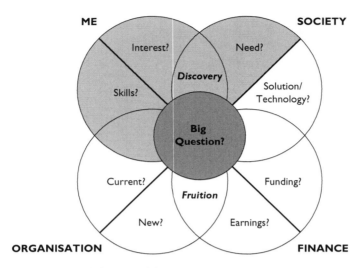

*Figure 8.1* The '9 Questions' for a Purpose-driven project, position or business

First, through the Discovery process, we figure out our central Big Question and define our Purpose, the action version of this question. We work mainly with three areas – our own interests, our skills, and if there is a need in society for what we are interested in solving.

Second, we move into making our Purpose reality – Fruition – and work with the other areas to build the business case for our idea: possible solutions, funding, income, and how it could fit in our organisation's strategy (how we could job-craft), or if it needs to be pursued outside our current employer. The latter means either extracurricular work for us and/or a transition out of the organisation.

## Discovery: just getting started is the important thing

Discovery is about exploring widely, gradually crystallising our future direction, through finding a Big Question that we want to help answer. This can guide our work and life for the next substantial stretch of time.

Discovery is the most critical part of the process. We have seen this already from many executives' stories. Yet over the years, I have observed that getting started on Discovery is where most executives struggle.

We are used to being the person who 'knows' and whose advice and decisions are being sought. Going Discovering means being a beginner again, a 'rookie', in a state of 'not knowing', vulnerable, needing help and potentially looking amateurish – all representing the antithesis of the image we are taught to adopt as leaders.

Finally, we are used to having well-defined goals already before we start a project. Starting a project where we have no idea where we are heading can be daunting.

I have also learned over the years that once executives get going past the first wobbly steps, they quickly get the bit firmly between their teeth and are unstoppable. It is about taking that first step, and then the next, and very soon we are running.

This was the experience of Mark (not his real name), a senior oil and gas technology and production executive from one of the oil majors.

After taking early retirement, in his mid-fifties, he became head of an energy-consulting firm's new oil and gas practice. After 18 months, the oil price tanked and client work started to dry up.

Mark wanted to think about what he might do if the firm closed down his practice. He was financially secure but wanted to work full-time for many more years to come. His low-energy body language exuded the message: 'I feel lost, but don't know what to do about it'.

When I suggested that he should go Discovering, he looked at me sceptically. Even more so when I suggested that instead of his idea of sitting down to make a plan and execute it, he could set up a coffee meeting per week with a 'new, weird and wonderful person' that he would not normally meet, recommended by others (to rapidly move beyond the 'lazy' networks most of us have). His comment was, 'Can I count you as the first weird and wonderful person?'. Fair enough . . .

I had noticed that Mark had an interest in supply chain issues. After our meeting, I sent him a link to an article that, by complete chance, popped into my Twitter feed on the potential for blockchain guaranteeing provenance in supply chains.[2]

I heard nothing back for several days and thought, 'Oh well, another executive without manners'. When Mark's thank you note finally arrived, I could feel the excitement radiating from the screen. 'That article was amazing. I have been happily "lost" on the Internet for two days following one link after another in different directions. I had no idea so much is going on out there! This is so EXCITING!'. And off Mark was on his Discovery process. Unstoppable.

The point of this story is that you don't need to know up-front exactly what to go and explore. Pick anything that interests you and start reading, meeting people and exploring. Just getting going is the key, as Mark Zuckerberg told us in Chapter 7.

On the way, you will discover other topics that intrigue you and you might shift direction. This is OK – we are Discovering.

Don't discard topics as not serious or worthy enough. All learning is valuable, and it helps you make connections between disparate areas where you might have a unique possibility to make an impact with your particular transferrable skills.

This is particularly important at this time when sectors and technologies are converging. At the edges and in the grey zones in between established areas is where the new technologies, solutions, policies and programmes are being created, and this is where the really exciting opportunities for work are emerging.

To illustrate the power of reading widely and extrapolating between fields, let's use Elon Musk, the founder of Tesla and Space-X, and two more billion-dollar companies. Since his early teenage years, he has reportedly read up to two books per day on widely differing topics – studying in many different fields, understanding the underlying principles and then applying these principles elsewhere.[3,4]

By reading widely, we have a better chance of understanding fundamental principles that can be applied cross-sector, where our core speciality can create Impact. Reading leads to more reading, identifying organisations, events and people you could learn more from and problem-solve with. And off we go to build networks and have new experiences. In principle, Discovery is really as simple as that.

### The Big Question: a guiding light

A 'Big Question' – converted into our Purpose – once found, works like a lighthouse guiding the direction of our solution development.

Big Questions are in the line of: 'I wonder if . . . ?', 'What if . . . would be possible?' or 'Wouldn't it be amazing if . . . ?'

Finding a Big Question is like a finding a lighthouse just beyond the summit of a hill; you can't actually see the lighthouse before you reach the top. The road there is through a maze, but you know instinctively that as long as you are moving uphill, you will at some point get to the top. You'll likely take dead ends and a longer route than necessary, but you will learn a lot on the way. Once you reach the summit, you see the lighthouse – the Big Question – that lights the route downhill clearly, including potential obstacles and opportunities.

To illustrate, let's go back to Richard Gillies, who we met in the previous chapter. Richard's purpose was not to become Chief Sustainability Officer of M&S; he was doing his normal job as Chief Procurement Officer, wondering for years how he could have a major impact on environmental issues – his maze.

He had an epiphany one morning when he contemplated that he had spent more time worrying about not littering with a stray small plastic bottle on the street than how M&S electricity was produced before he signed their monthly invoice.

His Big Question became: 'What if we could procure 100 per cent green energy for M&S?'.

This question in action mode (Purpose) became: I want to help M&S become a 100 per cent renewable energy user. This Purpose guided

Richard's further Discovery and Fruition process that over the next seven years resulted in 100 per cent renewable energy for M&S. As his knowledge of what could be done increased, he widened the scope of his Purpose, and subsequently became Chief Sustainability Officer for M&S, and continued building a career in this area.

### Can we be in Discovery mode for too long?

Theoretically, we can be in Discovery mode for too long; however, I have found the opposite to be true – executives normally spend too little time on Discovery. Discovery is exciting but often uncomfortable, and we are impatient to get to the goal and have *the* answer to stop the anxiety of not knowing where we will end up and how we'll earn our living. If we stop quickly, we deprive ourselves of learning things that might transform our lives.

The process often resembles what Yanos Michopolous experienced.

Yanos worked many years for Shell, and after a spell as CEO for Greece's national railways TrainOSE he became MD Southern Europe for Vestas, the Danish wind turbine manufacturer.

While at Vestas, who were going through a turbulent time, Yanos wanted to figure out what he really wanted to do next. He was not sure what his next career stage might contain, so he gave himself a grace period encompassing 9 to 12 months to go and Discover.

When we met up towards the end of that period, Yanos said, 'I am having fantastic fun exploring, but I am going in so many directions. I feel I now need to focus and I can't choose'.

The varied areas were: build an eco-resort for executive well-being in his home country Greece – he had land and a potential investor; leadership development – he had been discussing with various organisations; teaching in higher education – he had done guest lectures and liked it; private equity – he had PE firms wanting him to be CEO for some of their energy and clean tech portfolio companies; plus the option of a return to the corporate world – as an MD of a business unit.

He concluded that the resort idea was really for a later stage in his life – as he still had some family commitments to take care of.

His heart was telling him that he wanted to focus on education of the next generation of leaders, and at the same time the return to the energy world was a real possibility due to remuneration, status and the fact that in a few years these opportunities might not be open to him. However, this meant going back to an industry in which he had already spent almost 25 years.

I asked, 'Could these be combined? There is a huge amount of private equity investment going into education, including leadership development and well-being'. You could almost see the hair stand up on his head . . .

While Yanos continues to build his network and track record in the education sector, he has become Managing Director for Europe, Oil & Gas for an American science and technology company that is part of a private equity firm!

This way, he is preparing for a future potential opportunity combining the two strands – education of the next generation of leaders in a private equity setting.

### The importance of grace periods

Going on a Discovery journey is like what Dr David Livingstone did when he set out to find the source of the Nile. Livingstone had an idea of what he was trying to do, but he had no idea what he was going to encounter on the way, where he would actually end up, or exactly how long time it would take. He accepted the new reality as he went.

As mentioned, we often don't explore wide enough or long enough to learn something radically new about the world and ourselves. Like explorers, setting an approximate date until which we are free to not decide or force focus on the activity is very helpful. The length of this grace period for Discovery is up to you. From my personal experience, 6 to 12 months, depending on how new this activity is to us, with a check-in point with ourselves every few months, works for most people to find a workable idea of their 'Big Question'. You could also see this in Yanos' story above.

Once our 'Big Question' is clear(ish), it normally takes another 6 to 12 months to figure out how this might be practically implemented.

*Question 8.1:*   What length of grace period would you like to set for your Discovery process and first check-in time?

### Scheduling project time

Understanding how we want to contribute to society and making it real requires dedicated time in the calendar.

This means for most of us, with our extremely busy lives, that we need to make decisions about what activities we'll give up to free up time for our Discovery process. How many hours do we spend just relaxing, watching TV, reading news on the Internet, or answering emails and messages that could wait?

We all have the same number of hours per day at our disposal as Gandhi, Marie Curie or Albert Einstein had – the question is how we prioritise to use them.

Once we get used to having our own thinking and exploration time, it becomes sacrosanct. It is often the most productive, creative and insightful time of our week, and increases our productivity.

Many of the most successful CEOs in the world reserve at least a day a week for thinking and reading. Warren Buffett, the famous investor, has spent 80 per cent of his time during his entire career thinking and reading.[5,6,7]

One solution, opted for by many CEOs and consulting Partners, is to work from home on Fridays, taking no calls or meetings, instead thinking and progressing important strategic projects.

Other executives arrive an hour earlier in the office and work on their project before colleagues arrive, or work on it an hour at home before starting their commute. For others, the solution has been to use their commuting time on trains and planes or spend an hour or two alone with a notepad each weekend in a café.

We all find what works for us. The point is to carve out regular time for you and your project, and schedule it in your calendar, so that it can be protected and becomes a habit.

Question 8.2:   How many hours per week do you want to spend on your Discovery project in the next three months?

Question 8.3:   What activities can you change to schedule this amount of time each week?

### Be prepared for extracurricular work

The experience by executives who have transitioned successfully is that in the beginning, your Discovery project will be mainly an extracurricular activity.

You will need to invest time to acquire knowledge, meet new people, start to experiment, and then build the business case – for why this should be part of your role – in order for the organisation to see value and accept that this new activity becomes a part of your job.

We are used to adapting our roles this way when the organisation requires us to take on new responsibilities and projects. Job-crafting for Purpose in our work is the same thing. It can feel different as it is on our instigation and often deals with topics the organisation is not yet used to addressing.

We need to gradually help our organisation see the link to the daily business or longer-term strategy; to help them change their 'filters' for how they see the world and understand that Purpose helps society and the bottom line.

## Takeaways

In order to discover our Purpose, we go on a journey to Discover where our skills and interest meet the needs of society.

We then formulate our 'Big Question' – 'What if . . . would be possible?' – and convert it to an actionable direction – Purpose.

Discovery is a process we should spend time on; we learn invaluable things on the way, and we need to continuously schedule time for this.

There is no 'right' starting point. The key is to just start, and let what you learn guide you.

## Notes

1 Martin, R., Osberg, S. and Huffington, A. (2015). *Getting Beyond Better: How Social Entrepreneurship Works*. Brighton, MA: Harvard Business Review Press, Kindle edition, locations 342–356.
2 Elkington, J. (8 March 2016). *How Technology Can Expose Bad Business*. Eco-Business. Retrieved from: www.eco-business.com.
3 Simmons, M. (15 April 2017). *How Elon Musk Learns Faster and Better Than Everyone Else*. Medium. Retrieved from: https://medium.com.
4 Simmons, M. (23 March 2015). *How One Life Hack from a Self-Made Billionaire Leads to Exceptional Success*. Forbes. Retrieved from: www.forbes.com.
5 Scudamore, B. (7 April 2016). *Why Successful People Spend 10 Hours a Week Just Thinking*. Inc. Retrieved from: www.inc.com.
6 Scudamore, B. (3 June 2016). *Why This CEO Takes Every Friday Off*. Wall Street Journal. Retrieved from: www.wsj.com.
7 Business.com (11 July 2014). *How the World's Top CEOs Manage Their Time*. Retrieved from: www.business.com.

# Chapter 9

# Discovery

## Opening our eyes, hearts and minds to the world

*In this pivotal chapter of the book, we will work practically towards formulating our Big Question – the societal issue we would like to help solve – using three of the '9 Questions': societal needs, our interests and our skills.*

*There are three distinct – and very different – parts:*

- *Understanding our own interests and values, and identifying societal needs we are interested in helping address.*
- *Learning to use our Career Transformational Assets – self-knowledge, openness to new experiences, and building strategic and dynamic networks – to find out if and how this could be possible.*
- *Practising formulating our Big Question.*

*As the pivotal chapter, it is longish, mainly due to many executives' stories illustrating key aspects of the Discovery process and the inclusion of some exercises.*

*A quick read-through is recommended, then a return to pick exercises that appeal to you, depending on where you are on your Discovery journey – or design your own inspired by your reading. Do what feels right for you.*

### Three areas for discovering our Big Question

The three aspects of the Discovery process are, as seen in Chapter 8: exploring what we are interested in; what society's needs are; and what our transferrable skills are. See Figure 9.1.

Through the Discovery process, they come together to help articulate our Big Question, which we turn into our action-oriented direction – Purpose.

This was beautifully expressed by the novelist Frederick Buechner as 'where your deep gladness and the world's deep hunger meet'.[1]

This chapter is mainly focused on finding 'our heart's gladness and the world's deep hunger'. In my experience, the hardest task for most senior leaders, aiming for a career change with Purpose, is to figure out what area they would like to contribute to, not what their skills are.

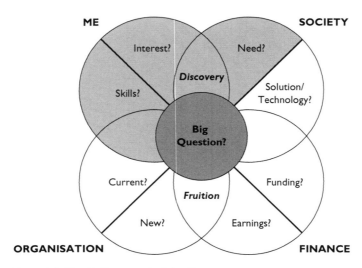

*Figure 9.1* The '4 Questions' of the Discovery process

We covered the topic of transferrable skills in Chapter 6, but if you wish to take a look at transferrable skills in a structured fashion, you can find exercises in Appendix 2.

This chapter is written so that readers who have never looked at changing careers, have no concrete ideas of what they would like to pursue, or like a bit of structure can start their Discovery journey with confidence.

If you roughly know the area you are interested in, but not how you could contribute, you can focus on the section 'What interests me deeply' to ensure your values and dreams for your future are incorporated into your Purpose.

If you know quite well what and how you want to contribute, but not in which area you could express this with Impact, focus on the section 'What societal need engages me'.

Alternatively, read through and pick the exercises that speak to you. There is likely to be at least one or two where you think, 'I have never considered that'.

If you are not an 'exercise' person, I would still encourage you to do Exercise 1, as it is often life-changing – and then let the topics inspire you to use whatever method suits you.

Let us kick-start the Discovery process by uncovering skills and abilities we are unaware of, creating a fresh lens for our lives and careers.

### Creating a new frame of reference: what do you appreciate about me?

Before doing anything else, I recommend you ask a few people the question: 'What do you *appreciate* about me?'. We rarely get to hear what unique abilities we bring – we all have positive blind spots, like we have negative blind spots.

Remember, from Chapter 5, how I would never have found out that I was good at coaching if I had not been told that I am good at asking questions that make people think deeply?

When I asked a trusted business friend the question above, the astonishing (to me) reply was, 'You take people as they come. You don't care from what background they come or what they do for work; you don't judge people'.

Putting these two insights together, coaching became a natural direction to explore. This would never have occurred to me without these two pieces of input; they literally reframed my view of myself and changed the direction of my life.

If we ask 'What do you think I am good at?' or 'What do you think I should do next?', we normally get told what professional tasks or skills we are good at, or extrapolations of what we are currently professionally engaged in. We can figure most of that out ourselves, but we can't see our positive blind spots.

---

## Exercise I   What do you appreciate about me?

Ask five people who you trust and know reasonably well (not your closest, long-standing friends, colleagues or family members) *three things* that they appreciate about you.

Don't specify or clarify anything, just listen and note down.

---

## The semi-structured 'Dump–Sort–Contemplate–Choose' process

To do our work to discover our interests and society's needs, we will use a semi-structured process with the four stages named in the title above.

There are two reasons for the semi-structured approach: first, in a fast-changing world, it is more effective to pursue broad themes than precise plans; second, we get to use the creative part of our brains.

This way of working might feel uncomfortable to start with, but hang in there and you will discover how much you already 'know' – but were not consciously aware of.

### Focus and unfocus is the key to creativity

If we are focusing in with too much structure, we don't get to use the creativity of the rest of our minds.[2] Srini Pillay, Assistant Professor at Harvard Medical School and the author of *Tinker, Dabble, Doodle, Try*, says:

In keeping with recent research, both focus *and* unfocus are vital. The brain operates optimally when it toggles between focus and unfocus, allowing you to develop resilience, enhance creativity, and make better decisions too.

When you unfocus, you engage a brain circuit called the 'default mode network'. Abbreviated as the DMN, we used to think of this circuit as the Do Mostly Nothing circuit because it only came on when you stopped focusing effortfully. Yet, when 'at rest', this circuit uses 20% of the body's energy (compared to the comparatively small 5% that any effort will require).

The DMN needs this energy because it is doing anything but resting. Under the brain's conscious radar, it activates old memories, goes back and forth between the past, present, and future, and recombines different ideas. Using this new and previously inaccessible data, you develop enhanced self-awareness and a sense of personal relevance. And you can imagine creative solutions or predict the future, thereby leading to better decision-making too.[3]

### Pursuing themes is effective in a fast-developing environment

In an environment where sectors and technologies are converging and new initiatives and coalitions are announced almost daily, pursuing a narrow or linear exploration process is not the most effective way.

You might also find that your Purpose is to help answer a question on the edges of two or more areas. Pursuing themes also allows you to become aware of – and visible to – your perfect opportunity, even if it does not exist today.

To illustrate, how many of us could have put the following topics or organisations on our list to explore, even a few weeks before they were announced?

That in September 2016, Mark Zuckerberg and his wife Priscilla Chan would pledge US$3 billion for breakthrough medical research with the aim to eradicate or manage all disease by the end of the century?[4]

That Public Investment Fund (PIF) of Saudi Arabia, known for its low-risk investments, would in 2016 first invest US$3.5 billion in Uber and then announce a JV with Softbank of Japan to create the US$100 billion Softbank Vision Fund, to create the largest tech fund in the world?[5]

Or a few years ago, that the distributed ledger technology behind the cryptocurrency Bitcoin, blockchain, would be the hottest technology in town for banks, governments and the music industry, even for proving ethical or sustainable provenance or reduce modern slavery?[6]

Or that within a couple of weeks of the White House announcing their intention to withdraw the USA from the Paris Climate Change Agreement, over 2,000 American mayors, governors, universities and companies would decide that #wearestillin?

Yet these initiatives will have been discussed and planned for a considerable time, as Mark Zuckerberg commented when he announced the new US$600 million Chan Zuckerberg science research centre and its new leader Cornelia Bargmann, a neuroscientist at Rockefeller University.[7]

This reinforces what we discussed earlier – in the tri-sector area, new positions mainly show up through referrals via your connections. The Discovery process allows you to learn to know the networks where these new initiatives are created and get known by them.

By pursuing a few themes, you increase your chances of being in the right place at the right time to be considered for these new exciting Purpose-driven opportunities. Just starting to explore is the key – the answer develops over time – in your new networks.

### The 'Dump–Sort–Contemplate–Choose' semi-structured process

The major task in our Discovery process is to discover new things we do not know today and use them as fuel for our contemplation and developing insight into where we need to go next to find new knowledge and answers.

To be able to make discerning choices, we also need to surface our own inner wisdom – all the ideas and thoughts that have floated around in our minds for a long time. You will be amazed at how much you already know about what you want.

This process described can be used for both the original 'surfacing work' and for digesting external learnings on the way. We will use it in many places going forward, and each exercise has its own guiding questions:

- *Dump.* We write down whatever topic surfaces without worrying about anything being relevant, possible, orderly, complete or perfect. Whatever tumbles out is fine; it does not matter if it is a 'what', 'why', 'how', 'who' or 'if' . . . until we feel empty (for now). (Unfocus)
- *Sort.* We sort our jumbled thoughts into themes. Post-it notes or mind mapping can be useful. Keep the 'discarded ideas' in a pile – they often turn out useful later! (Focus)
- *Contemplate.* We see where there are patterns, clarity, overlaps or gaps. We might need to sort the topics several different ways before a pattern emerges. (Unfocus)
- *Choose.* We pick two to four themes that intrigues us most – we are making our emergent ideas actionable through creating a loose focus. (Focus)

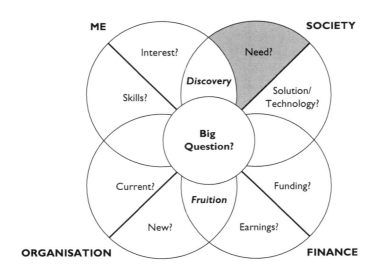

## What societal need engages me: using the SDGs to start Discovery

Our Big Question addresses a need in society we feel energised to fill. We can start from any topic that we feel drawn to or we can use the Sustainable Development Goals (SDGs), the Paris Climate Change Agreement, or any other framework we like, to get started.

*Figure 9.2* The UN Sustainable Development Goals (SDGs) – Routledge supports the SDGs

The approach below is aimed at executives who have not yet significantly explored their potential role in solving societal issues.

If you are deeply steeped in the SDGs, you might use this exercise to contemplate how they could play out in your organisation if you went for a '10X versus continuing like now' strategy (10X = a 10-fold improvement versus what we are doing now), as this might trigger some ideas for your business and your personal longer-term career strategy.

Even if you are not very familiar with the SDGs, a couple of them probably intuitively attract you. Start your Discovery process with them, and if you realise that an area is not right for you, try another. The learning you have gained is never wasted and, as already mentioned, many exciting new opportunities are being created on the edges of overlapping systems, and many SDGs influence each other.

Each SDG is a broad category with many subtopics, and the task is to find in which particular subtopic you are likely to be effective, have impact, enjoy contributing towards and, if needed, earn a living.

To illustrate, let's look at Goal 3 – good health and well-being – as described on the UN SDG Knowledge Platform:

> Goal 3 seeks to ensure health and well-being for all, at every stage of life. The Goal addresses all major health priorities, including reproductive, maternal and child health; communicable, non-communicable and environmental diseases; universal health coverage; and access for all to safe, effective, quality and affordable medicines and vaccines. It also calls for more research and development, increased health financing, and strengthened capacity of all countries in health risk reduction and management.[8]

Inside this definition is everything from paediatric to geriatric healthcare to medical research, community health, health financing, and much more.

Inside 'healthcare' alone there is a breadth of activities and technologies that will suit one person and not another. You could, like entrepreneur Rajan Pandahare, spend your time investing in hospital care in India;[9] like Oliver Harrison (who we met in Chapter 6), be CEO for the Spanish telecom company Telefónica's Innovation Health Moonshot[10] (part of the company's future-oriented digital R&D investment of over €1.1 billion);[11] or work on making vaccines affordable for the bottom billion like Dr Manica Balasegaram, Executive Director for Médecins Sans Frontières' Access Campaign.[12]

### It is about finding a concrete topic where what you bring can make a real difference

Remember Jan-Willem Scheijgrond in Chapter 6. In his and Philip's case, they make a real difference, with their knowledge and resources, working to improve the healthcare for an underserved segment – late childhood and young adults – in developing countries.

A further subsegment of healthcare is mental health. Geoff McDonald, the ex-Unilever Group VP of HR, discovered that removing the stigma from mental health in the workplace is his Purpose.

Geoff was instrumental in helping Paul Polman instil Purpose into Unilever's organisation. Their Sustainable Living Plan, aimed at 'significantly improving the well-being of a billion people by 2020',[13] triggered the realisation that Unilever needed to focus on their own employees' well-being as well.

Although Unilever had great mental health amenities in place to support employees, they were not utilised, as employees worried about divulging mental health concerns.

Geoff co-created a pilot project in their London office around mental health in the workplace that was so successful that Paul Polman gave his public support for a programme that has now gone global.

Geoff had 'job-crafted' a project in his area of passion that he found a way of positioning inside Unilever's overall strategy. This was good for him, Unilever and society.

After leaving Unilever, apart from helping companies embed Purpose, he is now focusing most of his time and passion on helping remove the stigma from mental health in the workplace in the UK and beyond.

We will hear more about what Geoff has created in Chapter 10.

### How to practically work this way with the SDG's

Using the 'Dump–Sort–Contemplate–Choose' technique, we will do three 'Dumps' before we 'Sort–Contemplate', and then two rounds of 'Choose'.

*Dump* – first, we pick a couple of SDGs that interests us and record all our associations; second, we combine them to discover what shows up at the edges of the system – interesting new areas, gaps and overlaps; and third, we combine our chosen SDGs, in turn, with our background (industry, business, technology or finance, etc.) and start identifying what kinds of *issues* our background might help solve.

We then *Sort* all this into themes of issues (and other important themes that can be used later) and take time to *Contemplate* what all this means and *re-Sort* if needed.

*Choose* – first, we sort the themes on the *impact* a solution to this theme would have (the world's need); and second, we sort them on *what excites us most* to work on (our heart's gladness), and we pick three or four themes.

These three or four themes create the basis for our Discovery process in the outside world. Structured stepwise exercises can be found below.

Why combine SDGs and your experience? SDGs and major practical issues often intersect with each other like in UNDP's collaborative initiative for sustainable healthcare procurement. This was created as public and healthcare professionals all over the world are exposed to risks when heathcare is delivered – from waste management to persistent organic pollutants (SDGs 3 and 12).[14]

Hence, if you are of a procurement background and put the two topics 'healthcare' and 'procurement' together, you can probably identify a number of areas for further fruitful exploration, and the same for HR, etc.

Skoll Award winners Riders for Health was born from such a combination insight, as described on their Skoll Award winner's web page:

> Andrea and Barry Coleman share a passion for motorcycles. Andrea is a former racer and Barry is a journalist and author. Through the racing world they became involved in fundraising for children in Africa. Visiting the communities served by the charities they supported, Barry and Andrea noticed broken vehicles everywhere many that could have been returned to service with minor repairs and maintenance. They saw women in childbirth being carried to the hospital in wheelbarrows, one of whom died during their visit.
>
> Frustrated that aid agencies abandoned vehicles rather than commit to basic repairs, the Colemans decided to fix the problem themselves. They re-mortgaged their house and founded Riders for Health to ensure delivery of essential healthcare services to rural Africa.[15]

Motorbikes and other light vehicles are vital components of delivery of essential healthcare to rural locations in Africa, if they are operable, and these two motorbike enthusiasts put the two together to amazing and measurable effect.[16]

Finally, if you are in a full-time position and would like to 'job-craft', a further powerful lens to use for exploration is Ben & Jerry's mission statement, which we mentioned in Chapter 1: 'We are a social justice organisation that happens to be making ice-cream'.[17]

Substituting 'ice cream' for what your organisation is supplying, and then contemplating all the things your business could do in your local community, in communities in your supply chain and wider society, can allow you to find a 'job-crafting' project that you are passionate about, as well as unleashing a tremendous amount of innovation in the organisation.

---

## Exercise 2    Using the SDGs to start Discovery

Pick a couple of SDGs that you feel attracted to, and go through the following questions for each individual SDG:

*(continued)*

*(continued)*

- What sub-sectors can you identify?
- What related issues, thoughts, questions or associations come to you, looking at this topic?

Don't aim for completeness or great accuracy; you will find facts later, and add and revise as you learn.

Transfer the individual answers to Post-it notes, and sort in themes or mind map them. You might need to sort them a couple of times.

What themes can you see emerging? Write them down.

---

## Exercise 3    Combining SDGs to find intersecting areas of interest

Take two of your SDGs and look at them together:

- What thoughts, ideas and opportunities come to mind that could be affected by both these issues being addressed together?
- What topics, ideas, opportunities or issues fall in the space between the two?

Transfer the individual answers to Post-it notes, and sort in themes or mind map them. You might need to sort them a couple of times.

What themes can you see emerging? Write them down.

---

### *Your background as a catalyst: a call to functional leaders*

Before moving on to Exercise 4, looking at the SDGs from the lens of your professional background, I would like to also call on functional leaders – before you settle for classic NED or trustee second careers – to explore how your experience could affect wider change, even exponentially on whole systems – 10X.

How could you, as a CFO in retail, insurance or chemicals, become 'a force for good' in affecting a major issue in the world outside your organisation? How could your skills help change the situation in avoiding corruption, ensuring fair tax payments around the world, enabling small companies in developing countries to get access to the right type of finance, helping to devise new finance models for insurance for low-income families, etc.?

To date, I see few senior HR leaders involved in big societal issues. HR is instrumental in embedding Purpose and values in organisations, as well as driving the leadership development programmes that will shape the next generation of leaders everywhere.

Technology is part of the solution in every SDG, so if you come from any technical background, whether software, digital or 'physical technology', there are enormous opportunities to find an area that could interest you.

With the speed the world is changing, Discovery journeys are useful for all of us, no matter where we are in an organisation.

Nick O'Donohoe is an example of an originally 'functional' leader who, via 'job-crafting', created a career working on system-wide change.

For many years Global Head of Research at J.P. Morgan, Nick was intrigued when, in 2007, a young MD in New York returning from a year-long sabbatical with Ashoka wished to start a social finance business in the firm. A senior executive was needed to supervise her in this position, and Nick agreed.

Although this might have turned out to be a distraction from his normal work, at least in the short term, he was intrigued as he had had some earlier exposure to microfinance. He spent a considerable part of his time on this 'side project' internally.

Externally, he became involved in the early stages of the Global Impact Investment Network (GIIN) – which aims to set out good standards for Impact investing, including how to measure Impact – and orchestrated the Impact Investment Report in 2010 with the Rockefeller Foundation.

When Big Society Capital was created – with the purpose of creating social investment firms to fund new front-line social organisations – Nick was asked to help set it up and be the first CEO.[18] He jumped at the chance as he felt the time had come to do something different.

Nick helped create this 'world first' financial institution, operated by a trust, funded by £600 million from the UK Commission on Unclaimed Assets and a few hundred million pounds of equity from leading banks,[19] which has been visited and studied by many government representatives from all over the world.

After almost five years, when Big Society Capital was up and running, Nick decided it was time for someone else to run the bank, and left to become Senior Advisor to the Bill & Melinda Gates Foundation in January 2016.

In March 2017, Nick was named CEO of Commonwealth Development Capital (CDC), the UK's development finance institution, continuing to work on global systemic issues through innovative finance solutions.

## Exercise 4    Matching my experience with ideas from the SDG exercises

Looking at the SDGs above with your professional background in mind:

- What issues come to mind that your background might help solve?
- What other ideas or associations come to mind?

To clarify: If you are a banker, what associations come up if you look at the SDG and think of your banking experience? If you are an HR director, what associations come up from a people perspective?

- How could you, as a functional leader, help your function become a force for good inside and outside your organisation?

Transfer the individual answers to Post-it notes, and sort in themes or mind map them. You might need to sort them a couple of times.
What themes can you see emerging? Write them down.

## Exercise 5    The 'Ben & Jerry's' exercise

Ben & Jerry's consider themselves as a 'social justice organisation that happens to be making ice-cream'.

- If you substitute 'ice-cream' for your organisation's products or services, what could you provide, solve, contribute to in your local community, communities in your supply chains and wider society?

What themes and ideas are coming out?

## Exercise 6    Identifying areas to pursue: drawing conclusions from Exercises 2–5

Looking at all the ideas above, it is time to do some sorting and choosing:

- Look at all *issues-related* themes collected above.
   o   Are some major themes standing out?
   o   How would you describe these themes?
- For whom are these themes or topics relevant?
   o   The inhabitants in my town? For all 7 billion world inhabitants today? Some 9 billion in the future? The bottom billion?

> Sub-Saharan Africa? Deprived urban communities? Urban old in 2050? Unemployed youth in India? Etc.
>
> - Which themes would have the biggest societal impact?
> - Which themes speak stronger than the others to you personally?
> - *Pick your top four themes.* Keep the rest for later consultation.
>     - What do you need to find out next about these four themes?
>     - Who might know, and how could you find this out?

If you answered the last questions, you are starting your first action plan on your Discovery journey, and starting to identify and build your new strategic and dynamic network (more about this below) – a significant milestone!

### The reason for choosing four themes to pursue during Discovery

It is easy to wish to hedge our bets by keeping many options open, but the advice by Margaret Lobenstein, in her 2013 book *The Renaissance Soul* – for people with many passions they wish to follow – is to pick four scenarios for exploration, and if they are not for us, they can be replaced as we learn. This is why you are advised to keep your 'discarded' themes in the exercises.

Picking only one option is too narrow as there is no guarantee that this option will turn out possible or practical, at least in the short to medium term. More than four means you spread yourself so thin that you are unable to build and maintain knowledge and networks in each area. These networks are what enable you to gather deep enough knowledge and identify future career opportunities.[20]

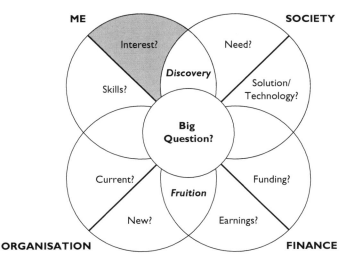

## What interests me – deeply?

This section is aimed at drawing out our ideas, values, motivations and what gives us happiness. After some short descriptions of some areas that can be used as food for thought, we will work in the same semi-structured fashion as before – 'Dump–Sort–Contemplate–Choose'.

### One day I would like to . . .

Even if we have no concrete idea of what we would like to focus on, all of us have a lot of insights simmering in our subconscious regarding our lives, work, careers, private lives, the world . . . what we dream of, hope for, 'if we had time', 'one day I would like to', interests, what upsets us in the world, etc.

This is invaluable input to our Discovery journey. Exercise 7 allows us to get all this wisdom out in the open. You will likely be amazed at how much valuable insight you already have.

### Values

Being a leader in today's world means we have to face many issues and need to know what our values are to have a compass to steer by. This is also vital input for seeking our future direction. Exercise 8 helps you think about your values through a range of structured questions.

### What makes me happy?

When we aim to change careers, it is easy to extrapolate from where we are right now. But looking back over our career and life to see when we were the happiest also gives valuable insight. We do this in Exercise 9.

How this works is illustrated by Laurence Mulliez. After many years working with BP, including being CEO for Castrol Industrial Lubricants and Services, Laurence created a new career, first as CEO for Eoxis (a private equity-backed solar developer), and now as non-executive director for a number of organisations, including the Green Investment Bank in the UK. In her own words:

> I wrote down what activities I had been doing, with whom and in what kind of organisational structure, when I was the happiest and least happy in my career, and when I and my family had been the happiest and least happy. I realised that running a P&L business was when I was professionally the happiest and renewables was the most rewarding sector. Hence, I started the exploration for such a position, which materialised at Eoxis.

Laurence had already worked in renewable energy in BP, and thus knew she enjoyed this industry (societal need). We might not have such specific background experience, and start with no real idea of what we want to do, but going through the thinking Laurence did, we gain understanding of what circumstances make us happy and productive.

### What motivates me?

In Chapter 6, we saw that we need to know what our motivations for doing Purpose-driven work are. As Nicholas Lovegrove remarked in *The Mosaic Principle*:

> Do you want to save the world, to make lots of money and be recognized and rewarded for your achievements, to change the organisation in which you work, to have power and influence over others, to enhance your skills and capabilities, to do things that interest and excite you, to work with enjoyable colleagues, or to have a lifestyle that suits you?[21]

We will explore this in Exercise 10.

---

### Exercise 7   Surfacing my less conscious ideas and thoughts about myself and my career

Do an unstructured 'Dump' of all the topics and ideas you have about your life, career, Purpose, dreams, hopes, interests or issues you have been thinking of pursuing.

Just keep writing until you are 'empty'. You can add new ideas as they arrive later.

---

### Exercise 8   What matters to me?

Write down your answers to the following questions:

- What are your values?
- What do you stand for as a leader?
- What do you stand for as a human being?
- What matters to you?

*(continued)*

*(continued)*

- What outrages you?
- What would you change if you were in charge – of this organisa-tion, this country or the world?
- What would you pursue if you had time and no financial constraints?
- What did you love to do when you were younger?

Transfer the individual answers to Post-It notes, and sort in themes or mind-map them. You might need to sort them a couple of times.
    What themes can you see emerging? Write them down.

When we stand at this pivotal point in our lives and careers, it is important to take stock of what motivates us *now*. If we don't, it is easy to continue in the type of work, work-style and lifestyle we have had during our younger adult years. This might not at all be what our 'heart's gladness' is now, but we don't know anything else. Spending significant time to contemplate our own interests, work- and life-wise, is very important.

### Exercise 9    When was I the most/least happy in my life and career?

Write down your answers to the following questions:

- When were you the happiest in your professional career?

    o   What were you doing? With whom? What kind of role, team and organisation were you working in?

- When were you the least happy in your professional career?

    o   What were you doing? With whom? What kind of role, team and organisation were you working in?

- When were you the happiest in your life?

    o   What were you doing? With whom? What kind of role, team and organisation were you working in?

- When were you the least happy in your life?

  o What were you doing? With whom? What kind of role, team and organisation were you working in?

What themes are coming out here? Write them down.

---

## Exercise 10   What motivates me?

What motivates you? Record your views on the following motivations (and any others if you think of them):

- To do good.
- To do well (financially).
- To have power (over people and resources).
- To have influence (over directions and outcomes).
- To drive change.
- To do interesting work.
- To have enjoyable colleagues.
- To improve yourself and learn.
- To have a lifestyle you enjoy.

What themes are coming out here? Write them down.

---

## Exercise 11   Personal guiding principles: drawing conclusions from Exercises 1, 7, 8, 9 and 10

Take the themes and observations from Exercises 1, 7, 8, 9 and 10, and contemplate them. What do these themes say about you and how you want to contribute *as a person* going forward?

*Try to write down in a few sentences a set of 'guiding principles' for yourself that encapsulate your findings.*

Don't forget the private part of your life . . .

Exercise 12 brings 'My interests?' and 'Social needs?' together.

---

### Exercise 12   Matching your ideas with your values: drawing conclusions from Exercises 6 and 11

Take the four themes from Exercise 6, and, one by one, compare them to your guiding principles above.

If you already had ideas in mind, but did not do Exercise 6, use them to compare with your guiding principles.

- How could you potentially express your guiding principles in the fields you are interested in?
- Which look the most promising – in terms of combining potential Impact and your own interests?
- What would you need to find out to discover if this is possible?
- Who might know, and how could you find this out?

---

You are now starting to develop an action plan – for information-gathering and network-building – that takes into account society's needs as well as your own interests and values.

It is now time to turn to the outside world to gather external input to contemplate, to be able to formulate our Big Question and convert to Purpose – our direction.

### Openness to New Experiences: creating opportunities for Big Questions to emerge

(Please refer to the Figure on page 147)

Whether we have started from scratch and created our four themes above, or we have been 'noodling' on a societal issue we would like to address for a long time, we need to experience new things to be able to formulate what Big Question we are trying to solve, and how – our Purpose. We do this by exercising our Career Transformational Asset 'Openness to New Experiences'.

As we mentioned in Chapter 5, adults learn best by experiential learning. That we also become more creative and 'smarter' by working and learning with socially diverse people was shown through the research of Professor Katherine W. Phillips, Professor of Leadership and Ethics at Columbia Business School. She showed that when we meet and work with diverse people, we expect to not understand each other fully, and therefore prepare better, become more open-minded and more diligent at sharing information, compared to when we work with known and similar people, and therefore create better solutions – we become 'smarter'.[22]

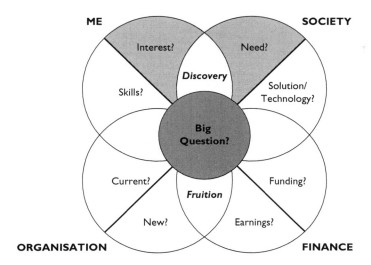

To be able to deeply understand issues and create truly new solutions, we need to learn to see the world through other people's eyes, the people we are trying to create solutions for and with. We need to immerse ourselves at 'the edge of the system', suspend our judgement, and learn to listen deeply with open minds, hearts and wills.

Engaging with marginalised communities does not mean that we have to do high-risk activities; it means that we need to find ways of exposing ourselves, in a considered and respectful way, to people and issues that might make us feel quite uncomfortable and vulnerable to start with.

We can do this gradually, and some of the ways to create opportunities for new experiences include: attending leadership development programmes focused on sustainability or social issues; pro bono work in local communities; volunteering; or guided on-the-ground immersion programmes. We will explore all of these, and how a few executives used them to have time away from 'the fray', to deeply experience new things and contemplate what their direction forward could be.

### Leadership programmes

Many universities and business schools all over the world run leadership programmes exploring societal issues. Here are three executives who got their Big Question, their 'aha' moments, while attending such a programme.

Nina Skorupska discovered her 'Big Question' – 'I wonder if I could impact the policy on renewables and the role of community energy in the UK?' – during Cambridge University's Prince of Wales Business and Sustainability programme.

Nina was wondering what to do next when leaving her senior executive position with the German power giant RWE. She knew she wanted to do something that had future impact on sustainability, energy and communities, and women's participation in science, technology, engineering and mathematics (STEM) education. After exploring further large corporate energy opportunities and realising it was not for her anymore, she became the CEO for the Renewable Energy Association (REA) in the UK, representing many organisations involved in renewable energy vis-à-vis the government and influencing the country's energy policy and beyond, and a board member of the Women in Science and Engineering (WISE) campaign. This has led to a non-executive director position on the board of Transport for London (TfL), transport being a major component of energy policy.

Virginie Helias, at P&G, got her insight while she was Marketing Director for a P&G business unit. In her own words:

> Six to seven years ago, while implementing sustainability projects in my business, I educated myself on the topic, as part of my job. I saw that the proposition was truly win/win when you build sustainability into the products. I then attended a course at IMD Lausanne co-organised with WWF called One Planet Leader.[23]
>
> I had an 'aha moment', realising that unless we bridge the 'science' of sustainability with the business needs, we will never make any significant progress. Sustainability needed to be embedded in everything we do, from strategy to innovation and brand building. It needed to be built in, and not a separate programme, and we [P&G] needed to do more on this, the 'big stuff'.
>
> What P&G needed was someone to translate this and be a bridge to the organisation. I realised that because of my background in business – 23 years in brand and innovation – I could be this bridge, and that I wanted this job. I went to the CEO with a job description . . . and I have never looked back.

Virginie is now VP Global Sustainability for P&G.

Her Big Question was: 'I wonder if we can combine the business need and the sustainability science for impact on "big stuff" in society?'.

James Wambugu, now Group Managing Director, General Insurance at UAP Old Mutual Group, had a similar experience while Strategy Manager for UAP:

> While doing my strategy job, I attended the 'Fast Forward Program',[24] which is about 'Level 5 type leadership'[25] and how to connect personal, family and professional life. There, I formed a view of how I could combine these things, which I still refer back to.

The question we were asked was: 'How can you contribute to your society?' In Kenya, insurance was badly organised. Society, especially low-income families, was not well served, and if an accident happened it had catastrophic consequences in people's lives. I had the dream to transform our society through insurance. I set about doing this.

After a huge amount of extracurricular reading and work, I convinced the organisation to go for this strategy.

In 2010, after five years in my strategy job and two years after attending the 'Fast Forward Program', I was asked to become CEO for the company when our then CEO retired. Our new strategy led to becoming the most well-recognised insurance company in Kenya, from having being almost unknown, and then it led to first an external equity investment, and ultimately the acquisition by Old Mutual.[26]

*Question 9.1:*    If the idea of immersion via leadership programmes for societal impact idea draws you, what universities or business schools near you have similar programmes to the above?

*Question 9.2:*    Might it be possible that your organisation could pay (or part-pay) for such a programme for you?


### Volunteering and pro bono work

Volunteering our time in organisations that are addressing issues we care about is an obvious way to explore at the edge – if we experience them on the ground.

Many executives planning to transition into a second career take board positions in charities or NFPs to gain board experience, as well as supporting their chosen organisation.

The advice from executives from the NFP and charity sector to executives from the other sectors is to work as a volunteer in the organisation before you agree to go on the board. This way, you will truly understand who the organisation serves and get to walk in their clients' shoes as close as you can. You will learn how the organisation serves their community, any associated issues and risks, and if this particular organisation is right for you.

If you have not done this, and later realise that this organisation's culture or issue is not right for you, stress aside, it is difficult to step down before at least two to three years have passed.

A new trend in major organisations is to create focused pro bono programmes (in addition to individual employee volunteering days) fitting with the organisation's overall strategy, core capabilities and where they can make significant impact on selective issues, rather than fragmenting resources and efforts through uncoordinated programmes.

IBM's 'Smarter Cities Challenge'[27] is an example of this, as are Intel's efforts in increasing the education and technical training for young people globally – especially girls – which also helps the company as they need highly educated recruits in emerging markets.[28] This includes their support for the highly acclaimed film *Girl Rising*, and the accompanying global campaign.[29]

Another example is Accenture's technology-driven 'Skills to Succeed' corporate citizen programme equipping over 3 million people around the world with the skills to get a job or start a company by 2020.[30]

*Question 9.3:*   Does your company have a pro bono programme that you might enjoy contributing to and learning from?

*Question 9.4:*   If not, would it interest you to start one?

### Exploring at the edge: immersion programmes on the ground

Another way to explore at the edge with marginalised communities is through on-the-ground immersion learning programmes or working as a volunteer. This is, of course, the model of organisations such as the Peace Corps and Volunteer Services Overseas (VSO). Many other organisations exist that coordinate volunteering all over the world, including organisations providing 'volunteering holidays' if you can't devote a long stretch of time for volunteer work.

Another model that is becoming increasingly popular is community immersion learning programmes in marginalised communities at home or abroad for executives. Examples of two different types are the programmes offered by organisations such as Leaders Quest and PYXERA Global.

Leaders Quest organises 7- to 10-day-long learning trips for groups of individual executives or entire corporate leadership teams, meeting business leaders and local community leaders.[31]

PYXERA Global helps companies create pro bono learning and service programmes of 10 days to 6 months in length. They identify and liaise with NGOs that can help their client organisation identify appropriate projects to work with the local community on that will have real impact.[32]

This 'time out' in new environments outside our normal comfort zone, where we don't know 'the rules', where we have to suspend judgement and listen deeply, helps us face our own questions regarding what leadership and business is actually about.

Being in 'listening mode', instead of our usual 'action mode', allows our own wisdom – which rarely has the chance to get heard in our busy task-driven lives – to surface.

IBM, Dow, SAP, EY, GSK and many other organisations are using these programmes as fast-track learning solutions, particularly for mid-career leaders. Once trialled, these programmes often become part of the core leadership programmes, such as the IBM Corporate Service Corps above, and they benefit employees, the company and society.[33]

In Chapter 11, we will discuss why it is important that older senior leaders are included in these types of programmes.

CEOs who wish to take their company in a Purpose-driven direction are increasingly using the shorter programmes. Immersing themselves together with their executive teams, exploring at the edge, is a life-changing experience, and they develop a deep insight into what leadership means today and what their business can contribute.

Paul Fletcher, while Chairman of the Private Equity firm Actis, which invests in sectors that support development of countries in emerging markets, wanted his Partners to personally deeply understand the communities they invest in.

Hence, their annual Partner meeting, instead of taking place in a fancy resort, was spent immersing themselves at the edge of the system – through a Quest – and meeting business and community leaders, each year in a different developing country.

Not only did he take his Partner team on these immersion weeks, they also included spouses. This way, they could personally experience where their spouses spend their time away from home, and the impact their work has on real people's lives.

An executive whose immersion experiences at the edge resulted in a career to help other leaders experience at the edge is Laura Asiala.

Laura Asiala worked most of her career with the Dow Corning Corporation in Midland, Michigan. Laura held various positions in the company, and when we worked together she was in charge of our global marketing learning and development programmes. Laura and I spent many fun hours together creating fresh approaches and strategies for new products and services, business development, and marketing excellence.

Later, Laura became Dow Corning's Director of Corporate Communications, and then Director of Corporate Citizenship. Laura helped Dow Corning arrange their first overseas immersion programmes in collaboration with PYXERA Global, with the objective to gain insight for innovation to serve the so-called 'Base of the Pyramid'[34] – the market of some 4 billion individuals with less than US$1,500 per annum purchasing power parity.

This included an initial programme in 2010 that gave 10 employees from Dow Corning locations across the globe an opportunity to volunteer for a month in Bangalore, India. These employees worked with three non-governmental agencies, two of which had a direct link to clean cook stoves: one to develop quality control systems and improve the supply chain for manufactured energy-efficient cook stoves, the other to research and analyse the needs and demands of rural customers when buying energy-efficient and environmentally friendly cook stoves in order to develop a more effective marketing and sales plan. The participants also engaged colleagues in their home locations to work on these programmes, and the company remained committed to the effort long after the individuals returned to their home locations.

As Bob Hansen, then CEO of Dow Corning, said in 2011: 'Dow Corning gained a fresh perspective and first-hand experiences through the work of our colleagues, including insights on how to fuel further innovation, and an understanding of how we can grow while addressing our social and environmental commitments'.[35]

In 2013, Laura was offered the post as Vice President of Public Affairs for PYXERA Global, and started out on her Purpose-driven second career.[36] She is now also a board member of Net Impact, a global community of over 100,000 students and professionals who use their skills and experiences to make a lasting social and environmental impact throughout their careers.

We can clearly see the impact above of being open to new experiences by exploring at the edge of the system for catalysing 'Big Questions' – how we get to personally really understand world issues and their consequences. This gives us a more humble and insightful way of creating solutions 'with people' rather than 'for people'.

*Question 9.5:*    Would an immersion on the ground be valuable for you in your business or personally to develop a strategy that connects with communities and issues relevant to you?

*Question 9.6:*    Does your organisation have these kinds of immersion programmes? If they are only for younger leaders, could you find a way to participate or instigate a pilot for you and your peers?

### Exploring at the edge of our self-knowledge: 'no regrets at 95'

Exploring at the edge of the system includes the understanding of ourselves and what our heart's wishes are. As we mentioned earlier, there is a lot of wisdom hiding just below the surface, if we take some time to 'unfocus'.

One of the most insightful exercises I do with executives – and myself – is the 'no regrets at 95' exercise.

Close your eyes, breathe calmly and deeply, and fully imagine yourself being 95 years old, with an aged, maybe not so healthy body, wrinkly skin, weak joints, eyesight and hearing, etc. Now look back from the perspective of the 95-year-old you. Imagine that you have lived a life where you have no regrets at 95. What would you be grateful for, and what have you done that makes it feel like a full and well-spent life?

Now imagine that you are continuing your life's trajectory as it is now, without any real changes – same type of work, same family and friends, same hobbies, same routine, maybe retirement and friends gradually leaving the world, etc. What would you regret at 95 that you didn't do in your life? What advice would the 95-year-old you give to your current you?

This might sound a bit 'radical', but it is a beautiful exercise that can give unexpected insights and great gratitude for what we already have in our lives. At this mid/later career stage, most of us have to admit that we are entering, or living, the second half of our lives, even though we all like to think we will live forever and keep on putting off life-changing decisions.

We have no guarantee for how many more days are afforded to us. Having lost my closest woman friend at age 63 due to a sudden stroke, my father at age 72 due to a post-operative blood clot and my closest male friend at age 78 after a short period of wasting away, I am forced to ask myself: What if I have only 2, 11 or 17 years left?

The question becomes: How can I make any remaining years count, whether they are 4 or 40? Why put off what I dream of doing until it might be too late? As the famous saying goes, 'It is not years in your life that counts, it is the life in your years'.[37]

Bronnie Ware, an Australian palliative care nurse, reported in her book *The Top Five Regrets of the Dying* that they are, in order:

- I wish I'd had the courage to live a life true to myself, not the life others expected of me.
- I wish I hadn't worked so hard.
- I wish I'd had the courage to express my feelings.
- I wish I had stayed in touch with my friends.
- I wish I had let myself be happier.[38]

A Discovery journey is a great first step to start to live a life that is true to ourselves, and in service to society. It is not about throwing out our entire life from one day to another, it is about developing a gradual understanding of what makes us content and at peace with ourselves, and learning to make choices that promote this well-being.

Let us close this section with some wise and light-hearted words by the Indian philosopher and mystic Osho. In a discourse on the topic of how to live your life, he says:

A friend has sent me a clipping from a paper. An old woman, eighty-five years old, was asked by a journalist that if she had to live again, how would she live? The old woman said – there is a great insight in it, remember it – 'If I had my life to live over, I would dare to make more mistakes next time. I would relax, I would limber up. I would be sillier than I have been this trip. I would take fewer things seriously. I would take more chances. I would take more trips. I would climb more mountains and swim more rivers. I would eat more ice cream and less beans. I would perhaps have more actual troubles, but I would have fewer imaginary ones.

'You see, I am one of those people who lived sensibly and sanely hour after hour, day after day. Oh, I have had my moments, and if I had it to do over again I would have more of them. In fact, I would try to have nothing else – just moments, one after another, instead of living so many years ahead of each day.

'I have been one of those persons who never go anywhere without a thermometer, a hot water bottle, a raincoat and a parachute. If I had to do it again I would travel lighter than I have.

'If I had my life to live over, I would start barefoot earlier in the spring, and stay that way later into the fall. I would go to more dances. I would ride more merry-go-rounds. I would pick more daisies'.[39]

The following wise quote from Mahatma Gandhi seems like a perfect summary for the need to go and Discover: 'Live as if you were to die tomorrow. Learn as if you were to live forever'.[40]

*Question 9.7:*   If you knew you had only a few years left to live, what would you spend your energy in creating?

*Question 9.8:*   If you knew you had only six months left to live, what would you start doing today? How would you reprioritise your 'to do' list?

## Acquiring knowledge about our chosen areas

Once we have a few themes we are curious about, it is time to learn more about these topics.

As we discussed in detail in Chapter 6, tri-sector leaders have an 'intellectual thread' in their knowledge; they have both generalist and expert skills. In single-sector leadership, we tend to become more generalist as we rise in the hierarchy and leave expert knowledge to others.

At this stage of the Discovery journey, it is time to read, watch, listen, and meet people who can help us understand our chosen areas and expose ourselves to new experiences.

As we discussed in Chapter 6, following organisations and people involved in our areas of interest on Twitter is an efficient way of starting to learn about an area. We are fed the latest news, links to relevant articles, deep research, seminars, events, TED Talks, books and people.

This helps us begin to shape our ideas and identify what kinds of people we need to speak to in order to define our Big Question. As we gradually hone in on an area, our reading will become more specific, and over time we develop a level of expertise in our chosen field.

*Question 9.9:*   What 5 to 10 people or organisations involved in your areas of interest can you start to follow on Twitter or get e-newsletters from?

## Building a strategic and diverse network: to learn and problem-solve

In Chapter 6, we discussed how building strategic and diverse networks are absolutely vital when we want to work tri-sectorially.

When we have some initial themes or ideas for what we want to work on solving, we need to find other people who are interested in solving similar problems, sharing knowledge and in introducing us to further contacts; we need to build a new network, exercising the third Career Transformational Asset – building strategic and diverse networks.

In my experience, strategic networking is another area executives often find hard to start. Even very senior executives frequently have internally or industry-focused networks that they haven't really spent effort growing or maintaining ('lazy networks'). To ask for help and favours from the network – what is called leveraging – also often feels uncomfortable.

Once we start practising, in a step-by-step fashion, networking becomes as natural as anything else we do. I promise. I have worked with executives who initially were hesitant to contact even their previous colleagues, and a few months later did not hesitate to contact anyone they wished to speak with.

If you are a hesitant networker, take it at your pace and gradually learn to network in a way that works for you.

Remember that *you are looking for other people interested in solving the same problems as you are* – there is no need to feel embarrassed.

### Gradually extending our networking comfort zone

A simple, practical and effective way to gain confidence and network reach is to first contact alumni of the organisations we have worked with – *who are now doing things that we find interesting*, and can give us information, insights and introductions.

The use of alumni connections comes naturally to most executives in consulting and tech firms. This is deeply ingrained in their way of operating, and alumni networks are well organised and easily accessible. MBA graduates are also used to alumni networking. Organised alumni networks are less common in the corporate world and most other types of organisations.

Alumni connections fall into four groups (for MBA alumni, substitute 'worked' with 'studied'):

- previous colleagues we worked closely with;
- previous colleagues we briefly worked with or know in passing;
- previous employees who were there at the same time that we don't know; and
- previous employees that worked there before or after us.

This is effective, as having worked in the same organisation – even if not at the same time – automatically confers a feeling of kinship when we approach others or are approached.

If your networking skills are really rusty, starting with ex-colleagues that you worked with who have gone on to do something different is an effective way to start to practise networking. They will be happy to hear from you and take time to help.

As we get comfortable with this, we can move on to ex-colleagues we did not know well, and then general alumni. You can then extend to alumni in organisations you have had partnerships or volunteered with. As people then introduce you to people in their network, your network grows naturally.

As you become comfortable contacting people, writing introductory emails and conducting meetings, moving further away from your comfort zone becomes easier and easier to do. And before you know it, you are without hesitation contacting anyone you wish to speak to.

A note on emails requesting meetings: they need to be short (one computer screen), clear (no typos and the recipient's name correctly spelled!) and upfront with what you are asking for, and give people a chance to opt out if they wish. No one wants to feel obliged to help. Making clear that your request is optional means they are free to choose for themselves and they are more likely to agree.

It is a real skill to write good introductory emails. You might want to ask a great networker to edit your first efforts. This can up your chances to get meetings by multiples!

---

### Exercise 13    A gentle start to networking

Which five previous colleagues of each group below who are now doing new and interesting things will you start off contacting?

- Previous colleagues you worked closely with?
- Previous colleagues you worked briefly with or know in passing?
- Previous employees who were there at the same time that you don't know?
- Previous employees who worked there before or after you?

---

### First conversations are about wide exploration – and new introductions

At this stage, it is about being curious, having exploratory conversations without trying to get a particular answer, and getting introductions to more people you can learn from.

If we try to be too end-result-focused (our next 'job'/career) early on, we will neither be able to identify areas unknown to us today that we might find really exciting, nor discover skills or abilities in ourselves that we are today not aware of as unique.

Many early conversations will be about topics such as:

- How did you end up doing what you are doing?
- What new and interesting things are going on in this area?
- What does your typical day look like?
- What are the things you think are unique about me, what I do and how I do it?
- What could you see me do if I was not doing what I am doing?
- Who do you think could give me more advice?
- Who is the most interesting person you have met recently?
- What is the most interesting thing you read recently?
- What networks or events do you find useful?
- What newsletters or publications do you find most useful?

You might be surprised by some of the questions above; I think you will be even more surprised by the answers you will get.

After each meeting, it is important to contemplate what we learned, increase our self-awareness and adapt our approach for the next meeting – we are in effect trying on a new identity – and gradually our confidence will grow in presenting our ideas and ourselves.[41]

As we learn more about the areas we are pursuing, our conversations become increasingly specific, and more of a dialogue between equals with the players in the space we want to work in. We are gradually establishing ourselves in the new area, and others can start to see us as potential employees or collaborators.

### Introductions are precious – value them and understand the risk to the giver

Anyone who has worked in business development or sales knows that the best way to learn to know new people is by being introduced by a mutual contact.

If someone we know well introduces another friend or business contact, we are highly likely to agree to meet and help as much as we can. Conversely, the less the person knows the introducer, the lower the likelihood they will go out of their way to help. This is why cold-calling and 'cold-emailing' has such a low chance of success, and the best way to extend your network is via other people's *'warm' introductions*.

If you can't get a warm introduction, a *'lukewarm'* introduction (such as LinkedIn second-level contacts) is still better than contacting someone 'cold'.

Introductions represent a risk for the introducer as they put their personal reputation at risk – often after meeting you very briefly.

Many executives, especially when the Discovery process is new to them, don't understand the sensitivity and time effort involved in giving introductions.

How you communicate with the introducer and the person they introduce you to *will reflect back on the introducer and yourself*. A misstep with someone's trusted contact can seriously damage the introducer's reputation and their relationship with their contact. For you, it will likely mean that this particular door to contacts and opportunities is closed – *forever*.

Good introductions take time. They have to be personal and – this is critical – set out an area of common interest between the two people being introduced. This gives an incentive to the receiver to agree to give their precious time to the unknown person to whom they are being introduced.

### Generosity, paying forward, courtesy and a few fatal faux pas

When we are used to operating in a network where we are well known, people will give us leeway etiquette-wise. When we are building a new network, understanding networking etiquette is a success or failure issue.

Good networkers are not smoochers; they are *good relationship-builders*. They are generous, pay forward into their networks, they return favours, and they are respectful and courteous to everybody, whether they see them as immediately useful or not.[42] Some basic good practices are as follows:

- *Paying forward* means building a positive goodwill balance with people for the day you might want to ask a favour from them. This is the best strategy for success, as Wharton professor Adam Grant proved with his research published in his seminal 2013 book *Give and Take*.[43]
- *Courtesy*, in its simplest form, means sending polite, short, well-worded requests to people you want to speak with and a 'thank you' via email for introductions given, and to let the introducer know what has happened with their contacts. This goes a long way, and most of the time nothing else is required. Other ways are to send interesting articles and invites to events, or make useful reciprocal introductions.

The number of times I have spent hours to do introductions for executives to never hear from them again, not even a two-word 'thank you' email, is quite shocking. Equally shocking is when they are rude when the introductions don't happen as fast as they want them to. The introducer is spending their precious time – for free on your behalf – risking their own reputation. Imperiousness is not a recommended strategy; you can be fairly assured that this will result in no further assistance today or in the future. Why should the introducer risk that you behave similarly with their contact?

Another shocker is very common: not informing the introducer of what happened with an amazing contact they put you in touch with. This is also a sure recipe for being on the introducer's blacklist.

These might look like minor issues, but they are really fatal faux pas if you are looking to build a network in a new area – you are dependent on the goodwill of people who can only judge you from the short interactions they have with you.

People in a sector know each other, and *you can quickly make yourself a* persona non grata *in the space you want to work in.*

*Research every person you are meeting.* Few executives would arrive at a business meeting without preparation. Yet when they are looking for a new career and are referred to me, very few bother to look at my background on LinkedIn, and even less my website. But they expect me to have read theirs in detail, with great interest, and be willing to give them advice and numerous introductions, for free.

Apart from being discourteous, it is a serious mistake. The other person is not going to be keen to introduce you to their valued contacts if you can't be trusted to observe professional courtesy 101 with them.

That person with an unconventional background you were introduced to might just be one of Bill Gates' closest friends and advisors. Assuming we know who is important and not is an especially fatal mistake when we are exploring new areas unfamiliar to us in the tri-sector space. Being extra courteous to everyone you meet is the best strategy.

*Not remembering who introduced you* shows how little you value the person who introduced you, who is probably very close to and highly valued by the person you are now speaking with. By being lazy, you have just made the person you want help from question your integrity and become hesitant to help.

*Don't cold-call.* The age of cold-calling is truly over. The etiquette for how to initiate contact has completely changed in business, and is now done almost 100 per cent by email. Organisations are even starting to abolish their voicemail systems.[44,45]

Emailing has two advantages. It allows the recipient to decide if you are genuine, and if they then take the call or meeting they are fully committed to it. Calling someone's mobile randomly risks catching them at a really inconvenient moment, which is not conducive for future help.

NB: This advice also includes headhunters. Contrary to popular belief, we do not sit at our desks not knowing what to do with our day. We speak with 1,000 to 2,000 executives every year, meaning 5 to 10 per day, in 30-minute exploratory discussions to two-hour deep interviews. Cold calling means that you will be disturbing us on another call, in the middle of a candidate interview or in a client meeting. A polite email is the way to get our attention.

And . . . *do pay for coffee.* I am frequently left with the bill after giving my time, insight and asked for numerous introductions – the ingredients for how I make my livelihood – for free. Few people are inclined to help when we behave like this, and it might seriously hamper your search for a new career if the person you offended later turns out to be a linchpin contact in the space.

Finally, it is always safer to assume that *everyone will become useful in your life, at some point in time.* They deserve your respect and courtesy for taking the call or meeting, at their personal cost, for your benefit, no matter who they are.

### Do answer headhunters' approaches – speaking to them is very valuable

Even if you are not looking for a new job right now, you might be one day. If a headhunter that seems serious contacts you, do answer that email and take that call.

You will achieve several important things: first, you build a network who know you, and know what you are interested in, for when you do want to change; second, you will learn a lot about yourself and what in your background and skills is valuable to other organisations; third, you learn how to 'tell your story' and refine it as you learn from your meetings; fourth, you gather useful market information – they speak to lots of people in the area you are interested in; and fifth, by recommending other people – if what the headhunter is working on is not right for you or right now – you help friends and build goodwill with the headhunter, who will be more keen to go out of their way to help you, when you need a hand.

When executives have changed jobs once in their careers, or are some way into creating their non-executive portfolio, 9 out of 10 will answer a headhunter's email. They have grasped the role and importance of head-hunters (and other advisors and financial providers) in getting you where you want to, career-wise.

Conversely, if executives have worked only in one company, they hardly ever answer.

How can we suggest that brilliant trusteeship or CEO job to you if you don't speak to us? All you risk is 15 to 30 minutes of conversation.

Even if you feel that you are too busy with doing your tasks, your job and your family responsibilities, it should not be impossible to carve out 15 to 30 minutes every few weeks for a call with a headhunter who contacts you. You can then let them know about what kind of work with Purpose you would like to do – this small investment in your future can make an enormous difference. What boring task could you delegate to someone else to do to find that time?

## Why you really should be on LinkedIn and use it

If you are a LinkedIn power user, feel free to skip this section. However, in my experience, the majority of executives, even with LinkedIn network sizes of 500+ contacts, are mainly passive users, and few use LinkedIn strategically.

Whether you are a passive user or in the cadre of executives that still feel that they don't need to be on LinkedIn, let me try to convince to get active.

### People of my seniority are now on LinkedIn

Many senior people are on the system, and it is increasing exponentially. Nowadays, I find executive committee members from all except maybe the largest listed companies present on LinkedIn. For example, the executive committee of Sandoz (a Novartis company) use links to their LinkedIn profiles on their executive committee web page instead of biographies.[46]

In 2015, LinkedIn and I made an estimate that there are over 50 million senior executives (executive committee, first-, second-, third-level) in the world in all types of organisations. At that point, about half of them were on LinkedIn, with the younger leaders more prevalent, and the past two years have seen a rapid increase of senior execs on the site. This means that *you have access to at least 25 million decision-makers*, directly or indirectly, in every conceivable sector, who are interested in solving problems – just like you.[47]

### You can reach almost anyone in two or three steps

Knowing how to use LinkedIn second- and third-level connections strategically, and with proper LinkedIn etiquette, can get you to almost anyone you would like to speak to within two or three steps. The world really is that small now. Why do it the hard way when you can do it the smart way?

### LinkedIn is just part of multichannel communications

A few years ago, senior people were surprised when contacted via LinkedIn; now it is just another communication tool, like their business email or intranet. We have got used to multichannel communications. Have a try and you will see what I mean.

### I am not looking for a job – I don't need to be on LinkedIn

I hear senior executives express this view, especially if they have spent most of their careers in one organisation.

A real-life example: In 2015, I spoke on new leadership competencies to 30 of the top 400 executives of a major global corporation. They were exco first- and second-level, aged 40 to 55, and only four of them were on LinkedIn. The reason they gave was that 'they were not looking for a job'.

This is the norm, not the exception, for long-term senior employees, particularly from large organisations in traditional industries.

This is missing the point of LinkedIn. LinkedIn is now, in many ways, '*the* global business directory' and has over half a billion registered members.[48] In the next chapter, we will also discover some of LinkedIn's pilot projects, which should make anyone think about how the world of work will function in the not so distant future.

### LinkedIn is vital for managing your personal brand

It is the first place most of us check the background of someone we are meeting. When you Google someone's name, the LinkedIn profile is the first thing that comes up. If this profile is rubbish, this is what people see.

No one has time to go and find another bio somewhere. They might just move on and contact someone else from another company whose profile they can decipher as being the correct person to speak to – about that idea that might have made all the difference for your business or that dream board position.

Executives who are of the digital native generation are largely present on LinkedIn from most types of businesses and geographies. In contrast, executives who left their organisations before social media became prevalent are rarely present on LinkedIn or on any other social media.

As we mentioned in Chapter 6, digital skills will be vital for our ability to continue to create careers going forward, whether executive or non-executive – can you be a credible candidate going forward if you havn't mastered something as basic as LinkedIn?

### The way you get found once you leave a big brand organisation

Many executives don't realise that the moment they leave a branded organisation, people need their private email to be able to contact them. You can guess a company email quite easily, but you can rarely guess someone's private email. Hence, if you are not on LinkedIn or *very famous*, you risk falling off the 'professional map' when leaving your big brand organisation.

Another downside is that if most of your company's executive community is on LinkedIn, and you are not, they are the ones more likely to be contacted for 'that interesting opportunity', as they can be identified and contacted.

The speed of business is now such that no one can afford the detective work to try to dig up someone they have never heard about or chase their private email address, and the longer since you left a big brand, the fewer people will remember you and be able to recommend you when asked for recommendations.

We need to take charge of our digital profile if we want to work beyond the traditional corporate career stage, change jobs or change our career.

Remember that cross-sector opportunities come through our networks. Let's say someone is looking for a senior executive with your background for that dream chairman role in a charity that you really admire; they don't know that you would be interested or that you actually exist because your background is new territory to them. How would they find you if you have no digital footprint?

I have frequently heard from non-executive directors that they are easy to find and contact as they are on FTSE or Fortune boards. If they are not on LinkedIn and we don't have their private email, the only other option is to contact the PA to the chairman or CEO of the company on whose board they are on. That only works if the PA is able to be helpful.

In summary: a simple profile on LinkedIn, including what you would be interested in being contacted for, makes you discoverable to the world.

As you refine your own Purpose, you can start to adapt and supplement your profile with information supporting your new interest, including advisory and board positions and publishing blogs. Learning from profiles that impress you is a free and efficient way of developing a good LinkedIn profile, and if you look at the LinkedIn messaging system as just another email account it all becomes very natural.

### The importance of having a few uber-connectors in your network

Malcolm Gladwell pointed out in his book *The Tipping Point* that information, new ideas and social change happen through networks via three types of people with unique social gifts: mavens (information-gatherers), salesmen (promote the ideas) and connectors.

*Connectors* are the people in a community who know large numbers of people and who are in the habit of making introductions. They usually know people across an array of social, cultural, professional and economic circles, and make a habit of introducing people who work or live in different circles. They are people who 'link us up with the world . . . people with a special gift for bringing the world together'.[49]

Connectors are the embodiment of the dynamic and diverse network builder we have discussed. Some even connect networks with networks – uber-connectors.

Having a couple of uber-connectors in your network can be extremely useful to affect a career change – they are the human equivalent of the information superhighway. If you don't know any uber-connectors, ask your current network if they know any 'people who know everybody', and learn to know them. It is worth the investment as they give you shortcuts literally everywhere you want to go.[50]

Why do connectors spend time introducing others? We do it because we enjoy it, our networks gain value by being used, and we believe that in helping others create new business, more business will come to us eventually – we pay forward.

Adam Grant, in his book *Give and Take*, shows that the most successful people in business are givers who give strategically to make the pie bigger for everyone – more successful than reciprocators (who only give if they get something), takers (who take and rarely give), and indiscriminate givers (who help everyone and become doormats, neglecting their own work).[51]

A feature unique to connectors is that they *'take all meetings'*. This means that if a trusted contact suggests they should see someone, they will do their best to take this meeting, even if it might look somewhat random. They are not wasteful with their time, but they *suspend their judgement*, as they have learned that some of these meetings are what sparks entirely new connections and enables their networks to connect to new networks. This is part of the secret of how connectors are successful.

When we set out on our Discovery process, it is useful to learn from the connectors – suspend our habitual filters of what might or might not be useful to do or who to meet, no matter how far-fetched the suggestion initially might seem to us, and *be grateful to and appreciative of everybody we have the privilege to meet*.

In Appendix 3, you can find a LinkedIn DIY 'cheat sheet' for you to get the power out of LinkedIn for your job-crafting or career change.

*Question 9.10:*   Do you need to upgrade your LinkedIn profile? Do you know someone who has a great profile who can help you?

*Question 9.11:*   Do you know any 'uber-connectors'? If not, do you know someone who can introduce you to one?

## There is no right or wrong topic, size or activity – enjoy the journey

As we gradually learn more about our chosen topic or topics, through small iterations, we gradually develop ideas for which societal issues we might impact and how.

It is easy at this stage to compare our early ideas with other executives' projects and achievements, and feel that if we can't achieve what they have done, quickly, we are not successful. We have taken our competition mindset with us into our search for Purpose in our lives. This is neither useful nor necessary.

Looking at our Discovery journey as an artistic work in progress (WIP) is the way. It normally turns out much more beautiful and interesting than you could ever have imagined at the start. As you probably picked up from executives' stories, the journey keeps unfolding. Why fix your view of what Purpose 'should be' when you can instead enjoy what it actually is?

When we speak about 10X thinking, we do that in order to create different solutions and impact *versus continuous improvement thinking*, not size or scale of our own organisation or solution. Our aim is to shift equilibriums in society, as Martin, Osberg and Huffington say in their book *Getting Beyond Better*:

> They focus their attention not just on relieving the symptoms of a social problem, but on finding ways to get to the root causes and address them, bringing about positive change on a grand scale in ways others can replicate.[52]

Those last words are important – *in ways others can replicate* – this gives true scalability.

To illustrate how this plays out over the short and long haul, as we learn and gradually understand how we can have impact, let us use Eva Holmberg-Tedert and her orphanage in Nepal, Richard Gillies when CPO at M&S, and Paul Dickinson, the CEO of the Carbon Disclosure Project (CDP).

Eva Holmberg-Tedert, a Regional Coordinator at Arbetsförmedlingen (the Swedish Job Centre organisation), created the 'Association for the Street Children of Nepal'[53] after experiencing their plight on a visit to Kathmandu. Children end up living on the streets, being forced into prostitution or domestic slavery, often as a result of their mothers dying in childbirth and the ensuing extreme poverty in the family.

Eva decided to first create an orphanage for girls aged 6–16, giving low-caste and cast-less girls a safe home and education. She then created a second orphanage for smaller street children, of both genders. At a first glance, this seems to mainly have a 10X impact on the daily quality of life of more than 40 street children in Kathmandu.

But it also impacts the community in long-term ways – the true aim of her work – as the children are safe, they will become educated and economically productive citizens, and most of all they will also help solve one of the root causes of children living on the streets: the lack of midwives.

Eva's project gives the children basic schooling and then secondary training in healthcare and midwifery. In 2016, Chhiring Tamang became their eleventh Medical College student accepted (top student on entrant exams) for the three-year course to become a health assistant. The plan is to top this up with a Rural Medicine Skilled Birth Assistant course for her fourth year.[54] In total, they now have 15 students in Medical College. Recently, the organisation sent their first students to begin to qualify as midwives.

This approach supports Nepal's investment in human capital development, an important lever to achieve their vision to graduate from the least developed country level by 2022. The International Commission on Financing Global Education Opportunity has shown that US$1 invested in an additional year of schooling, particularly for girls, generates earnings and health benefits of US$10 in low-income countries.[55]

Eva's aim, through what she calls her 'small-scale' work, is to create a scalable model that can be replicated easily locally and eliminate root causes for the existence of street children.

Richard Gillies' exciting 100 per cent renewable energy project when Chief Procurement Officer at M&S helped transform a now £10.6 billion turnover and 88,000-people organisation. Proving this concept in addition inspired countless organisations all over the world to aim for the same, which enabled suppliers of renewable energy and technology to create replicable solutions that could be sold to other corporations.

This work enabled the RE100 coalition to inspire over 100 (as of August 2017) corporate partners to commit to procure and use 100 per cent renewable energy,[56] and according to the Rocky Mountain Institute's Business Renewables Center (BRC), US corporate renewable energy private purchasing agreements (PPAs) are doubling every year, and are the fastest-growing PPA category.[57]

This was an exciting and inspiring project for Richard and an important part of the M&S 'Plan A' strategy, but no one could foresee that it would enable a major energy shift in the world when they started out.

Paul Dickinson is founder and chairman of the CDP (we will hear his career journey in Chapter 10). His interest was to somehow incentivise businesses globally to lower their carbon emissions. He was from the start aiming for systems change – 10X.

He founded the Carbon Disclosure Project (CDP) in 2000, and 15 to 20 years later institutional investors and purchasers representing over US$100 trillion in assets support their approach.[58] The scope has, over recent years, been extended to cover organisations' water and forest footprints.

The CDP itself is a tiny organisation, in terms of actual people, but creating huge impact. They are increasing their impact through constant iterations of the concept and extensions of scope. Here, the replicator effect comes from companies competing for good rankings and exchanging best practices. Many of the world's largest corporations now prominently display these rankings alongside share prices and other key business data,[59] and their rankings are widely reported in both the trade[60] and financial press,[61] incentivising yet more organisations to join.

Finally, Andrea and Barry Coleman and Riders for Health, which we briefly discussed above, shows how a scalable solution and its increasing impact unfolds over a long stretch of time.

Their story is told in the book by Martin, Osberg & Huffington, *Getting Beyond Better*, and shows how from inception and the early 1990s pilots in Lesotho, by the mid 2000s Riders for Health had expanded this model in seven sub-Saharan countries. Then, after being active in the Gambia for over 20 years, they offered the Ministry of Health to take over the whole healthcare transportation operation for the country on an outsourced lease agreement, Transport Asset Management (TAM).[62,63]

### Focus on the Discovery process – not the outcome

We never know exactly what the result will be when we start, and, as we have seen above, most societal innovation that has real impact started small and was refined through many iterations before reaching scale.

If our happiness depends solely on results being delivered, by us, we will not be enjoying our lives on the way to the goal. Enjoying our lives *and* work is what most of us are seeking when we start looking for Purpose. Replacing one form of performance angst with Purpose performance angst, I am sure you agree, is neither useful nor wise.

One of Bronnie Ware's (who we mentioned above) palliative care clients 'Cath', who had led several charities and projects for troubled youths, expressed this as follows:

> We all have a positive contribution to make. I've made mine. But while I was searching for my purpose in life, I forgot to enjoy myself along the way. It was all about the result of finding what I was looking for. Then when I did find work I loved, work I could do with the heartfelt intention of contributing, I was still results-based.[64]

There is something else that is important to note in the stories throughout this book: no one really sets out on their journey with the *fixed* aim of ending up in a particular job, position or with a type or size of organisation.

They just pursued something important to them that was needed in the world. Their ideas about potential future positions were expressed more as, 'Here is an idea, and I am trying to figure out if this can somehow work in my present organisation. If not, I am open to other ways of working on this idea'.

This observation is supported by Stanford University Professor of Psychology Carol Dweck's research, reported in her book *Mindset*: 'Fixed mind-set executives hunger to be at the top, however, growth mind-set executives rarely set out to get to the top, but often end up there as a by-product of their enthusiasm for what they do'.[65]

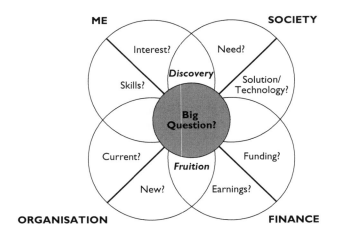

*Tentatively formulating a Big Question*

---

## Exercise 14    Practising formulating a Big Question

If you would have a first stab at your Big Question, what might it be?
Big Questions come in the form of:

- I wonder if we could . . . ?
- What if . . . would be possible?
- Wouldn't it be amazing if . . . ?

---

At this early stage, especially if reading this book is the first step on your journey, you are not yet likely to have formulated a Big Question, but if there is a particular topic that keeps surfacing, you might want to formulate a Big Question from this thought – just to practise. It can be set aside if you find a topic that engages you more.

## Takeaways

As this is the book's pivotal chapter, there is no real substitute for reading the text.

A few key areas we covered:

Asking a few trusted contacts what they *appreciate* about you can totally change the lens you see yourself through.

To formulate our Big Question, we work with three areas: our interests, needs in society, and matching these to the skills we are good at and wish to contribute going forward:

- You can use the SDGs or any other framework or topic to start. It does not matter where you start, just start.
- Using a semi-structured process is important; if we are too structured, we don't get to use the creative part of our brains.
- Choosing two to four areas for further exploration is practical; one is too narrow, and more than four stretches us too thin. Discard and add areas as you learn.
- Opportunities often emerge in the overlaps or gaps between existing areas.

Openness to new experiences is key to let Big Questions surface:

- We do this by gradually exploring as close to the edge of the system as we can.
- Management programmes, volunteering, pro bono work or immersion programmes on the ground are all opportunities for this.

Building new strategic and dynamic networks is the key for acquiring knowledge and understanding how we could impact an issue. These networks are also the conduit to new jobs:

- Networking means building relationships with people who are interested in solving the same problems as you are.
- Learn to network gradually and do it in a way that suits you. Learn networking etiquette and what constitutes faux pas!
- You really need to be on LinkedIn.

Practise formulating Big Questions – 'Wouldn't it be amazing if . . . ?'

Focus on the Discovery process, not the outcome. You have no idea, starting out, just how many exciting things are going on out there!

## Notes

1 Buechner, F. (1993). *Wishful Thinking: A Seeker's ABC*. London, UK: Bravo Ltd. Quote retrieved from: www.goodreads.com/work/quotes.
2 Long, J. et al. (2016). Distinct Interactions Between Fronto-Parietal and Default Mode Networks in Impaired Consciousness. *Scientific Reports*, 6(38866). DOI: 10.1038/srep38866.
3 Pillay, S. (12 May 2017). *Your Brain Can Only Take So Much Focus*. Harvard Business Review blog. Retrieved from: www.hbr.com.

4  Seetharaman, D. and Das, P. (2 December 2015). *Mark Zuckerberg and Priscilla Chan to Give 99% of Facebook Shares to Charity.* Wall Street Journal. Retrieved from: www.wsj.com.
5  Torchia, A. and Wilson, T. (14 October 2016). *Saudi Arabia, Softbank Aim to Be World's No. 1 Tech Investor with US$100 Billion Fund.* Financial Times. Retrieved from: www.ft.com.
6  Levitt, T. (7 September 2016). *Blockchain Technology Trialled to Tackle Slavery in the Fishing Industry.* The Guardian. Retrieved from: www.theguardian.com.
7  Seetharaman, D. (22 September 2016). *Zuckerberg Family Fund to Invest US$3 Billion in Research Technology.* Wall Street Journal. Retrieved from: www.wsj.com.
8  Goal 3 Target. Sustainable Development Knowledge Platform. Retrieved from: https://sustainabledevelopment.un.org/sdg3.
9  Rajan Pandahare LinkedIn profile: www.linkedin.com/in/rpandhare/.
10  Oliver Harrison bio. World Economic Forum. Retrieved from: www.weforum.org/people/oliver-harrison/.
11  El Economista (14 January 2016). *Nace Telefónica Innovación Alpha: La Operadora Quiere Impulsar La Transformación Digital.* Retrieved from: www.eleconomista.es.
12  Médecins Sans Frontières (25 May 2015). *Governments Take Decisive Step Towards More Affordable Vaccines.* Retrieved from: www.msf.org.
13  Unilever (n.d.) *Sustainable Living Plan.* Retrieved from: www.unilever.com/sustainable-living/.
14  Kumwenda, R. (20 October 2016). *UNDP Is Walking the Talk Towards Greener Healthcare Procurement.* Blog. Retrieved from: www.skoll.org.
15  Skoll Award winners 2006. Retrieved from: http://skoll.org/organization/riders-for-health/.
16  Mehta, K.M. et al. (1 January 2016) Systematic Motorcycle Management and Health Care Delivery: A Field Trial. *American Journal of Public Health*, 106(1): 87–94. DOI: 10.2105/AJPH.2015.302891.
17  Hurst, A. (27 January 2017). *Why Ben & Jerry's Founder Pushes His Company to Merge Ice Cream and Social Justice.* Fastcoexist. Retrieved from: www.fastcoexist.com.
18  Big Society Capital website: www.bigsocietycapital.com.
19  Martin, R., Osberg, S. and Huffington, A. (2015). *Getting Beyond Better: How Social Entrepreneurship Works.* Brighton, MA: Harvard Business Review Press, Kindle edition, location 880.
20  Lovegrove, N. (27 January 2017). *The Mosaic Principle: The Six Dimensions of a Successful Life & Career.* London, UK: Profile Books, Kindle edition, location 2102.
21  Lovegrove, N. (27 January 2017). *The Mosaic Principle: The Six Dimensions of a Successful Life & Career.* London, UK: Profile Books, Kindle edition, location 1413.
22  Phillips, K.W. (1 October 2014). *How Diversity Makes Us Smarter.* Scientific American. Retrieved from: www.scientificamerican.com.
23  IMD (21 June 2010). *IMD Partners with WWF to Offer Best in Class Sustainability Program for Business Leaders.* Retrieved from: www.imd.org.
24  Sunny Bindra – Fast Forward Program: www.sunwords.com/fast-forward/.
25  Collins, J. (2001). *Good to Great.* London, UK: Random House Business.
26  UAP Old Mutual website: www.uapoldmutual.com.
27  IBM (n.d.). *Smarter Cities Challenge.* Retrieved from: https://smartercitieschallenge.org.

28 Intel (n.d.). *An Investment in Her Is an Investment in Our Future: When Girls and Women Learn, We All Win.* Retrieved from: www.intel.com.
29 Girl Rising website: http://girlrising.com.
30 Accenture (n.d.). *Skills to Succeed.* Retrieved from: www.accenture.com/us-en/company-skills-succeed.
31 Leaders Quest website: https://leadersquest.org.
32 PYXERA Global website: www.pyxeraglobal.org.
33 PYXERA Global website, corporate partners: www.pyxeraglobal.org/partnerships/
34 Stuart Hart and CK Prahad first coined this term and explored this approach: www.stuartlhart.com/sites/stuartlhart.com/files/BoPProtocol2ndEdition2008_0.pdf.
35 Dow Corning (21 September 2011). *Dow Corning Pledges Support to Global Alliance for Clean Cookstoves.* Retrieved from: www.dowcorning.com.
36 PYXERA Global website: www.pyxeraglobal.org.
37 Adelai E. Stevenson quote. Retrieved from: http://quoteinvestigator.com/2012/07/14/life-years-count/.
38 Ware, B. (2012). *The Top Five Regrets of the Dying: A Life Transformed by the Dearly Departing.* London, UK: Hay House, Kindle edition.
39 Osho (n.d.). *Seven Kinds of Ego: The Heart Sutra, Chapter 6.* Discourse. Retrieved from: www.oshoworld.com.
40 Mahatma Gandhi quote. Retrieved from: www.goodreads.com.
41 Ibarra, H. (2002). *Working Identity: Unconventional Strategies for Reinventing Your Career.* Brighton, MA: Harvard Business School Press, Kindle edition, location 322.
42 Hoffman, R. (2012). *The Start-Up of You: Adapt to the Future, Invest in Yourself, and Transform Your Career.* London, UK: Cornerstone Digital, Kindle edition, location 1089.
43 Grant, A. (2013). *Give and Take: A Revolutionary Approach to Success.* London, UK: Weidenfeld & Nicolson.
44 Stanford, D.D. (22 December 2014). *Coca-Cola Disconnects Voice Mail at Headquarters.* Bloomberg. Retrieved from: www.bloomberg.com.
45 Glazer, E. (2 June 2015). *J.P. Morgan Hangs Up on Voicemail.* Wall Street Journal. Retrieved from: www.wsj.com.
46 Sandoz Leadership team web page: www.sandoz.com/about-us/who-we-are/sandoz-leadership.
47 Hoffmann, A. (2016). *Purpose Driven Leader – Purpose Driven Career.* Cranfield University's School of Management Doughty Centre for Corporate Responsibility, p. 60. Retrieved from: www.cranfield.ac.uk.
48 LinkedIn website: https://press.linkedin.com.
49 Gladwell, M. (2000). *The Tipping Point: How Little Things Can Make a Big Difference.* London, UK: Little Brown. Retrieved from: https://en.wikipedia.org/wiki/The_Tipping_Point.
50 Gladwell, M. (2000). *The Tipping Point: How Little Things Can Make a Big Difference.* London, UK: Little Brown, p. 19. Retrieved from: https://en.wikipedia.org/wiki/The_Tipping_Point.
51 Grant, A. (2013). *Give and Take: A Revolutionary Approach to Success.* London, UK: Weidenfeld & Nicolson.
52 Martin, R., Osberg, S. and Huffington, A. (2015). *Getting Beyond Better: How Social Entrepreneurship Works.* Brighton, MA: Harvard Business Review Press, Kindle edition, location 95.
53 Föreningen för Gatubarn i Nepal website: www.gatubarnnepal.net.
54 Här kommer vår 11:e Medical College Student. Föreningen för Gatubarn I Nepal blog: http://bit.ly/2g2miS4.

55 Jagannathan, S. (8 November 2016). *Why We Should Invest in Secondary Education in Nepal*. Asian Development Bank blog. Retrieved from: https://blogs.adb.org.
56 RE100 website: http://there100.org/re100.
57 Sustainable Cities Collective (7 September 2016). *Mutual Needs, Mutual Challenges: How Corporate PPAs Are Remaking the Renewables Sector*. Retrieved from: www.sustainablecitiescollective.com.
58 CDP website: www.cdp.net/en.
59 Heidelberg Cement website, rating und rankings: www.heidelbergcement.com/en/rating-und-rankings.
60 Caldwell, G. (27 October 2016). *L'Oréal Scoops 'A' Ranking in CDP Climate Change Charts for 4th Year in a Row*. Global Cosmetics News. Retrieved from: https://globalcosmeticsnews.com.
61 Mooney, A. (27 October 2016). *BlackRock Calls for Higher Carbon Price to Tackle Climate Change*. Financial Times. Retrieved from: www.ft.com.
62 Martin, R., Osberg, S. and Huffington, A. (2015). *Getting Beyond Better: How Social Entrepreneurship Works*. Brighton, MA: Harvard Business Review Press, Kindle edition, locations 95–1560.
63 Riders for Health website: www.ridersintl.org.
64 Ware, B. (2012). *The Top Five Regrets of the Dying: A Life Transformed by the Dearly Departing*. London, UK: Hay House, Kindle edition, locations 3533–3541.
65 Dweck, C. (2012). *Mindset: The New Psychology of Success*. London, UK: Robinson, Kindle edition, location 859.

# Chapter 10

# Fruition
## Making your Purpose reality

*In this chapter, we will cover how to turn your Big Question from Chapter 9 into action – Purpose – and start to explore how we can make this real.*

*We will work with the remaining five of the '9 Questions': a technical solution, funding, our need for income, and if you can execute your idea at your current employer by 'job-crafting', or it is better pursued externally.*

*We will cover the strategic and practical considerations, and take an investment portfolio approach around choosing what type of work to invest in – full- or part-time, executive, non-executive or advisory, etc. – and how we spend and get paid for our time.*

*As we refine our Big Question and our Purpose, and iterate the potential solutions, we cycle back and forth between Discovery and Fruition – it is normal to feel that you have one foot in each camp for some time.*

## Fruition: five areas for making our Purpose reality

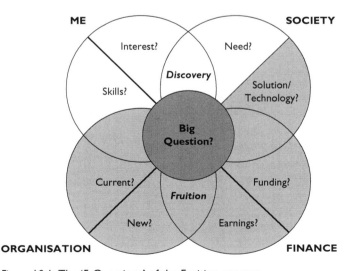

*Figure 10.1* The '5 Questions' of the Fruition process

How to find technical solutions and raise funding externally for projects is beyond the scope of this book – however, as we discussed earlier, digital business models can have 10X Impact, and exploring the potential of digital solutions is vital.

It will come as no surprise that the Career Transformational Assets – self-knowledge, building and leveraging your networks, and being open to new experiences – are the route to finding answers to these questions as well. Our new networks help us problem-solve, give us access to people and organisations interested in funding our project, and new experiences make us see new potential solutions.

We will now focus on three aspects of the Fruition process: the best organisational fit for your Purpose project job-crafting at your current employer; and how to think of work models and personal earnings when the time comes to exit and pursue your Purpose externally.

This will be illustrated throughout by the real-life stories of how leaders created these careers.

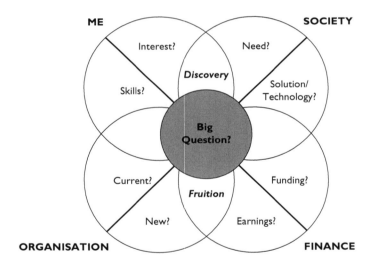

## Big Questions and Purpose: not complicated, just fuzzy

As we mentioned in Chapter 9, once we have an idea of a Big Question, we can turn this into an action statement – our Purpose.

Most of us are not used to trying to find an undefined destination, and this can make us feel unsure about if we will ever find our new direction – our Purpose. This feeling of being unsure simply means that we are in the middle of the uncomfortable Unknown Zone.

It is useful to remind ourselves that we are looking for a *direction*. Clarity arrives gradually through continuously learning and exploring, remembering that there are no absolute answers.

To illustrate, let us look at how finding Purpose played out for two people who started with no clear ideas – just an issue or two that intrigued them: Sola Oyinlola, whose story we heard in Chapter 7, plus the story of Paul Dickinson, the founder of the Carbon Disclosure Project (CDP).

Before Sola Oyinlola formulated his Purpose as 'technology investor for the bottom billion', he *spent a year figuring out* what he was interested in contributing to. With his background in technology and finance, his Big Question emerged as: 'What if we could make technology affordable enough to help solve major issues in Africa?'.

He then set off on a *five-year project* to learn and define how he, with his background, could make a difference this way. Over time, this resulted in his clearly articulated Purpose and the manifestation of his portfolio of work when leaving Schlumberger.

Paul Dickinson, the co-founder and chair of the CDP, *was concerned about climate change for some time*. When in 1999 he saw that the $CO_2$ graphs from the Clinton White House and other sources were all showing the same trend, he decided *he needed to do 'something about $CO_2$'*.

His first Big Question was: 'What if UK investors could force $CO_2$ producing companies to reduce their $CO_2$ emissions?'.

He was advised that this effort must be global, and at the same time he realised that investors cannot simply force change. What was needed was a demand for disclosure, to 'force' emitters to change; no one wants to be at the bottom of league tables.

The CDP was born in late 2000 with the Purpose: 'Getting the world's largest corporations and their largest supply chain companies to disclose their carbon performance to force change through transparency'.

Over the past 15 years, this has expanded to include cities as well as companies, plus water and forest footprints, and their network of investors and purchasers now represent over US$100 trillion, with the Purpose: 'We motivate companies and cities to disclose their environmental impacts, giving decision makers the data they need to change market behavior'.[1]

As you can see from the above, we refine our Purpose as we learn. If you worry that you are not immediately 'finding Purpose', do not feel disheartened. You will find an issue or topic that captures your interest and energy, through Discovering – meeting people, reading and exploring – it is just fuzzy for quite a while.

It is now time to have a first try at turning our Big Question into an action statement.

At this point, you might not have a clear Big Question, but for practice you can pick any issue that interests you and formulate a Big Question (to formulate one, see Exercise 14 at the end of Chapter 9).

---

**Exercise 15   Articulating Purpose: turning a Big Question into an action statement**

Look at the examples above and try to turn a Big Question into an action statement.

It should contain: (1) what; (2) for whom; and (3) the intended impact in some form. You can see this in the CDP mission: 'We motivate companies and cities to: (1) disclose their environmental impacts, (2) giving decision makers the data they need to (3) change market behavior'.

If you had a preliminary stab at turning your Big Question (in however raw a form it is) into an action statement, what would it be?

---

*Question 10.1:*   What does this question and Purpose statement tell you that you need to find out to refine it and understand how it could be done in practice?

*Question 10.2:*   Who might know something about this, or who else to talk to? Who could you team with to make this have material impact?

*Question 10.3:*   Where can you learn more? Reading? Webinars? Events?

## Purpose-driven careers often unfold in three stages

As many of the executives' stories illustrate, Purpose-driven careers often have three stages. First, 'job-crafting', then a bigger in-house role reflecting our Purpose, and finally transitioning out when they were ready – having acquired the skills and networks needed.

We saw these aspects play out with Richard Gillies. First, job-crafting (100 per cent renewables project), being offered the Chief Sustainability Officer position at M&S, and – when he felt he had accomplished what he could for M&S – accepting the approach from Kingfisher. If you look at Richard's LinkedIn profile, you will notice that he has also been an advisor or NED to BSR, NERC, We Mean Business and Business in the Community for years.

He is clearly a valued contributor to sustainability issues, and this positions him to continue to contribute with greater scope and scale at each career stage – a very important point.

The stories often also show that a *major* career change takes around five years to implement.

The Discovery period is often at least a year, followed by a few years of 'job-crafting' while you establish yourself in this new area – in your current organisation and externally – to prepare the launch to your new career in the outside world.

If you start from scratch after leaving an organisation, in my experience, a career change still takes the same length of time. Not finding 'any job', but it takes this long from starting to figure out something new to being established as a serious player in the new field.

It is therefore a great advantage to learn, and establish ourselves in our new field, while we are still with our long-term employer. It allows us, when we are ready – or when forced by circumstances – to launch ourselves onwards with momentum, instead of doing a stop-start transition.

Think of it as a ski jump: you want to have controlled momentum launching yourself elegantly into your next career . . .

We can also deduct from the stories that leaders reassessed, around the five-year mark, where they needed to pivot next, doing a new Discovery journey to see how they could expand their Impact.

Purpose truly is a direction, and not a forever fixed idea. It keeps unfolding and expanding in the most astonishing ways – in a direction.

Another example for how Purpose evolves over time is Professor David Grayson, at the Doughty Centre for Corporate Responsibility at Cranfield University's School of Management in the UK.

David discovered an additional string to his corporate responsibility Purpose after caring part-time for his elderly dementia-suffering mother during the years leading up to her death in late 2015.

He got so interested and passionate about the topic of caring that he became the Chairman of Carers UK in 2013, and in 2017 published his book *Take Care*.[2]

With our increasing longevity, we will all be carers (or cared for) at one or more points in our lives, and our employers will need to know how to manage this fact. This will become an important aspect of corporate responsibility going forward – and a 'job-crafting' project for David . . .

## The business case: matching my Purpose and the organisation's strategy

(Please refer to the Figure on page 178)

The approach below applies whether we are currently employed in an organisation or not.

If you are employed, going through the Discovery process to find your Big Question and Purpose means that you will most likely be assessing if and how this can work in synergy with your current organisation's strategy, then creating your job-crafting project and a supporting business plan, as this is about personal learning while concurrently adding value to the organisation.

If you have already transitioned out, you would be trying to find an organisation with a strategy (and/or Purpose) where your Purpose can fit.

Organisations are at different maturity stages in terms of how they approach Sustainability and their role in helping solve societal issues. Below are a few scenarios reflecting this, with examples of executives who pursued Purpose-driven careers in various types of organisations, through 'job-crafting' internally or externally, and how their careers developed over time.

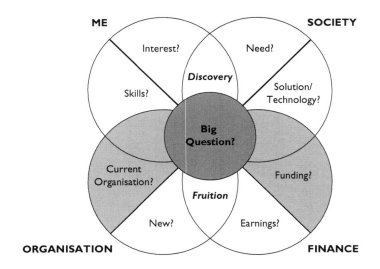

### When the company has a sustainability- or Purpose-driven strategy

If Purpose or sustainability is core to your company's strategy, you clearly have opportunities to discover how you can contribute to your company's Purpose and develop your Career Transformational Assets and tri-sector leadership skills as part of your job. Later, if that is the right thing, you might transition to another position inside or outside to pursue your Purpose.

If your company has recently started on a Sustainability strategy, signed up to the SDGs or a new CEO has arrived – aiming to change the company – you have an ideal situation to volunteer yourself, and have a tremendous opportunity for learning, job-crafting and career change.

The emerging interest by large corporates to aim for B-Corps status should aid this approach. B-Corps are companies who have been certified by the non-profit B Lab as being 'for benefit' to all stakeholders (beyond shareholders) and committed to making a positive impact on society.[3]

DanoneWave – the largest non-cheese dairy producer in the USA – is now the largest US registered 'for-benefit' corporation, and is working towards getting its full B-Corps certification by 2020.

Danone and B-Corps have also created an open-source cooperation agreement that aims to accelerate the process for large, publicly listed multinationals to become certified as B-Corps.[4,5]

Maybe you can become the catalyst for your organisation becoming a B-Corps?

To show how we can match our own Purpose inside the company's wider strategy, let us go back to Geoff McDonald, who we met in Chapter 9.

Geoff realised that his passion for mental health issues in the workplace could fit into Unilever's strategy 'to improve the health and well-being of a billion people by 2020'.

In 2013, Geoff had worked for Unilever for over 25 years and was Global Vice President HR for Marketing, Communications, Sustainability and Talent. He had been central to Unilever's journey, with Paul Polman, in embedding the Purpose-driven change programme throughout the company. This was a world first in such a large global organisation.

Unilever, at this juncture, took their top 400 executives through a leadership programme where they could find their own personal Purpose and how this aligned, or not, with Unilever's purpose, knowing that a few executives would decide to leave and pursue their own paths. This is central to their philosophy – if all executives feel aligned with the company's purpose, they will be much happier and engaged in their work.

One of the executives that started thinking at that time was Geoff. He had a very keen interest in employee well-being, particularly in the area of mental health. He realised that there is a lot of stigma attached to the topic of mental health issues in business, and he wished to remove this stigma in Unilever. He co-led a high-visibility pilot in the UK with keen support from his CEO, and it was quickly adopted in many other geographies. Geoff was soon asked to come and speak on this topic to other companies who wished to address the mental health topic.

Over the space of about a year, the decision ripened with Geoff that he really wanted to pursue these two topics – driving Purpose and mental health issues in business – on a larger canvas than one company, to help other organisations with what he had learned. He started exploring opportunities for doing so, and in July 2014 he left Unilever and joined the Bridge Partnership, who help shape the next generation of leaders.

In November 2015, Geoff, together with Georgie Mack, Managing Partner at the Made by Many digital innovation consultancy, started Minds@Work, a network to remove the stigma from mental health in the workplace.[6] By mid-2017, the network had grown from 10 people to almost 900 strong. Geoff had, among many other successes, engineered a meeting at 10 Downing Street with the then Prime Minister David Cameron and the CEOs of 10 major UK organisations on the 'mental health in business' topic.

He was now getting so much traction on the topic that in June 2016, he decided to leave his formal role with the Bridge Partnership to focus fully on his mental health work. Minds@Work has a quarterly get-together, and has also held a number of major events called 'This Is My Story', where senior executives – men and women – stand up on stage and speak about their own mental health challenges and support from their organisations. These have so far taken place in London and Glasgow.

As Geoff says, 'For the first time ever, we are seeing leaders from the workplace share their stories, and this helps normalise mental health, and this is what breaks the stigma'.

Geoff's story neatly illustrates how finding a way to fit you passion into your company's strategy and 'job-crafting' prepares you for transitioning out when the time is right.

Discovering Purpose means finding a direction, not finding *the final and only purpose in our lives*, which is a common misunderstanding. Over time, we develop a deeper understanding for what we can impact and contribute to in the world.

Geoff McDonald's first 'Big Question' was: 'I wonder if/how we can get a massive organisation like Unilever to live its Purpose?'.

Once that was well under way, the second question slowly developed, in sync with the 'well-being Purpose' of Unilever: 'What if we could increase the health and well-being of our own employees by removing the stigma around mental health in Unilever?'. This continued to develop into wondering how this could be done in all workplaces in the UK . . . and beyond.

### When the company does not have an explicit sustainability- or Purpose-driven strategy

Although many organisations still have to embrace sustainability or Purpose in their core strategy, most organisations have a corporate social responsibility (CSR), sustainability or environmental strategy of some form. You can start from there to see what kind of 'job-crafting' business case you could develop.

To illustrate this, we will use Gina Tesla's story. Gina has been since 2010 Director of Corporate Citizenship at IBM, and job-crafted while in the strategy practice before being offered this position.

In 2000, she decided to take a career break from her communications agency career and volunteered for the Peace Corps, working for two years on community economic developmental projects in Panama.

On her return, she joined IBM in the strategy consulting practice, and through her colleague Kevin Thompson, also a Peace Corps returnee, got involved with a leadership development programme he had created. This was originally created to prepare employees for working in a global environment.

The programme was built on the Peace Corps model, and is now the famous IBM Corporate Service Corps.[7] This was later expanded with the Executive Service Corps[8] for senior executives at IBM.

Both programmes are now flagship leadership programmes in IBM. The latter is now part of the 'Smarter Cities Challenge'[9] competition, which lends top IBM people to cities around the world, pro bono, to help solve major problems. The programmes are life-changing experiences, at the edge of the system, for leaders of all seniority levels.

Over time, these programmes have become central to IBM's 'Smart World' strategy that was conceived in the depths of the financial crisis in 2009.

Gina's 'Big Question' was: 'I wonder if we could create a global pro bono programme on the Peace Corps model in IBM for benefit to leaders, IBM and communities?' and turned it into action – Purpose.

*Question 10.4:*    What kind of sustainability- or Purpose-driven strategy does your current organisation have? How could you build a business case here?

*Question 10.5:*    If you are looking to join an organisation, what kind of sustainability- or Purpose-driven strategy does the organisation you are looking at have?

### If your Purpose has no fit with your company's strategy: extracurricular 'job-crafting'

You might find that what you are really passionate about pursuing is not compatible with your company's strategy or cannot fit into a job-crafting project.

The solution, then, is to pursue your topic of interest and learn outside work, often in the form of volunteering or board work. This, however, does not give you the same opportunity to develop skills and networks – *while helping to change your current organisation and adding value to them* – while you prepare for a future career.

An example of the 'extracurricular' scenario is Pallav Sinha, founder and CEO of MeraJob India:

> Moving back from the UAE to India in 2008, when asked by Temasek to set up Fullerton in India, meant that I connected back to my roots. Thoughts about a change had been brewing inside me since some time . . .
>
> I could see the issue around employability for the lower end of the pyramid in India. *One million people are reaching working age each month*, while job opportunities are far fewer and the education system does not prepare graduating students for employment.
>
> Candidates might be located in smaller tier 2 cities, just 50 km away from the main centres like Mumbai or Delhi, but they could not signal their presence and availability for employment to the employing companies.
>
> First, we thought about skill development to enhance jobseekers' skills, but gradually it dawned on me, from my experience in consumer financial services, that what we needed was a 'credit bureau of jobseekers'. This grew on me more and more.

While I was working at Fullerton, in our spare time, we completed our research and figured out our business model, and finally in 2012 we decided to give it a go on a full-time basis and I left my employer. We could see a big commercial potential and a way of making a real difference to this underserved segment and employment ecosystem.

MeraJob basically pre-screen employees for employers, coach them to interview and do basic job postings. We are developing content to coach jobseekers get entry-level jobs, via partners and even via our own videos on the website.

We now work with around 100 employers across over 20 Indian cities and have about 100 employees. We serve around 1.5 million jobseekers and are adding several thousand per day.

The first four years have been fantastic – as a personal experience and as an enterprise. It has also been frustrating due to the overwhelming demographics of India . . .

*Question 10.6:*    If you don't feel your current organisations strategy can house your Purpose, what could be the right organisational type of home for it (there might be several)?

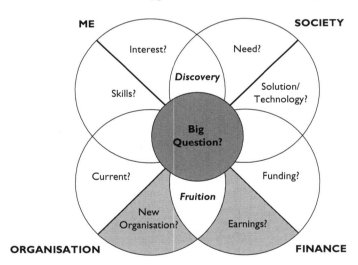

## Business models – for our external next stage career

At some point, it will be time to transition out of our organisation. We might wish to focus on our Purpose 100 per cent of the time, it might be time to 'retire', or a reorganisation creates the impetus to move on.

We now need to explore what kind of business models could work for achieving our Purpose, earning the income we need and the lifestyle we seek.

This could mean working in business, government, social enterprises, charities, NGOs, NFPs, institutes, associations, academic institutions, etc., in full-time, part-time, executive, non-executive, consulting or advisory positions, or any combination thereof – paid or pro bono. This can be quite confusing if we are used to working full-time for many years for one employer.

Before we continue to the strategies and practicalities for choosing options for creating our new career – *our career investment portfolio* – there is another important topic to discuss: how programmed and 'addicted' we are in terms of how and how much we work – we need to change this to achieve any work-life balance objective as part of our career change.

### Understanding our work addiction

In the middle of our ultra-busy full-time careers, we dream of another way of working and living, with less pressure to constantly deliver close to impossible results on a 24/7 schedule.

What we are not always aware of is our addiction to our work patterns, to work itself, and how we unconsciously perpetuate these patterns. The research by Alexandra Michel, a Wharton business school professor, illustrates this starkly. She conducted a 13-year study of four cohorts of investment bankers pushing themselves hard as they started out on their careers. Around year 4, they started to break down from overwork. Some of them realised they needed to work differently and left banking.

When Professor Michel followed these leavers at mid-career (years 9–13), the disturbing findings were that not only had they often chosen similarly demanding positions, but that *they brought their previous work habits with them*, even when they had rejected their previous employer's work culture.

*This included when they had left for what was considered lower-stress careers; they in fact intensified the pace of work for everyone else, role-modelling behaviours they were then forced to sustain.*[10]

I have also seen this happen with senior leaders – trapped in this pattern, always 'on', always available. This can be a legacy from our junior days, at the beck and call of our superiors, a 'need to feel needed', or fear of consequences if 'something happened' and we had not worked every hour possible.

It is important that we are aware of and consciously work on changing our work addiction patterns if we want to achieve a different quality of life in our next career stage.

A simple but effective habit that has literally changed the lives of many executives is to learn to *schedule private activities in your calendar before work is scheduled*. Work has a way of filling all available time, so we need to make some time 'unavailable' for work. Work finds a way of fitting in around private appointments, but the corollary is not true. If you don't schedule your private appointments (including time for your career change project), they will never happen – work will.

---

### Exercise 16    How to get to do 'the things I never have time for'

Pick one regular personal activity that you 'never have time for' (yoga class, wine course, concerts, volunteering, family dinner) and block out the required time in your calendar for the next six months.

Now make your first four appointments.

Check back in three or four months' time and see how many appointments you kept and how many you cancelled. How many activities would you have achieved without making these appointments?

---

### Thinking of our second careers as a 'project investment portfolio'

At mid/later career, once we leave the organisations where we worked for many years, our next employers are rarely organisations where we will work for more than a few years. This can sound both unfair and scary. Why would new employers not want us to stay longer?

As we reach senior levels, whether professional or executive, we are mainly hired into new positions to use *our experience in a particular field to help them solve a particular problem*. Turnarounds or strategy change processes are largely implemented in two to five years, and if there is not a longer-term hole in their succession planning that you are plugging, it will be time to move on when what you came to do is done.

If you want examples, have a look at the résumés of executive committee members of listed companies (which is public information) who were external hires, and the stories (plus the LinkedIn profiles) of, for example, Richard Gillies, Steve Howard (ex-IKEA CSO), Pablo Fetter, Nick O'Donohoe, Laurence Mulliez, Yanos Michopolous, Luke Swanson and Jay Koh in various chapters.

This might feel strange at first, but if you ask these executives how they feel about it, they like the freedom this gives them. Once a major Purpose-driven change project is embedded, most executives want to move on to either do the same thing in another organisation full-time, or find a way to help more organisations, moving on to an advisory career.

A listed company executive committee member once described his way of looking at this phenomenon very practically:

> I now look at every full-time 'job' I am hired into as '*a project that might last two to three years*'. If it lasts longer, great, but in case something unforeseen happens, I have made sure I have achieved everything I

needed to at the two-year point. This way, I can ensure I leave the legacy I was hired to create for the organisation, should I have to leave earlier than planned.

This is a great way to look at our mid/later career moves. So much can happen in short time frames: a financial crisis, a company scandal, or the ousting of the CEO who hired you. Planning to 'be done' in two years, if needed, is a sound strategy.

In the words of Reid Hoffman, the founder of LinkedIn, we should think of our employment as 'tours of duty'. The definitions for them are: rotational (to learn), transformational (to transform one's career and the company) and foundational (long-term). The transformational tour of duty applies here; it lasts two to five years, has a specific mission, and the person's résumé should look considerably more impressive afterwards.[11]

Corporations normally think of tours of duty for the up-and-coming '30-something' leaders. When we change careers mid/later career, we are again 'up-and-coming' – we literally have a second 20- to 30-year career to build. We can't rest on old laurels; we will need to continue to build our resumes for many years to come with new and relevant experience.

This means looking at our career as an investment portfolio. Just as with financial investments, we need to create *optionality* and *returns* short, medium and long term. We need to understand how to invest in skill- and network-building to create 'transformational tours of duty' in order to earn income at different stages of our later lives – and enjoy our work.

Starting out understanding that full-time employment with others might not be available forever, and keeping options open, will be vital, as we shall now see.

### Why going fully non-executive immediately can reduce your longer-term options

When executives start to think about transitioning out, they are mainly familiar with what previous colleagues have pursued – acquiring a number of non-executive director or trustee positions on boards – the 'classic' portfolio career.

Acquiring board positions seems to be the new standard to measure up to, and many mid/later career executives spend the last three to four years before exiting their long-term employer sitting on various company and charity boards. The bigger the organization, the better, to gain status in the non-executive director job market.

Learning about governance and becoming a good director is a growth and learning challenge, but after a few years directors can 'get bored with boards' and realise they would like to do something 'more executive' again – but find it close to impossible to return to the executive job market. They realise that they unintentionally closed off other potential career roads too early.

Due to our increasing longevity, at age 50–55, when most of us look at our 'next career stage', we might be looking at 20 to 30 years when we will need or want to work. Do we want to immediately restrict our options to only one type of work when we embark on this long, new and unchartered stage?

The job market is also, unfortunately, still very ageist. Trying to return to full-time executive work after four to five years of non-executive board work in our mid-fifties and beyond is difficult. After relatively few years away from the executive fray, you are seen as no longer being 'up to speed' in your sector or unable to catch up with the rapid progress of technology.

We spoke earlier about how executives who left 'corporate' life more than five years ago by and large have missed the social media revolution, which now highly affects working life, as well as company risk and strategy. Not being cognisant in this area is not going to be a good place to be if you plan to have a long working life. This applies to both executive and non-executive work. As mentioned earlier, digital experience is also now one of the non-executive director skills most in demand – for mainstream business as well as for trustee positions in charities.

My hope is that the ageist situation will change over time, but to keep options open, it is advisable to have a serious Discovery period before an exit decision is made, and to preferably start out with a variety of work.

This way, you can gradually choose what is right for you, and ideally 'try before you buy' your next main professional activity, without closing off many potentially interesting avenues by accident.

An example of this is Steven Howard, for 11 years CEO of BITC (Business in the Community – the Prince's Responsible Business Network) in the UK. Before going 'plural' – having a full-time NED portfolio, as the term is known in NED circles – he tried part-time and changed his mind. He recounts his experience as follows:

> After an executive career culminating in two CEO positions for Cookson Group plc and Novar plc, we sold Novar and I wondered 'what next?'. I had had various NED positions for over 10 years, and the logical direction would have been to have a 'portfolio career'.
>
> After spending all my time in committees for many years, I was not sure this was what I wanted to do . . . so when I was approached for the MD job in Business in the Community, that we had been members of with my previous company, I jumped at the chance.

There is nothing wrong with having a portfolio of only non-executive director positions, if you are sure that this is what you really want to do for the long-haul, but starting with a range of activities and 'trying before buying', we know what we are getting into, and in case we change our minds about full-time executive work, we have not accidentally closed that door.

Another benefit to having a couple of legs to your professional stool is that it helps to smooth out earnings – work streams do go quiet periodically.

## Full-time executive career choices

To express our Purpose in a full-time role, there are many options we can consider. We can join existing substantial for-profit or not-for-profit (NFP) organisations, small companies or start-ups, work for them interim or run our own organisation full time. Below, we will focus on the full-time executive work options, beyond the traditional full-time hire.

### Running our own business

Reading the press, we could believe that only young people start new businesses; however, recent research by the Kaufmann Foundation, surveying 500 successful high-growth founders in the US, showed that the typical founder is now 40 years old, and that twice as many successful entrepreneurs were more than 50 years old than under age 25.[12]

If you have always dreamt of running your own business, now might be the time. There are many options beyond creating our own start-up, but let us first contemplate this type of option.

### Starting our own Purpose-driven for-profit company

All the more well-known Purpose-driven for-profit companies once started out with a founder or a team of founders believing in doing business differently – doing well while doing good – and grew over time.

Most businesses started at the later career stage draw heavily on our previous experience, which minimises risk. An example of this is Rolf Fouchier, previously CEO of the energy company E.ON Vertrieb Deutschland and E.ON Netherlands, now the founder of Exceleration, an angel investor in early-stage energy tech companies, who we met in Chapter 5.

Sometimes our experience is translated into another, new, area. Examples are Pallav Sinha, who we met above, and Jay Koh, who we met in Chapter 6.

Pallav used his banking clearing house knowledge to create MeraJobs, a 'clearing house' for graduates seeking employment and their potential employers.

Jay Koh, the founder of the Lightsmith Group, uses his investing experience and groundbreaking climate resilience and adaptation finance research to create a world-first financial vehicle – the launch of the world's first fund focused on resilience and adaptation to climate change.

### Starting our own social enterprises

Social enterprise, 'for-benefit' corporations and 'B-Corps' companies (mentioned earlier) are other forms of businesses. The first focuses on solving a particular societal issue while making profit – normally more modest than for a 100 per cent for-profit; the second has adopted a legal framework that means it is mandated to balance the interests of all stakeholders, not just shareholders, and is required to create a positive impact on society; and the third are companies who have been certified by the non-profit B Lab.

There has been an upsurge in social enterprise-type organisations the past few years. Just in the UK, mid-2015, some 70,000 were operating, contributing a gross value added of £24 billion to the economy and employing nearly 1 million people and creating jobs at almost twice the pace of mainstream SMEs.[13]

Although the average size of a social enterprise is normally smaller than the average SME,[14] some are sizeable. Examples of sizeable social enterprises are Warby Parker, the online eyeglass seller in the USA, and Zambrero, the healthy Mexican food restaurant chain in Australia. Both use a 'buy one, give one' model, where for each unit sold, they donate one to someone in need.

At Zambrero, one meal is donated for each meal bought. The chain, started in 2005 by Dr Sam Prince, now has 135 restaurants across Australia, New Zealand, Thailand and Ireland.[15]

At Warby Parker, for each pair of glasses purchased, the company pays for the production of another pair of eyeglasses for the NFP VisionSpring. They in turn sell the glasses to consumers or companies in developing countries as a way to encourage entrepreneurship. Warby Parker turns over 'well over US$100 million', and was Fast Company's number 1 most innovative company in 2015.[16,17,18]

Magnus Pousette decided to start a social enterprise – that can become sizeable – after 'trying before buying' a portfolio career. He decided to start a business similar to the one he had spent many years running for a major corporation, but on a social enterprise model. Magnus says:

> After 14 years working in ABB's €600 million turnover outsourced technical maintenance business, called the 'Full Service' business, I – as the CEO – recommended and led a divestment process that culminated in the unit being sold to a private equity fund in 2014.
>
> As I did not join the spun-out company, I spent a couple of years testing out a lot of different exciting avenues, from tech to TV production, and promoting technical education, non-executive work and consulting.
>
> I had never imagined going back to my 'old business', but I kept getting approaches from previous customers, partners and employees. Hence, I started exploring how this could be done, but at the same time I wanted a 'different' business model, for both how and why we would do this.

During my 'trying out' period, I realised that my Purpose in life is 'reducing industrial waste', and my Purpose couldn't be achieved without an opportunity to do it in real life. VOEE[19] is the platform to achieve this Purpose.

Industrial waste is composed of: people – due to lack of education on the job, poor safety, un-engagement, poor planning, poor processes/methods/tools, bad culture, 'uber-control', environmentally – due to low overall equipment effectiveness (OEE), no continuous improvement of equipment, sloppiness, no risk-based thinking, poor discipline, prioritising cost versus value and other short-term thinking, no 'everyday innovation', cross functional rivalry, etc., plus capital waste . . . and it goes on, becoming a scarily long list . . .

In 2015, we registered VOEE services, an outsourced technical maintenance business, founded on vested outsourcing principles – developed by Kate Vitasek at the University of Tennessee.

Vested® is a business model, methodology, mindset and movement for creating highly collaborative business relationships that enable true win–win relationships in which both parties are equally committed to each other's success. A hybrid business model of such in which both parties (the company and the service provider) focus on shared values and goals. In summary, 'What's in it for WE'.[20]

We decided to extend this concept to our financial business model, and will split our profits four ways between owners, employees, employee development and our local communities.

This makes creating this business so much more exciting and fun! Living your Purpose.

### Buying a company

If you would like to run your own Purpose-driven business, have capital to spare, but don't fancy doing a start-up, there is the possibility of acquiring an existing business.

We will not cover this in detail as it is a straightforward concept. Few executives, in my experience, think about this as an option when leaving their long-term employer, unless they have previous experience investing their own funds. If this option has appeal, learning how to be an angel investor while we are employed – like Sola Oyinlola and Katarina Elner-Haglund (below) – is a good way of building comfort around investing our private capital.

### Working with private equity and venture capital or their portfolio companies

If you are not ready to start or fully own a business, it is possible to take on executive leadership roles for private equity (PE) or venture capital (VC) owned businesses, or work in their investment teams as industry partners or advisors. PE normally invests in more mature technologies and established businesses, and VC in earlier-stage technologies and businesses, including start-ups.

Working for PE/VC can be quite intense work, but it can provide serious wealth creation, on exit, if the company has grown well. In Chapter 9, we met Laurence Mulliez, who built the solar developer Eoxis with the backing of PE firm Platina Partners.

Another interesting option, often overlooked, is to be a 'deal introducer'. The lifeblood of PE and VC is access to deals, preferably before they become public – these are found through trusted relationships.

Senior executives can create interesting and lucrative second careers by using their industry networks to introduce PE/VC firms to deals, help acquire the company, and take an executive, non-executive or advisory position in this business – if wished.

Corporate executives rarely think of their industry network as a real financial asset, or might feel they are too 'senior' for this kind of work. However, after leaving big brand corporate life, a business card with the title of 'Senior Advisor' to a well-respected PE or VC firm, and a mandate to talk about deals, opens many doors.

An increasing number of PE- and VC-owned companies are active in environmental and social impact investing space. In addition, major PE and institutional investment is going into healthcare, education, water and renewable energy around the world, at 'industrial scale' as well as at 'community scale'.

One example of such an investor is the PE fund is Actis. With around US$8 billion under management, they invest in emerging markets, focusing on products and services needed for growing countries sustainably.[21] This includes renewable energy, healthcare, insurance and consumer-oriented financial services, such as mobile transaction services in Africa or solutions for ATM networks in India, in addition to industrial applications.[22]

### Working with Impact investing firms or their portfolio companies

Impact investments are made 'into companies, organisations, and funds with the intention to generate a measurable, beneficial social or environmental impact alongside a financial return', as the Global Impact Investing Network (GIIN) defines the practice.[23]

This area has attracted a lot of investors over the past few years, including diversified financial institutions, pension funds, private foundations making programme- and/or mission-related investments, insurance companies, development finance institutions (DFIs), family offices, fund managers and individual investors.[24]

Even major institutions such as Goldman Sachs now have Impact investment units, and since 2001 their Urban Investment Group has committed approximately US$5 billion to underserved American communities. They partner with local leaders and non-profits, focusing on community development, social impact bonds and financing for small businesses.[25]

At the other end of the organisational size spectrum, husband and wife team Nadia Sood and Varun Sahni co-founded Impact Investment Partners (IIP LLP) in 2010.

> With over 20 years of experience in investing across emerging markets, with a strong focus on social change and positive impact, we set up IIP to act as a holding company identifying gaps within markets and sectors, and in turn incubating, operating and building companies to address these gaps.
>
> At present, we have been building companies that use data analytics to address the credit gap for small and medium enterprises globally, as well as other companies that use virtual and augmented reality along with gamification for serious brain injury rehabilitation.
>
> Across our businesses, we have a strong focus on disruptive and scalable technology, and as a holding company have a very different model and view than most investors, which is operational, entrepreneurial and long-term in nature.

### Running a foundation

Most major corporations and many SMEs have or are creating foundations for social investment. In addition, there are foundations created by ultra high net worth individuals' (UHNWI) family offices, such as the Bill & Melinda Gates Foundation, and foundations created by sovereign wealth funds (SWFs).

That they have serious money to spend is clear from the fact that the Bill & Melinda Gates Foundation has an annual budget twice the size of the World Health Organization,[26] the Chan Zuckerberg Initiative for disease eradication pledging US$3 billion over a decade[27] and the Ford Foundation pledging US$1 billion in the same time frame for 'mission-related investing'.[28]

Foundations are increasingly developing their grant giving into impact investment-style portfolios, leading to career opportunities for leaders with the right transferrable skills, as can be seen from the story of Clare Woodcraft, the CEO of Emirates Foundation in the UAE.

Clare's career has spanned roles in Shell, Visa and Burson Marsteller after an early career in journalism and sustainable development. In her own words:

> My role in Shell in regional communications ended up being a huge learning experience, as I stepped up to help redirect the social investment portfolio of Shell in 14 countries in the region (Middle East and Africa) away from short-term branding-driven opportunities towards long-term commitments to building human capital in the region. We did this via

social investment, moving Shell from traditional PR/communications to more business-based initiatives with measureable outcomes.

These outcome-oriented impact investing skills, combined with my background in sustainable development, allowed me to be a CEO candidate for Emirates Foundation, the national foundation of the UAE focused on youth, and develop it into a high-impact social investment portfolio rather than a short-term grant-giving operation.

### Being an interim executive

Yet another route to continue executive work is as an interim executive, taking on a full-time leadership position for a period of a few months to a couple of years, helping a company through a particularly tricky period or providing cover while full-time recruitment is being done. In between these projects, executives often take an extended period of leave.

An example of this is Nick Brooks, who after a long career in Shell's downstream business has been a serial CEO in the biofuels industry, with a particular focus on Africa. He is currently CEO of FutureBlends a biofuels company focusing on pyrolysis of biomass as a route to fuels, and a board member of Sunbird Bioenergy, who recently acquired a majority stake in Addax Oryx Groups's massive bioethanol plantation and bioenergy project in Makeni in Sierra Leone.[29]

### Running not-for-profit and public organisations

We can of course take up full-time executive positions in charities, non-grant-giving foundations, NFPs, NGOs, IGOs, institutes, think tanks or governmental organisations.

Luke Swanson, since 2015 CEO of Chance to Shine, a not-for-profit organisation with the mission of helping young people to learn and develop through sport, is an example of this.

Luke started his career in the NFP sector, with Business in the Community (BITC) and the Prince's Trust, where he saw first-hand the role that business could play in pressing social issues. He wanted to explore further how business and the NFP sector could work together, joining Diageo and later Pearson (the global education company, at this point owner of the *Financial Times* and Penguin Books). At Pearson, he was a member of the executive committee, in his dual role as Corporate Affairs Director (with responsibility for Pearson's global community programmes) and Transformation Director.

Meanwhile, he was also an active volunteer in the sporting world, coaching young people and seeing the impact that the opportunity to play sport could have on their outlook, confidence and skills. Ten years down the line, this personal passion led to his position as CEO of Chance to Shine.

As Luke says:

Although I currently have the privilege of working for a fantastic not-for-profit, my experience is that if you choose carefully, you can find purpose-driven work in any sector. Pearson is a company with a very powerful sense of purpose. We saw profit not as an end in itself, but as the by-product of producing high-quality journalism, books and education services that helped people get on in their lives. And we were passionate about that mission – just as we are at Chance to Shine about using sport as a vehicle to help young people develop and learn.

In the end, my own fundamental choices have been about finding the Purpose I want to dedicate myself to working towards. It has taken many different forms – and changed repeatedly over the course of a rich, rewarding and very fortunate career.

### Starting your own not-for-profit (NFP)

If there is no NFP addressing the area your Big Question aims to answer, you can start your own. Before taking this route, it is worthwhile checking if an organisation already exists as the past 30 years has seen an enormous upsurge in NFP organisations, and the 'third sector' is now a major employer worldwide.

In 2015, in the USA, there were nearly 1.6 million registered *non-tax-paying organisations* and over 105,000 foundations managing over US$3 trillion in assets, and their wages and salaries represented 9.2 per cent of all wages paid in the country.[30]

In the UK, there were 162,965 registered *charities* in 2013/2014, and a few thousand new ones get registered every year. These UK charities had a total income of £43.8 billion and net assets of £105.8 billion and employed 827,000 people, whereof 62 per cent were full-time employees.[31]

In 2012, the Johns Hopkins Center for Civil Society studied 13 countries' NFP and volunteering sectors. They found that 7.4 per cent of the workforce in these countries work in NFP organisations, around 75 per cent in salaried positions and the rest as volunteers.[32]

This means that the NFP sector, in terms of employment figures, *is similar in size to the global construction sector*. Chances are that an NFP already exists in the area you wish to pursue.

If there truly is an unmet need, creating a new charity, NFP or NGO can be the right thing to do, as we heard from Eva Holmberg-Tedert with her orphanage in Nepal (Chapter 9) and Paul Dickinson and the CDP (earlier in this chapter).

We will end this section with Max Robinson's story of how he made this decision to create his charity – Rainbows4Children – while working at Dow as their Global Director for their Customer Technical Service Centre. Max now lives in Ethiopia, where he runs his charity with wife Kathryn, and he is MD Growth Projects Ethiopia for Dow on a (very) part-time basis.[33] Max recalls:

> My charity (Rainbows4Children) was created in memory of my son Nicolas, who died at age 5 in October 1996.
>
> During the summer of 1996, I had been contemplating how to change my life and work, to be more complete, and a plan was coming together. In the aftermath of Nicolas' death in October 1996, I went back to this plan. I asked people to give money, instead of flowers, to build a school in memory of Nicolas, but I was not yet ready to make this a reality.
>
> A few years later, through my new wife Kathryn, I met an Ethiopian travel guide who had once been living in exile in Sudan during the civil war in Ethiopia. During his time in exile, he was helping war veterans who had lost arms or legs to use prosthetic limbs. He told me he knew of an organisation that would be interested in support for a school, and we realised through this experience that we would focus on the education of children of disabled war veterans in Ethiopia, as they are among the most disadvantaged members of society.
>
> At this stage, I visited Ethiopia once per year as part of my annual leave. I did not ask for any help from my employer. Ninety per cent of funding was from fundraising, which I could do in my free time.
>
> We used our business skills to create the vision of building the best in educational excellence in Ethiopia. This meant building one school and one technical/vocational training college. Our goal is to prove that standards as high as the best in the world are possible in Ethiopia, and then to work towards making it scalable for someone else to then fund and implement the scaling. We are halfway through this 20-year vision. The school is already fully managed by local Ethiopian staff, and in 10 years' time we aim to have accomplished the same for the college, with both being financially sustainable.
>
> My charitable work was only visible to my colleagues through the annual fundraising event for which Dow kindly provided the facilities. We did a sponsored walk that over the past 12 years has raised around US$600,000. This event turned into a social day out for families and a great learning opportunity for the children about those who 'don't have'.
>
> Each year, many colleagues and friends come to Ethiopia, to contribute to developing the skills of the school staff and take 'time out'. For example, one of my colleagues lost her job, and while looking for new employment came out to Ethiopia to teach practical science (Ethiopians have good theoretical knowledge but not always practical knowledge) to teachers as they built graduate laboratories. She then did some consulting work, and has a new job now, for which her work as a volunteer and with me as a reference was an important factor in being selected.

Another colleague, whose husband worked in the solar power industry, helped us install and connect a solar panel to power the school's underwater well-pump. Yet another volunteer, a CEO from a healthcare company, asked me what he could do . . . my advice was: 'You are a business leader – you can teach business skills to our school management team . . . others have taught English, science, sports, music and arts'.

*Question 10.7:*    Which of the options above were new to you or more substantial than you previously thought?

*Question 10.8:*    Which of these options attracts you? What would you need to find out to assess if they could work for you?

## Portfolio, hyphen, slash and gig careers

Let us now turn to the part-time work model options, which are changing and multiplying rapidly, as the cryptic title above reflects.

The past 5 to 10 years have dramatically changed how and with whom we work – technology-driven and increasingly in loose networks with external partners. The next 5 to 10 years will see an even more dramatic change in how and with whom we work, so staying flexible is vital.

As already mentioned, having a variety of types of work when starting our later career stage is a good strategy. We can 'try before we buy', build work in a few areas, and pivot to another area if work dries up in our major area of business. And we don't risk closing doors to some types of work – especially executive work – before we are ready.

Let us now have a look at the many versions of 'part-time' careers currently on offer, which can be combined in any fashion you fancy.

### Creating a non-executive director (NED) portfolio career

Most executives still mainly think of the post-full-time executive career as 'the portfolio career' – a portfolio of mainly paid non-executive director (NED) and pro bono trustee positions.

This route can still work fairly smoothly if you have been a very senior executive from a famous brand, as they are desirable as candidates for high-profile, public and private company boards, or high-profile charities, etc. However, if we don't develop digital skills, even very senior executives cannot in the future expect to automatically become prime NED candidates for major listed boards, as we saw in Chapter 6.

If you had a more general middle management career and/or are not financially independent, making a living from exclusively non-executive work could be a tricky project. This is due to a combination of modest remuneration on smaller company boards and the time available in your calendar.

Board meeting schedules normally run on a rolling annual basis, and board governance requires a certain level of attendance by NEDs – which prevents you from accepting many paid board positions. The governance and investor community also frown on NEDs serving on many boards, particularly with listed companies.

In the start-up area, equity-only payment is common for NEDs, and many start-ups are exclusively looking for NEDs who can invest a serious sum in the company and then hold an investor board seat.

Finally, being a NED on the board of a larger private equity owned company is different to serving on listed company boards. The NEDs are often asked to take a more active role in the operational activities of the company, which in listed companies is strictly divided from the responsibilities of the board.

Mixing and matching NED work with other paid work, fitting around board meeting schedules, can be a more practical way of approaching a 'portfolio'. It is also worth pondering if you will be content with uniquely engaging in board work for 20 or 30 years going forward . . .

### Creating a 'hyphen' career

In the tri-sector skills section in Chapter 6, we heard about the importance of having an 'intellectual thread' when pursuing Purpose-driven work. It is also important to have an 'intellectual thread' between the different roles in your portfolio. If the different parts of your work are too disparate, keeping up to date with all of them becomes draining, time- and energy-wise.

Katarina Elner-Haglund's experience is a good example for creating a portfolio of different types of work held together by an intellectual thread.

In 2015, Katarina, at age 61, took up a new part-time academic position at Lund University's Mechanical Engineering Section, lecturing in Designing with Plastics and 3D Printing Design or Additive Manufacturing Design to use the correct technical term, as part of her entrepreneur-communicator-mentor portfolio. How did she achieve this?

After graduating from Lund Technical University with an MSc in Polymer Engineering in the early 1980s, Katarina chose to spend her career in polymer and technology journalism as the technical editor of the polymer industry publication *Plast Nordica*, while running her own B2B technical communications business on the side.

Keeping herself at the forefront of technical developments in the polymer area, she kept a particular eye on 3D printing, which has the potential for creating low-weight, high-strength structural parts in a low-asset-intensive way that can revolutionise many industries and save huge amounts of raw materials and energy.

To grasp the potential of 3D printing: start-up Dextra in Canada will start shipping mechanically activated 3D-printed hand prostheses to amputees in Lebanese refugee camps in 2018 – at the price of US$20 – where advanced robotic prostheses with a similar mechanic capability might cost up to US$25,000 to make.[34] Think about the impact when this technology can be applied on location . . .

In addition, Katarina has taught and mentored young entrepreneurs based at IDEON – the university's innovation centre – for some years. This meant that when she felt it was time to do 'something else', she had the knowledge, credibility, positioning and connections to make this happen.

She describes her thought process for arriving at her mix of work as follows:

> There was a long period of exploration, trying to figure out what I wanted to do, and questions to answer like:
>
> - What of the things I had been doing up to now do I want to keep, expand or reduce?
> - What new things do I want to add?
> - How could the bits fit into a whole that is interesting and has synergies – in terms of impact and time – to allow for a different lifestyle?
>
> The three threads in my career, entrepreneurship, polymer technology and communications, led to my new combination of activities:
>
> - A part-time academic teaching and research position in Additive Manufacturing at Lund Technical University – I had to take a teacher qualification!
> - Co-founder and board member of the Swedish Additive Manufacturing Association (SVEAT) – where I am in charge of communications and events, etc.
> - Technical communications consultant through the business I have owned since my university days.
> - Mentor to young entrepreneurs at IDEON – the innovation centre at the university.
> - Angel investor – I occasionally invest in these entrepreneurs' businesses.
>
> I am an entrepreneur-communicator-mentor in the polymer materials area.

Katarina's approach is an illustration of a 'hyphen career', where your different roles hang together thematically. This is efficient time-wise and you can easily explain to other people what you do, 'with a hyphen in between the roles'.

Presenting yourself as a 'mentor-coach', 'advisor-consultant' or 'executive chairman-advisor to private equity' makes a lot of sense to people you meet, as they are similar enough to be tagged together.

### Creating a 'slash career' – for the medium or long term

The 'slash career', on the other hand, is when one part of your work is very different to another part – they are, in effect, parallel careers. Examples are marketing director/chef, lawyer/film producer or accountant/social entrepreneur.[35]

The slash career is often in place during a period while we are transitioning into a very different field, and the two parts stay in place on our business card until we have established ourselves in the new field and can make a living there. Or, they can be permanently in place if this is what we want to do, or might need to do to maintain our earnings – such as the lawyer/film producer above, earning money from their legal work to be able to pursue their love of producing films, an occupation they could not live from if pursued on a full-time basis.

### Creating a 'gig career'

A 'gig career' means to work in a number of temporary positions as an independent contractor on short-term engagements. The 'gig economy' is the new shape our economies are expected to be heading in due to the 'on-demand' economy.[36]

This 'on-demand' trend will be important for us in two ways: the effect on the organisations we are involved with, and the effect on our own opportunities to find work.

The organisations we will engage with professionally will be affected positively or negatively by the 'on-demand' technology trend. There will be operational issues and governance issues – including a number of ethical issues around transparency in the 'work supply chain' – that need insight and understanding.

For ourselves, if we understand how this new phenomenon works, we can find interesting work, if we understand how these organisations work – and are identifiable by organisations that could use our skills.

A study by Intuit estimates that by 2020, 40 per cent of American workers will be independent contractors, driven by the 'on-demand' economy.[37] VCs are pouring money into 'on-demand' technology – US$17.4 billion in 2015, and US$1.2 billion in HR tech start-ups for 'on-demand work' in the first half of 2016.[38]

Is this another crazy VC 'dot-com' boom with lots of small start-ups that will go under in another 'tech bust'? The proof that this is not the case is mounting. One example is as follows.

In June 2016, Microsoft announced their US$26.2 billion acquisition of LinkedIn.[39] With the massive resources of Microsoft behind it, two of LinkedIn's pilot projects should give us pause for thought. These are for placement and recruitment services in India, for graduates and for SMEs, respectively.[40] If successful, this will then be rolled out globally.

Why is this important to me as a senior leader from a large organisation looking to create a new career? Looking at the LinkedIn matching service above, we have to wonder when they will start to offer matching services for executives, executive chairmen (part-time CEOs), interim executives, non-executive directors, trustees, advisors, consultants and mentors?

Three examples illustrate 'gig economy' careers: Mudbrick, Bain & Co. alumni consultants, and GLG.

Nick Jepson, the founder of Mudbrick Consulting, got the idea for *a new community-based outsourcing model* outside London when he could not commute into the city on a daily basis while recovering from a serious operation.

This community-based model will allow highly qualified professionals (accountants, lawyers, consultants, etc.) to work from home when they need to work very flexibly (e.g. having caring duties for children, parents or spouses, recovering from illness or accidents, or retirees wishing to work from home rather than commute into cities). Having a large number of people in a network means they can quickly cover for each other on projects if a child is ill suddenly, you don't feel well, etc.

Currently, it is difficult to stay employed by a big firm if you need this amount of flexibility.

Bain & Co. see alumni as part of their extended workforce. If alumni wish, they can be called on to work on projects just like any other colleague, either in the normal Bain & Co. setting or on projects for Bridgespan, their large pro bono consulting firm. Employees can also move between the two firms to learn new skills and contribute differently.[41]

Gerson Lehrman Group (GLG) is a New York headquartered global membership network of 'experts for hire' who describe themselves as 'a technology-enabled learning platform that connects top professionals with experts'. The engagements can range from one-hour phone discussions to in-house long projects. In July 2017, according to their website, they had '425,000 thought leaders and practitioners, including business leaders, scientists, academics, former public sector leaders and the foremost subject matter specialists' as members.[42]

Many investment firms use senior executives who are 'between jobs' or 'retired' when they need quick access to expertise on a particular topic for a potential deal or to solve an operational issue.

It does not take an enormous intellectual leap to have an inkling that something fundamental is going on and that it will be very important going forward to be present in new electronic channels – for all generations of leaders.

There is another trend that makes the gig economy interesting for second careers. Big cities attract start-up firms, particularly in the tech space, who in turn attract highly educated younger people – creating what is known as knowledge clusters or knowledge hubs.[43]

There will be an enormous amount of interesting work to be done, in all forms, with these high-tech start-ups, as they will require experienced executives to help them flourish. A lot of this work will be part-time due to the early stage of these companies' financing. If we have a speciality we want to serve this part of the economy with, we can create very nice businesses working for a number of companies on parts of our time.

To be able to be effective directors or advisors to them, we need to understand the world they live in (technology), how they work (technology), how they communicate (technology) and how they recruit (technology!).

---

## Exercise 17    Building a mix of work with a common thread

Which of the things I have been doing up to now do I want to keep, expand or reduce?

What new things do I want to add?

How could the bits fit into a whole that is interesting, with synergies – in terms of impact and time – to allow for a different lifestyle?

---

### Getting paid market rates for your work – and the power of fractional capital

We spoke earlier about taking an investment portfolio approach to later-stage career development – in terms of creating optionality. Now we have to think about returns – properly valuing our time and knowledge, and investing it wisely in our portfolio of work.

If we are not used to charging for our services, or are fairy financially secure, it can be easy to give away work for free – because we are too embarrassed to ask.

Selling our service is a skill that takes time to develop, and before we get used to this it can be very difficult to ask for payment, but we must learn to ask for the market rate for the services we are providing.

This is important for two reasons. First, work that is free is never valued the way paid work is. In this scenario, there are no consequences for your client cancelling a project you are working on. Second, by not asking for payment, you are in effect depriving someone else from earning a living, unless the work is truly pro bono.

#### Create a portfolio of IOUs

If you are asked to work for free because the organisation doesn't have the funds to pay in the short term, there are ways to solve this.

You can agree a lower ongoing cash fee and payment of the balance when the next funding is raised, a combination of smaller cash fee plus a small stake in the business, or if no cash is available and you still want to do the work, settle for payment by a small equity stake in the business.

If the business one day takes off, you will have a nice payback on the risk you took, and if not, you are no worse off than you were if you would have given the work for free. Your client having some skin in the game changes how they value your work and how they treat you.

We are aiming for a risk-balanced portfolio of our time investment – with a mix of the above payment options.

In the future, many of us are likely to manage large portfolios of such micro-stakes – *fractional capital ownership* from our invested time – in addition to our traditional financial portfolios, as Amy Whitaker wisely points out in *Art Thinking*.[44]

As we are likely to need to earn a living for much longer going forward, learning how to convert our effort into cash and a fractional capital portfolio – some are likely to pay out big and others creating a flow of steady micro-streams of income – could be a financial lifesaver long term.

*Question 10.9:* Which of the work models above intrigue you? How can you find out more? Which ones would give you the freedom – time, geography, regularity – that you would like to have?

*Question 10.10:* If you could pick three or four things you would like to mix in terms of work models, what would they be?

*Question 10.11:* Who would be able to give you ideas and advice on how to understand the different models and identify potential organisations you might contact?

## And the journey never really has to end . . .

As we have discovered, most executives' journeys to find Purpose in their career are not one-off transitions. We keep on learning and our work keeps morphing into new expressions – as the world changes and new opportunities to contribute and engage emerge.

This is the beauty of going on our journey of Discovery. Once our curiosity is kindled and we realise just how much we can contribute to help solve issues in the world, this flame is very hard to extinguish. It becomes a lifetime quest to learn, share our experience, and contribute to society and coming generations – in ever-shifting ways. Learning is never wasted, and has a funny way of turning out useful at a later stage, to which I can personally attest.

Let us now meet some leaders of different ages and at different stages of their lives, who keep learning, contributing and creating inspirational new careers.

Babette Pettersen is now Chief Business Development Officer at Capricorn Venture Partners, whom she joined after a long career as an executive in the speciality chemicals industry, and she is busy raising a Green Chemistry fund:

> The common thread throughout the years has been marketing and business development of new products.
>
> I spent over 20 years working at Dow Corning, and I really enjoyed this, as every few years there were new interesting things to do and new markets to explore. I did not one day decide to leave, but in 2007 as I turned 50, I was headhunted by DSM as VP New Business Development.
>
> Through this, in a way by chance, I got to learn about life sciences and biotech, which led me to sustainable chemistry.
>
> I did not seek out the position at BioAmber (NYSE: BIOA), it came to me through my network. Networks are key to changing careers. You never know which conversation could lead to a job.
>
> The BioAmber experience allowed me to build a broad network in the biotech area, as in my role as Chief Commercial Officer I was often the external brand-building face of BioAmber.
>
> In early 2016, when our strategic partner Mitsui & Co took over the commercial activities of BioAmber, our team stepped out. I knew I wanted to continue in the Green Chemistry area, and by being a panellist at some major conferences, without a company identity, just as Babette Pettersen, I learned that my brand could stand on its own, and I thus accepted the position as Chief Business Development Officer at Capricorn Venture Partners to help them raise a Green Chemistry fund.
>
> Earlier in my life, careers felt like a funnel narrowing in towards the top, and now it feels the opposite; it is as if there is a funnel of opportunities opening up as I am turning 60.
>
> It's almost as though I had lived my career back to front, with all the change and start-up experience at the end rather than the beginning.[45]

Jean-Claude Larréché, who just turned 70, is the Alfred H. Heineken Chaired Professor of Marketing at INSEAD, and a world-leading marketing and strategy consultant to major corporations around the world and the author of *The Momentum Effect*. He is the founding Chairman of the consulting firm StratX, whose sophisticated simulation business game *Markstrat* many of you will have played during leadership development programmes.

To give back, Jean-Claude decided to sponsor a three-year INSEAD research programme to create a low-cost, high-quality business game giving access for anybody – regardless of income level, and without the need for a university degree – to rapid, high-quality learning of business skills.

From this research, Jean-Claude created the *Discovery Innovation Growth* (DiG) game, a fast-paced, hands-on, digital business learning solution, which can be used by business, academia or any organisation at a fraction of the cost of traditional business games, for all, including leaders from low-income countries.[46]

Jean-Claude and Yvette Roozenbeek, CEO and co-founder of DiG Business Learning, are now busy making this into a Purpose-driven business. They are building a global network of consultants and coaches, as well as creating Centres of Excellence. (Full disclosure: I am the leader for the Centre of Excellence: DiG for career change work.)

Jean-Claude is a living example of executives 'scaling up' rather than 'slowing down' in our later careers – using his core skills of marketing, growth strategy and digital business simulation to give back at 10X scale.

Dr Israel Klabin, now in his nineties, decided many years ago to spend his life supporting sustainable development rather than running his family's forestry business.

First, he was mainly active in Brazil, and then gradually on a global stage. He was one of the Brazilian organisers of the United Nations Conference on the Environment (Rio 92).

He is a former Mayor of Rio de Janeiro, and founded, along with 24 national and international corporations, the Brazilian Foundation for Sustainable Development (FBDS), which he has presided since its creation in 1992. He is a member of the board of directors of Klabin Irmãos & Co., a family holding that controls one of the largest forestry companies in Latin America. He is a member of the board of governors of Tel Aviv University, and was a member of the Inter-American Development Bank's Independent Advisory Group on Sustainability. He is the author of the book *The Urges of the Present*, launched in September 2011.

Currently, Dr Klabin is working with the Brazilian government, advising them on a massive reforestation programme and a groundbreaking agricultural policy that would see Brazil being able to, in principle, feed the entire world by 2050, producing 450 million tons of food. Dr Klabin is a key member of the United Nations Sustainable Development Solutions Network (UNSDSN).[47]

Clearly, Babette Pettersen, Jean-Claude Larréché and Dr Klabin have no intention of 'retiring'. Their insights, knowledge and networks are invaluable to companies and change initiatives all over the world, and all of them say, 'My life has never been as exciting and I have never been happier than I am right now!'.

The key to keeping your career going for as long as you want is, as you might have guessed, to keep learning, building and maintaining your network, and constantly being open to new experiences. Reading, writing, speaking and contributing knowledge and introductions to your network will keep you positioned as a valuable collaborator.

You are then able to choose how you want to contribute, in ways that suit how you wish to live and work, at that particular time in your life, becoming the captain of your own ship – able to create exciting work and have time to 'smell the roses' on the way.

There really is no time when we 'have to stop' working, unless there are health issues or we want to, as the inspirational Dadi Janki shows us.

Dadi Janki is the spiritual leader of the Brama Kumaris, a non-religious organisation promoting meditation for peace.

Dadi Janki, who turned 102 in December 2017, is still working full-time, and took up her new position at age 92. Her job takes her around the world, and in her 100th year she clocked up 49,418 business air miles.[48]

An article for her 100th birthday quotes the first of her top 10 secrets for staying young:

> Sense of Purpose: Dadi has a very clear vision for the future of humanity, which she feels she is working towards and will continue to do so. Retirement is not a word in her vocabulary. When you have passion for what you are doing, why would you want to stop? This passion and sense of purpose gives her energy, drive and commitment.[49]

This passion, captured in 140 characters in her 100th birthday tweet, seems an appropriate ending to this chapter: 'Let the past be the past. Whatever you want to do, do that now! There R many good things 2do. Just continue to move forward. #DadiJanki100'.[50]

*Picture 10.1* Dadi Janki – Spiritual Leader of the Brama Kumaris[51]

# Takeaways

Purpose-driven careers often develop in three stages – job-crafting, a move inside our current organisation to a role more geared towards our Purpose, then a transition out of the organisation to pursue our Purpose.

It is useful to think about our later careers as investment portfolios, where we need *optionality and returns* for the short, medium and long term.

We create optionality in two ways. First, if we aim for full-time employment, we need to understand that new full-time roles tend to last two to five years. It is thus useful to think about our next 'jobs' as 'two- to five-year projects' and continue to Discover, to be able to pivot if needed to our next 'project'.

Second, when we are looking to create a 'portfolio of work', by starting out engaging in a range of different activities, we avoid accidentally closing doors too early in the still ageist and fast-changing job market.

To create *returns* from our portfolio, we need to learn to ask to be paid professional rates for the work we provide, unless it is bona fide pro bono work.

Asking for a micro-equity stake in lieu of, or for part of, our fee will become more prevalent in the emerging 'gig economy'.

Learning to manage such a 'fractional capital' investment portfolio of your time and work could make a major difference in your long-term financial health – some 'IOUs' will pay out big.

Technology is rapidly changing what work we do, how we do it, and how recruitment for all types of work will happen, and digital skills are already a highly sought-after expertise for non-executive and trustee positions in large and small organisations.

Once we learn how to Discover and create new career options for ourselves, we can continue until we decide to stop – age is no barrier.

# Notes

1  CDP website: www.cdp.net/en.
2  Grayson, D. (2017). *Take Care: How to Be a Great Employer for Working Carers*. London, UK: Emerald Publishing.
3  B-Corps website: www.bcorporation.net.
4  Kowitt, B. (25 April 2017). *This Dairy Company Says Its Business Model Is the Future of Corporate America*. Fortune. Retrieved from: http://fortune.com.
5  B-Corps (17 December 2015). *Partnership Agreement with Danone Opens Doors for Multinationals to Measure What Matters*. Retrieved from: http://bcorporation.eu.
6  Minds@Work Movement website: www.mindsatworkmovement.com.
7  IBM Corporate Service Corps: www.ibm.com/ibm/responsibility/corporateservicecorps/.
8  IBM Executive Service Corps: www.ibm.com/blogs/citizen-ibm/category/executive-service-corps.

9  Smarter Cities Challenge: https://smartercitieschallenge.org.
10 Michel, A. (2016). Dualism at Work: The Social Circulation of Embodiment Theories in Use. *Signs and Society*, 3(S1), DOI: 10.1086/679306.
11 Hoffman, R. and Cashnocha, B. (2014). *The Alliance: Managing Talent in a Networked Age*. Brighton, MA: Harvard Business Review Press, Kindle edition, location 326.
12 Holly, K. (25 January 2015). *Why Great Entrepreneurs Are Older Than You Think*. Forbes. Retrieved from: www.forbes.com.
13 Grene, S. (1 October 2015). *UK Social Enterprise Booms as Founders Try to Save the World*. Retrieved from: www.ft.com.
14 BMR Research (May 2013). *Social Enterprise: Market Trends Based on BIS SME Survey 2012*. Retrieved from: www.gov.uk.
15 Zambrero website: www.zambrero.com/zambrero-au/story.
16 Wikipedia: https://en.wikipedia.org/wiki/Warby_Parker.
17 Warby Parker website: www.warbyparker.com.
18 Chafkin, M. (17 February 2015). *Warby Parker Sees the Future of Retail*. Fast Company. Retrieved from: www.fastcompany.com.
19 VOEE Services website: www.voeeservices.com.
20 Service Futures (May 2015). *Why Vested Outsourcing Is the Next Big Thing*. Retrieved from: http://servicefutures.com.
21 CDC website: www.cdcgroup.com.
22 Actis website: www.act.is.
23 GIIN website: https://thegiin.org.
24 GIIN website: https://thegiin.org/impact-investing/.
25 Impact Investing. Retrieved from: www.goldmansachs.com.
26 Grayson, D. (2017). *Take Care: How to Be a Great Employer for Carers*. London, UK: Emerald Publishing, Kindle edition, location 3475.
27 Chaykowski, K. (21 September 2016). *Chan Zuckerberg Initiative Promises to Spend $3 Billion to Research and Cure All Diseases*. Forbes. Retrieved from: www.forbes.com.
28 Field, A. (5 April 2017). *The Ford Foundation Is Committing Up to $1 Billion to Mission-Related Investments*. Forbes. Retrieved from: www.forbes.com.
29 Ayemoba, A. (3 October 2016). *AOG Transfers Ownership of Pioneering Bioethanol and Green Electricity Operation in Sierra Leone*. Africa Business Communities. Retrieved from: http://africabusinesscommunities.com.
30 National Centre for Charitable Statistics (April 2016). *NCCS Business Master File 4/2016*. Retrieved from: http://nccs.urban.org.
31 NCVO (2016). *UK Civil Society Almanac 2016: Fast Facts*. Retrieved from: https://data.ncvo.org.uk.
32 Salamon, L.M., Wojciech, S. Haddock, M.A and Tice, H.S. (2012). *The State of Global Civil Society and Volunteering: Latest Findings from the Implementation of the UN Nonprofit Handbook*. Baltimore, MA: Johns Hopkins Center for Civil Society Studies. Working Paper No. 49.
33 Max Robinson bio, Rainbows4Children website: www.rainbows4children.org/index.php/about-us/the-founders/.
34 Shikh Hassan, M. (29 July 2017). *3D Printing for Social Good*. Blog. One Young World. Retrieved from: www.oneyoungworld.com.
35 Alboer, M. (2012). *One Person/Multiple Careers: The Original Guide to the Slash Career (Volume 1)*. Retrieved from: http://heymarci.com.
36 Rouse, M. and Wigmore, I. (May 2016). *Gig Economy*. Retrieved from: http://whatis.techtarget.com/definition/gig-economy.

37  Sharpe, S. (13 August 2015). *Intuit Forecast: 7.6 Million People in On-Demand Economy by 2020*. Retrieved from: http://investors.intuit.com.
38  Coppola, G. (30 August 2016). *Explosion of Gig Economy Means There's an App for Juggling Jobs*. Bloomberg. Retrieved from: www.bloomberg.com.
39  Microsoft (13 June 2016). *Microsoft to Acquire LinkedIn*. Retrieved from: www.microsoft.com.
40  Khedekar, N. (13 September 2016). *Microsoft's LinkedIn Three-Step Strategy for India: Here's Why It Makes Sense*. Retrieved from: http://tech.firstpost.com.
41  Hoffmann, A. (2016). *Purpose Driven Leader – Purpose Driven Career*. Cranfield University's School of Management Doughty Centre for Corporate Responsibility. Retrieved from: www.cranfield.ac.uk.
42  GLG website: https://glg.it.
43  Rizk, C. (14 August 2015). *How Tech Clusters Form*. Interview with Rutgers professor Brett Gilbert. Strategy+Business. Retrieved from: www.strategy-business.com.
44  Whitaker, A. (2016). *Art Thinking: How to Carve Out Creative Space in a World of Schedules, Budgets, and Bosses*. New York: Harper Business, Kindle edition, location 1794.
45  Wittenberg-Cox, A. (2016). *What Work Looks Like for Women in Their 50s*. HBR April issue. Retrieved from: www.hbr.org.
46  DIG website: www.digbusinesslearning.com.
47  Dr Isaac Klabin, UNSDSN bio: http://unsdsn.org/about-us/people/israel-klabin/.
48  Brama Kumaris (30 September 2015). *Dadi Janki – Spiritual Leaders of the Brama Kumaris – 101 Years Young and Still Working Full-Time*. Retrieved from: www.dadijanki.org.
49  Brama Kumaris (30 September 2015). *Dadi Janki – Spiritual Leaders of the Brama Kumaris – 101 Years Young and Still Working Full-Time*. Retrieved from: www.dadijanki.org.
50  Janki, D. [@DadiJanki]. (28 March 2016). *Let the past be the past. Whatever you want to do, do that now! There R many good things 2do. Just continue to move forward. #DadiJanki100* [Tweet]. Retrieved from: https://twitter.com/DadiJanki/status/714464221757632514.
51  Reproduced with the kind permission of the Brama Kumaris.

# Part IV

# What leading organisations are doing

*This part of the book explores the role of organisations in helping mid/later career leaders acquire new skills, to become effective leaders for the world we now live in, and learning how to create future career options for themselves.*

# Chapter 11

# Career development skills
## What organisations can do

*This chapter summarises the main findings of the paper* Purpose Driven Leader – Purpose Driven Career *produced for Cranfield University School of Management's Doughty Centre for Corporate Responsibility in 2016, with a few additional notes.*[1]

*To ensure that readers who might have jumped directly into this chapter can contextualise the recommendations, there is first a short summary of the main arguments for why organisations should invest in this topic.*

### Long lives mean several transitions in our careers

As discussed throughout the book, our increasing longevity means that most of us will have to or want to continue to work long past what is today considered retirement age, for economic or other reasons.

If we take a step back and think of the combination of increasing longevity and the rapid change in work and business models, it becomes clear that most of us will have to change careers, and the types of work we do, many times during our much longer working lives.

Knowing how to develop our careers and generate options for ourselves will become a foundational skill we all need to have, throughout our careers. In the future, we should all learn these skills. Younger leaders are already used to career and job changes, but older executives have often spent many years in a single organisation or one industry.

There is a particular urgency around the mid/later career executives of the 'boomer generation' leaving corporate life in the next 5 to 10 years, the first post-war generation whose pensions are likely to run short and run out.

The urgency is for the executives, their organisations and society. Society needs capable leaders to help solve major issues, organisations need capable and motivated leaders, and both need economically productive older leaders rather than burdens on social systems. Executives themselves need goals and meaning – even after they leave their executive positions.

Of course, the same applies to all employees in the company, but as this book focuses on leaders and their development we will restrict ourselves to this cadre.

## Tri-sector skills development – not only for millennial leaders

We covered earlier (Chapter 6) that in order to develop careers with Purpose and Impact in society, we need to develop new leadership skills – tri-sector skills – to work effectively in fluid collaborative partnerships across sectors, with the aim to create exponential impact solutions for societal issues – 10X.

These skills are essential for *all* leaders going forward, as society is increasingly asking business to be involved in solving societal issues. As a bonus, we also learn the skills needed to generate tri-sector-oriented career options for ourselves. This benefits leaders, their organisations and society.

We also discussed that adults learn best through experiential learning. That real understanding of what is needed in the world, and innovative solutions for this, comes from experiencing the reality of, and creating solutions with, the marginalised communities we are trying to assist.

Such 'world view changing' tri-sector type of leadership development has become increasingly common in the past 5 to 10 years for early/mid career leaders. Originally conceived as retention tools to enthuse the 'millennial' generation, the power of this approach has gradually become apparent. These programmes are moving from 'pro bono personal motivation programmes' to becoming key components for organisations' development of the next generation of leaders.

To date, few organisations extend such tri-sector-type leadership development training to their mid/later career senior executives. One of the reasons for this was found to be that if the programme was originally created for junior leaders, there could be significant resistance from both senior levels and the HR organisation to incorporate them into the senior leadership curriculum. If it was initiated from the top – started by the CEO, often to aid a changed strategy – senior leaders were included and the programme quickly embraced by the whole organisation.

One example of tri-sector leadership development programmes that is aligned with the company core strategy is IBM's Corporate Service Corps (early/mid career) and Executive Service Corps (mid career), where teams work for four weeks on the ground with local government, NGOs and NFPs on joint community projects as part of the Smarter Cities Challenge – where cities compete to get senior IBM teams to work with them for three weeks. This is aligned with the IBM 'Smarter' strategy all the way from the top.

Actis, the emerging markets private equity firm, and Bain & Co. are examples of organisations who periodically take their entire senior cadres (around 40 for Actis and 400 for Bain) on week-long immersions in developing countries, meeting senior business leaders, politicians, social entrepreneurs, community grassroots leaders and activists.

Grant Thornton, with new CEO in the UK Sacha Romanovitch, took executives on such an immersion programme in Greece, as her tweet said on 11 October 2015: 'Thought provoking day with fellow CEOs & leaders in Greece. Met with banks, unemployed grads & start ups to understand context of economy'.[2]

You don't need to go to another country to experience the edges of the system; some of the UK and USA's largest financial services institutions are now immersing their leaders in marginalised communities in inner cities.

One company that realised they were unintentionally underinvesting in their senior people's development is Total, the major French oil and gas producer, who in 2015 created a special leadership programme for the top 400. This included immersion days in inner-city communities and social enterprises, etc.[3]

NB: The oil and gas industry has had to fast-track younger leaders, as in the 1990s during the very low oil price, they did not recruit graduates for a decade or more, and have thus been dealing with the situation for the past 10 years that one-third of their workforce could retire, and they needed to keep experienced executives and professionals in the companies as long as possible.

Many other firms are slowly expanding these programmes from their original organisational homes, often in the CSR team into the mainstream leadership development curriculum. This is happening in organisations such as SAP, GSK, P&G, Dow, EY, Becton Dickinson, Microsoft and Credit Suisse, among others.

## Career development programmes: tech and strat consulting lead the way

Dedicated career development skills programmes are unusual in most sectors except tech and strategy consulting firms, and pre-retirement programmes are becoming a trend in wider professional services, but are still rare in corporates.

What tech companies and some consulting firms have realised is that alumni are incredibly valuable.

For tech firms in Silicon Valley, alumni are a 'life and death' matter in terms of their business. To achieve this, employees need to be seen as having a 'lifetime value', and need investment from the day they join the firm until they leave, and through all their following careers. These companies embrace the concept of 'lifetime careers', and the approach by tech firms is to train and develop their people in the skills for their current and any *future* position. They train their employees to be a great candidate somewhere else if the right job does not show up at the right time in their own organisation.

Tech firms train people in building productive networks, and encourage people – as part of their job description – to work on projects of their own choice that help solve world problems (i.e. they automatically get to practise Purpose-driven career development skills as part of their jobs).

Their workforce is obviously on average still very young, so they don't have programmes focused on older leaders wanting to transition to their next careers per se, but as employees learn this automatically we can assume that these practices will continue as these organisations mature and become mainstream.

Consulting firms – particularly the larger strategy houses such as McKinsey and Bain – have for a long time realised that alumni are their most favourably disposed client base. The McKinsey Talent Network and the Bain Executive Network both help Partners transition into client-side careers when they feel their time with the firm is coming to an end. This includes in-house 'placement services' as well as coaching and support.

Bain & Co. are also the founders of the Bridgespan Group[4] – the world's largest pro bono consulting group – which allows employees at all levels to rotate in and out of Bridgespan, learning tri-sector consulting skills on the way. Retired alumni can also opt to be called in on projects for the firm in both for-profit and pro bono work.

## Pre-retirement programmes: professional services gaining momentum

A 2014 study by the Conference Board found that 27 per cent of the surveyed (91) companies in the USA had pre-retirement programmes and 5 per cent had Purpose-focused retirement programmes (encore programmes).[5]

In Europe, this is harder to determine as retirement policies are more driven by individual countries' legislation than by companies' policies. In Germany, you can 'save time' during your career, enabling you to work part-time coming up to retirement, and other countries have rules around workers' rights to 'fade-out periods' when you can work increasingly part-time.

This is all well and good, but to date most policies aim at facilitating people's *exit* from the employment market, and very few policies support remaining in the workforce. In some countries, your pension can get seriously penalised if you continue to work. Yet in others, employers cannot insure a post-state-pension-age employee. These policies force people to leave the workforce and become a burden on the pension system, even when they could – and want to – work.

Therefore, to date, individual companies had little need to create their own late career or pre-retirement programmes. With the changing demographics, this is now becoming a priority.

A number of professional services firms started pre-retirement programmes a few years back. They normally have two components, a 'fade-out period' (up to five years) and a course that prepares Partners for post-firm and retired life, financially and work-wise, mainly aimed at board director and trustee positions.

Professional services firms have large cadres of senior leaders coming up to the age when they want pursue other careers, thus the topic has now come to the fore and firms are looking to create still mainly 'pre-retirement' programmes, whilst slowly starting to realise that this is not a 'retirement' issue only; it is a wider 'career' development issue, as the work of consulting firms is changing rapidly due to changing technology.

An additional incentive for learning how to create new careers, particularly in the professional services sector is the fact that AI is expected to severely hollow out the careers of many traditional knowledge jobs. One example: by October 2016, six law firms – BakerHostetler, Dentons, DickinsonWright, Latham & Watkins, von Briesen and WombleCarlyle – were already using the IBM Watson-based technology called ROSS to provide research support to lawyers.[6] At Baker Hostetler, ROSS provides the research for 50 lawyers . . .[7]

That this trend might have significant influence on the professional services industry is demonstrated in the July 2017 article in the *Harvard Business Review* by Barry Libert and Megan Beck, aptly named: 'AI Might Soon Replace Even the Most Elite Consultants'.[8]

## Corporate pre-/post-retirement programmes emerging: mainly technical

The corporate organisations active in creating retirement programmes and alumni programmes are mainly industrial firms that need access to experienced technical personnel, professional or middle managerial.

The insightful report by the Conference Board and Encore.org in 2014 shows how, for example, Intel, IBM and HP have year-long programmes, mainly in the USA, for transitioning to for-profit and not-for-profit careers – what they call 'encore' careers' with a partly paid year-long secondment to NFPs. Some also have train to teach (T2T) programmes, where employees get teacher training certification paid by the employer.

It also shows how P&G, Eli Lilly and Boeing created YourEncore, a virtual consulting firm consisting of retired experienced experts in research, product development, brand management, marketing and other vital areas that can be hired by any of the three companies on a per project basis. They also invite clients' retirees to join YourEncore.[9]

Traditional corporations largely struggle with the alumni concept. In many cases, once you leave the organization, it is as if you never existed. There are alumni efforts, as per above, aimed mainly at valued technical personnel, but few programmes focus on the executive side. For senior executives, outplacement is the most common second career transition service.

In contrast to corporates, consulting firms highly value their alumni – as great routes to market – and also have a tradition of hiring and rehiring people, and working with external subject matter experts on a project-by-project basis. They are used to working with different people on every project, either part-time or for a limited period. This makes it easier for them to get their heads around the idea of 'alumni as extended employees' and the 'alumni consulting' concept.

## The 'career for life' concept: being seen as employees also when we leave

Looking into the not very distant future, there will be more people over age 40 than under age 40,[10] and already traditional sectors find it harder to attract young people. This means that organisations need to creatively rethink succession planning, start to think of alumni as our extended workforce, and we should start to think of 'careers for life' – here or elsewhere – for all age groups.

This means investing in professional development throughout leaders' careers – *also when they become alumni* – including career development skills and creating flexible work models for alumni of all ages – not just late career alumni. (NB: Not using the word 'retiree' is deliberate; this puts people in an odd – and 'old' – bracket in other employees' minds.)

If leaders can keep knowledge, leadership and professional skills up to date and know how to develop career options, they will continue to be valuable employees for our organisations, if they and we wish, long past what is today considered retirement age.

Knowing how to develop our career options means that unexpected downsizings or industry disruptions become less disruptive psychologically and practically.

For organisations, the alumni concept would also mean more flexibility and freedom in staffing projects short and long term, more predictable succession planning, and less trauma when downsizing is needed.

While outplacement services can be great, the loss of self-esteem associated with being suddenly let go, especially if we have never changed jobs before, can be devastating. By learning career development skills, having to leave is no longer such a trauma, and the loss of confidence is minimal; we already know our value in the outside world and can relatively smoothly move on.

As Martin Swain, previously Vice President, Global Employee Relations, Inclusion & Diversity, GSK, UK, expressed it so succinctly: 'I have always wondered why we wait until redundancy to give the best possible career advice to our people'.[11]

Although the 'career for life' concept and associated career development skills development applies to all ages of leaders, the mid/later career group needs to be addressed with some urgency as they are the group about to exit their mainstream careers in large numbers.

Additionally, executives rarely leave corporate life at age 65. They normally decide in their early or mid-fifties that they need to go somewhere else, to be CEO, or 'do something with meaning'. Professional services firms' 'pre-retirement' programmes often start at age 55, at the height of the executive's professional power, with 15 to 25 years of good health and energy to find an outlet for.

If the only thing these very capable executives do is to sit on a few boards, in my view we are wasting an enormous amount of human potential that could be used for economic and societal progress.

If we trained our senior leaders in tri-sector and career development skills, we could see a step change in how organisations engage with society and enable leaders to transition over time into influential second career positions in the cross-sector partnerships forming across the world to address major societal issues.

This is a worthwhile investment for organisations, as we get senior leaders fit for dealing with a world that increasingly demands 10X thinking and who know how to embed societal impact into the core of organisational strategy. At the same time, they learn to build networks and partnerships for the organisation and their own futures.

## How do leading organisations do this?

Leading organisations embrace the 'career for life' concept and value alumni highly. This means that they look at everybody as employees, whether they are still formally inside the organisation or not.

They invest in them while they are formally employed for a future point when they wish or have to leave, through the transition, and also when they are alumni. This includes technical skills, leadership skills, and career development skills and services.

At the heart of this philosophy is the ability to have open and adult conversations about careers, between the executives and the organisation, without fear on either side that the conversation will precipitate an exit. In many organisations today, when executives express thoughts about longer-term aspirations or that they are even thinking of 'one day' a career outside their organisation or industry, they are seen as less committed and frequently put on the 'to be exited' list of the organisation.

When open and adult conversations can take place, succession planning becomes an exercise based on reality, and not on wishful thinking – still often the case – as in many organisations both parties feel they need to keep a mask of 'employment forever'.

At the leading edge of Purpose-driven leadership and career development, companies have the following processes and practices in place.

More details can be found in the 2016 Cranfield University School of Management Doughty Centre for Corporate Responsibility study *Purpose Driven Leader – Purpose Driven Career*.[12] This forms the components of a framework for organisations to develop practices around mid/later career development, for the organisation and for individual leaders.

## Integrated career development practices for mid to late career executives

The organisational practices focus around how the organisation puts practices and processes in place that enable mid/later career development to become a process highly integrated with succession planning, enabling executives to truly own their careers.

### (a) Purpose: development of company and executive Purpose

*How much attention are the board and executive committee devoting to societal Purpose? How does the company enable executives to develop their own purpose?*

- The strategy is driven by social Purpose, and the company believes they will deliver value for their stakeholders in society and profit for their shareholders this way.
- How well we are delivering our Purpose is a key board and executive committee topic.
- Processes are in place for executives to go on their own Purpose journey.
- Mid/later career executives are included in the company's tri-sector and on-the-ground programmes in an appropriate and effective manner.

### (b) Board attention to mid/later career development as strategic issue

*How much attention to and understanding does the board have of the benefit to the company strategy of developing executives' longer-term internal and external career ambitions?*

- The board discusses individual succession-planning candidates and their career development needs internally and externally.
- They discuss how assisting the executives in developing for their future career ambitions externally can be of benefit to the company and their strategy short and long term.

### (c) Mid/later career issues included in succession planning

*How does the succession planning process take into account and allow for changing motivations by executives as they mature?*

- Understanding of the changing needs and motivations of senior executives individually and as a group is used as the basis for succession planning.

### (d) Mid/later career development process and skills

*When and how does the company introduce executives to the process of and skills to own their own careers?*

- Starting at age 40, executives receive training, coaching and support to develop career development skills, which is a career-long process.
- Refreshment of career development skills done every five years.

### (e) Career development review

*How and for what is the annual or six-month progress review used?*

- One hundred per cent focus on career development, performance reviews are done separately.
- The discussion is around the aspirations of the executive, short, medium and long term, internally and externally.
- Open discussion of any critical decision points, including how the executive is progressing their internal and external career development understanding.

### (f) Open adult conversations about careers

*How explicitly do conversations about the executive's future take place?*

- Adult discussions throughout the executive's career around, 'If one day you were not working here, what might other opportunities be, and how can we prepare you for them?'.

### (g) Exit policies

*How much assistance and fluidity exists for executives to tailor their exit process and support to the benefit of both the company and their new direction?*

- The executive is allowed to create a high-profile customised position that benefits the company and sets the executive up for their next career in two to four years.
- The company has an in-house executive transition team that supports executives in their new career creation.
- External support also available as part of executive's development budget.

### (h) Pre-retirement preparation

*How long before retirement does the preparation process for second careers start, and what kind of support is available?*

- Programme starts four to five years before retirement eligibility.
- Regular workshops/peer work groups over the years to retirement.
- The programme explores a full range of career options from NED to social entrepreneurship, NFP careers, government postings, investing, etc.
- Transition coaching support throughout.
- Funds are available for certification training for next careers or 'exprenticeships' – e.g. part payment of NFP salary or secondment possible to tri-sector organisations.
- Possibility to work in social purpose parts of the company, part- or full-time (e.g. CSR, new technology venture investing, etc.).

### (i) Post-retirement policies

*How does the company link to the executive post-retirement for mutual benefit?*

- A lively post-retirement community in place.
- The company reaches out to retirees for problem-solving, mentoring, etc.
- A post–retirement 'job centre' exists where retirees can be matched with suitable jobs and projects and training.

### (j) Alumni processes

*How does the company keep in contact with alumni for mutual benefit, particularly alumni leaving before retirement age?*

- Alumni seen as a critical asset to the company's innovation and success.
- Different levels of alumni groupings exist, including a 'by invitation only distinguished alumni network'.
- Alumni seen as an extension of the company, and it is natural for employees to reach out to alumni, and tools to make this easy exist.
- Alumni social media groups sponsored and maintained by company exist for alumni to connect and interact with each other.

*Question 11.1:* Where is your organisation on the above topics?

## Practices for developing new leadership (and career development skills) for mid/later career executives

The practices below are focused around the development of the individual executive.

Many of the new externally focused leadership competencies are identical to what an executive needs to learn to successfully own and develop their career on both the inside and the outside of their current company (see Appendix 1).

### (a) Finding a focus area

*Are executives encouraged to find social purpose opportunities and projects in their own business area?*

- Aligned Purpose goals and projects are part of the organisation's strategy, and thus of the goal-setting process.
- Training and support programmes are in place to help make this happen.

### (b) Pro bono/community/tri-sector work experience

*Are senior executives part of the company's pro bono work on the ground in communities or across stakeholder sectors?*

- Early, mid and late career leaders can all be part of the community pro bono programmes and the tri-sector secondment programmes.
- Returning leaders from the programmes mentor other leaders and are called on to contribute to the company strategy.

### (c) Building strategic and diverse networks

*Are executives encouraged, trained and incentivised to network outside the organisation?*

- Building external networks across all stakeholder constituencies is seen as a vital executive skill in the company.
- Training as well as mentoring in place around networking.
- Executives have earmarked budgets for networking.
- Sharing the knowledge gathered from networks is an established process.

### (d) Partnership-building

*Are executives encouraged, trained and called upon to create high-level partnerships for the organisation on the outside?*

- The ability to build partnerships with a multitude and diverse set of organisations across constituencies is vital to our strategy, and this topic is discussed at the board/executive committee.
- We have an 'executive exchange programme' with NGOs and government.
- We have development support for this and peer-sharing on best partnership practices.

## (e) Technology

*Are executives kept up to speed on how to use new technology?*

- Technology will change business and work radically in the coming years. We have a Digitalisation strategy and a company wide reskilling strategy.
- To be able to assess the risks and invest in opportunities, executives are routinely updated on an engaged in technology innovation in the company.
- Tech 'savviness' is part of our performance system.

## (f) Mentoring

*Are there intergenerational and reverse mentoring opportunities?*

- Programmes are institutionalised and include:
  - o Reversed mentoring of junior and senior leaders.
  - o Intergenerational mentoring programmes with senior executives working with Gen X, Gen Y and millennial leaders for mutual mentoring.
  - o Dynamic duo system in place: moving well beyond traditional mentoring, 'dynamic duos' are intergenerational (and often cross-disciplinary) collaborations operating top-down and bottom-up, outside-in and inside-out, to the benefit of both partners – while driving innovation and creating significant new value for their organisations.

## (g) Support

*Is there development support for the executive to go on this journey?*

- We have a dedicated programme and support function with business/HR and CSR actively leading them.
- We have both internal and external coaches supporting our executives.

*Question 11.2:*   Where is your organisation on the above topics?

## Takeaways

When organisations adopt the 'career for life' view of their employees, the point of view shifts from 'How do we invest in people most efficiently to perform their duties in the organisation the next 5 to 10 years?' to 'How do we invest in people most efficiently so they help us deliver our business strategy in the next 10 to 20 years, inside or outside our organisation?'.

When there is openness and transparency around career questions, it becomes a normal part of a company's way of operating, and greatly improves succession planning. Organisations who practice this reported that their employees become more loyal and engaged than when there is fear around discussing career thoughts openly, as we shall hear shortly from Bain & Co.

As time goes on, we are likely to see more and more organisations migrate towards the 'career for life' concept.

Young industries such as tech, who are growing exponentially and constantly have to compete for the best talent, teach us about the value of alumni and how to invest in them. They do not yet have large cadres of people retiring, but will likely carry over their current philosophy to this group as they transition out of the organisation in the future.

Strategy consulting firms are gradually adopting the 'career for life' concept, and finding great benefit from this. We are now seeing professional services firms develop from short pre-retirement programmes to longer and deeper pre-retirement programmes beyond finding board positions.

Corporates are only at the starting point, with some creating 'post-transition' consulting opportunities for technical personnel, but otherwise little engagement once executives leave the organisation. As there are fewer – especially technical – graduates interested in working in these industries, organisations are starting to wake up to the fact that having access to their technical experts post-exit is important. Over time, this should change when these sectors find it harder to attract graduates or keep early/mid career leaders keen on working with Purpose and societal Impact.

Courtney della Cava, Head of Global Talent & Leadership & Global Bain Executive Network, summarises the above perfectly:

> The Bain Executive Network (for Partners and senior executives) and the Bain Career Advisory (for more junior consultants and alumni), involve a significant investment from Bain. They reflect our philosophy of 'career for life' and reinforce our heavy focus on our people – current Bain consultants, alumni, and others connected to the firm.
>
> Early in Bain's history, there was at times a resistance and even some fear in having open career conversations as we thought this would encourage people to leave, but we quickly learned it's quite the opposite.
>
> Our people have tremendous internal and external career choices, and we want to actively engage them in a broader 'how to thrive' career and life planning dialogue, and ideally and actively choose to stay. In some cases, our people pursue outside roles and return a few years later with additional experience and perspectives that are helpful to solving our clients' most critical business issues.
>
> What used to be formal performance appraisals one to two times per year are now more fluid and holistic career development conversations around 'How can we help you achieve what you want to achieve at Bain and beyond?', 'How can we help you thrive broadly in your life?'.

Bain & Co. has one of if not the highest Partner retention rates in the industry, and loyalty has only increased with more transparent and active career and life planning conversations. We have found that the more open and supportive we are, the more engaged and happy our people are. And if they leave, Bain continues to support them along their broader career path, with access to career resources and individual coaching – as we say, 'Once a Bainie, always a Bainie'.

## Notes

1 Hoffmann, A. (2016). *Purpose Driven Leader – Purpose Driven Career.* Cranfield University's School of Management Doughty Centre for Corporate Responsibility. Retrieved from: www.cranfield.ac.uk.

2 Romanovitch, S. [@romanovsun] (11 October 2015). *Thought provoking day with fellow CEOs & leaders in Greece. Met with banks, unemployed grads & start ups to understand context of economy* [Tweet]. Retrieved from: https://twitter.com/romanovsun/status/653296032542027781.

3 Hoffmann, A. (2016). *Purpose Driven Leader – Purpose Driven Career.* Cranfield University's School of Management Doughty Centre for Corporate Responsibility, p. 23. Retrieved from: www.cranfield.ac.uk.

4 The Bridgespan Group website: www.bridgespan.org.

5 Piktialis, D. et al. (October 2014). *Second Acts in Prime Time, Helping Employees Transition to Post Retirement Careers.* The Conference Board and Encore.org. Retrieved from: www.conference-board.org.

6 ROSS Intelligence website: www.rossintelligence.com.

7 Turner, K. (16 May 2016). *Meet 'Ross', the Newly Hired Legal Robot.* Washington Post. Retrieved from: www.washingtonpost.com.

8 Libert, B. and Beck, M. (24 July 2017). *AI Might Soon Replace Even the Most Elite Consultants.* Harvard Business Review. Retrieved from: www.hbr.org.

9 Pitikalis, D., Gottemoeller, M. and Brayboy, R. (October 2014). *Second Acts in Prime Time: Helping Employees Transition to Post-Retirement Careers.* BSR & Encore.org. Retrieved from: http://encore.org.

10 Parker, J. (2014). *The World Reshaped, the End of the Population Pyramid, the World in 2015.* The Economist. From print edition retrieved online. Retrieved from: www.economist.com.

11 Hoffmann, A. (2016). *Purpose Driven Leader – Purpose Driven Career.* Cranfield University's School of Management Doughty Centre for Corporate Responsibility, p. 3. Retrieved from: www.cranfield.ac.uk.

12 Hoffmann, A. (2016). *Purpose Driven Leader – Purpose Driven Career.* Cranfield University's School of Management Doughty Centre for Corporate Responsibility, pp. 47–58. Retrieved from: www.cranfield.ac.uk.

# End word

I hope you have enjoyed your reading and gained some useful insights for your own Discovery and Fruition journeys to create a Purpose-driven career.

Once we get going and start learning and meeting insightful people, a whole new world opens up to us. Working together in partnerships across organisational sectors – in Impact Coalitions together with community leaders – means that solutions can be developed for the many urgent issues we need to address in society.

The time for creating solutions *for* people is over; the time for creating solutions *with* people is here.

I also hope you have discovered how vital it is to develop our *Career Transformational Assets* – self-knowledge, building strategic and diverse networks, and openness to new experiences. They will help you become an externally effective collaborative tri-sector leader, and help you continuously develop new career opportunities.

With job security decreasing the older we get,[1] and our need to work longer increasing, career development will be a vital life skill going forward, and individual executives need to acquire these skills. With our ageing workforces, organisations are increasingly realising that they need to help their executives acquire these skills, at a minimum from mid-career.

Open and honest career development practices help succession planning to become a real exercise, not wishful thinking, and it keeps valued leaders wishing to stay longer in the organisation. If it really is time for them to move on, giving them the skills to create new careers creates immense goodwill towards their employer and they can become highly valuable alumni employees.

To ensure later career leaders can lead effectively in this open collaboration age, where society is asking business for increasing help to solve issues, they also need to be included in tri-sector leadership development programmes, today aimed mainly at the early/mid-career leaders.

Leading organisations are putting such practices in place, both leadership development and career development wise. Often this is precipitated by the start of a Purpose- or sustainability-led strategy journey, or when they realise that they have large cadres of later career leaders starting to think of 'retiring' or starting 'second careers'.

We have seen that by going on a *Discovery* journey, working with the '9 *Questions*', finding our *Big Question* (the issues we wish to spend our time and effort impacting), we can turn this into an action statement – our Purpose.

Creating a Purpose-driven career normally happens in three stages. First, via 'job-crafting' – creating a Purpose-driven project that fits within the organisation's strategy – which helps us learn new skills and understand how to materially impact issues in society.

Second, we are often offered a new position in our current organisation where we can express our Purpose on a larger canvas, internally and externally, and further develop our skill and networks.

Finally, there normally comes a point when we wish to work on our Purpose 100 per cent of the time and we start to plan our exit. We then make this a reality by working with the *Fruition* process, creating a '*career investment portfolio*' that gives optionality and returns for the short, medium and long term.

Once we have learned how to continuously create career options, we can be as professionally active, with as much Impact as we wish, for as many years as we like, health providing. Age is no object when we keep developing relevant knowledge, skills and networks that value our contributions.

We have arrived at the end of this odyssey. I hope you have found the reading interesting, and that it has inspired you to start your own journey. As we said at the beginning, the hardest thing is to get going. Once we take a few steps, being out of our comfort zone becomes 'the new normal' and continuing to learn becomes a lifelong passion.

At this mid/later career stage, we have to face the fact that we will not be here forever, and there is no guarantee for how much time any of us have left. How are you going to make whatever years remain to you count? How will you live engaged with compassion and passion, totally and fully?

Wishing you deeply fulfilled days *Discovering* and making your Purpose into a passionate, Impactful and inclusive reality.

I end this labour of love as I started it: It's time to #LoveLikeJo.[2]

Anita

**Today I pledge to #LoveLikeJo. I will**

ANITA

Far more unites us than divides us

Jo Cox
1974-2016

@DrueKataoka

*Picture E.1* I commit to #LoveLikeJo[3,4]

## Notes

1 Thomson, P. (14 February 2017). *Older Workers See the Biggest Decline in Job Security Over the Last Decade*. Centre for Ageing Better. Retrieved from: www.ageing-better.org.uk.
2 Addley, E., Elgot, J. and Perraudin, F. (22 June 2016). *Jo Cox: Thousands Pay Tribute on What Should Have Been MP's Birthday*. Retrieved from: www.theguardian.com.
3 Reproduced with the kind permission of the Jo Cox Foundation and Drue Kataoka.
4 Portrait of Jo Cox by Drue Kataoka: www.drue.net.

# Afterword

'How', asked one of my good friends recently, 'can I work out what I want to do in life?'. My friend is of an age where in previous generations, that question would have been considered redundant: if he didn't know already, it was too late in life to start deciding. Now, as Lynda Gratton and Andrew Scott point out in their best-seller *The 100-Year Life*, we can expect to live and work much longer. So, my friend is nowadays in plentiful company. We quickly clarified that most of us will have purposes plural rather than a single one; the relative prioritisation of these purposes may vary over time and may indeed change entirely. Thus, rather than being a one-off exercise, the exploration of personal purposes will typically be *for the next phase of life* rather than for the rest of life.

What constitutes purpose is very personal. It is not just – or even necessarily at all – about paid work. One purpose for many will be to be a good husband or wife or partner. Another will be to be a good parent and a good son or daughter. Some may draw more of a sense of purpose from volunteering (e.g. as a youth club leader or as a campaigning activist) than in their paid work.

My friend is in the fortunate position of having a good job in which he is reasonably happy, and which pays well enough to provide financial security and a decent quality of material life. Like many others, though, he would like more out of life beyond material comfort and financial independence: a greater sense of purpose.

I encouraged my friend to identify one or more issues that he feels passionately about, to use his natural curiosity and eagerness to be learning new things to investigate these issues, to use his opportunities to travel, to meet some of the leading thinkers and doers in his chosen issue(s) that his research identifies, and perhaps then to get involved as a volunteer with an organisation working on his chosen issue. To keep open the option of making that a bigger part of his life in the future.

Now, my friend, and so many other purpose-seekers, has this wonderful new resource: Anita's book. I feel some proprietary pride in Anita's book. As she explains, the book grew out of her Occasional Paper for the Doughty

Centre for Corporate Responsibility at Cranfield School of Management, which itself was the result of a chance conversation at the launch of another book by a mutual friend of ours: Lindsay Levin, founder of the inspirational Leaders Quest. Little did I imagine that our chat would have such superbly productive outcomes: first the Occasional Paper, now this book, and – we intend – in future, workshops for purpose-seekers such as my friend who wants the later stages of life to have meaning and as much positive impact as possible. I am excited to be working with Anita to design and run these 'Exploring Purpose' workshops.

David Grayson CBE
Professor of Corporate Responsibility
Cranfield University School of Management

# Externally oriented leadership competencies

*In this appendix, we take a closer look at the externally oriented leadership competencies referred to in Chapter 6.*

Leaders of business organisations are facing a fast-changing, increasingly externally focused, multi-stakeholder, transparent, digitalised and socially accountable world, where collaboration across industries, across sectors (government, business and NGO/NFP), and across geography and culture is vital.

The leadership competencies needed for this environment are, by necessity, increasingly externally focused, compared to the traditionally internally focused operational and change management skills and competencies many organisations have used to recruit, develop and promote leaders.

In a late 2012 Executiva/BSR study, *Sustainability and Leadership Competencies for Business Leaders*, respondents (CEOs, group HR directors, CSOs and leadership thought leaders) were asked to rank the competencies they thought were the most important for leaders to be proficient at going forward. See Figure A1.1.

## The top six competencies and their definitions

### I External awareness and appreciation of trends

We need leaders who can interpret long-term societal trends and anticipate how governments, NGOs and society are likely to react to them. These leaders spend the majority of their time with different-thinking people, inside and outside the organisation, and understand the risks and opportunities these trends will bring for their organisation, and they must be able to develop strategic options for the business.

### 2 Visioning and strategy formulation

Resilient leaders can co-create strategies and effectively communicate the vision of what the company is aspiring to become – in other words, how the company will be profitable by addressing a societal need, internally and externally.

### 3 Risk awareness, assessment and management

Today's leaders need to address risks far beyond operational physical risks, such as risks to corporate reputation, stakeholder relations, business continuity, or even customer demand. Leaders need to focus particular attention on high-impact, low-probability risks that could jeopardise the company's future.

### 4 Stakeholder engagement

To be truly effective at stakeholder engagement, leaders need to learn to be comfortable listening to and engaging with people of varied backgrounds and points of view—and see them as true co-owners of the business' journey, not just a group of people to whom they are communicating.

### 5 Flexibility and adaptability to change

Resilient leaders demonstrate the ability to lead when there is considerable ambiguity about the best way forward. They listen carefully to voices inside and outside the company for new information that might require a change of direction, and they think creatively about new ways of doing things.

### 6 Ethics and integrity

All business leaders interviewed for our study named ethics and integrity as the overarching competency – without this it does not matter if a leader is good at the other competencies. Hence it was not ranked, but broken out of the ranking. It's not enough to have ethics policies; leaders need to show how ethics and integrity are embedded in company culture.

In the runner-up section, we also have *partnership-building* and *organisational buy-in*, two other competencies that have relationship-building and cooperation across silos at their heart.

A bit further down, we can see *political and policy orientation*, which in later studies have moved up in priority. For convenience, the definition of this competency is: 'Understands how to read the political landscape internally and externally, and how to build coalitions to bring the organisations voice to the appropriate decision-makers'.

**Top 6 competencies – Chosen by majority**

- External Awareness & Appreciation of Trends
- Visioning & Strategy Formulation
- Risk Awareness, Assessment & Management
- Stakeholder Engagement
- Flexibility & Adaptability to change
- Ethics & Integrity

**The close runners –up**

- Decision-making & Judgement
- Managing Innovation
- Partnership Building
- Courage & Persistence
- Securing Organizational Buy-In

**The classic competencies**

- Understanding of Global Impact of Local Decisions
- Effective Dialogue
- Political & Policy Orientation
- Passion & Optimism
- Analytical Thinking
- Creative Thinking
- Creating Internal Accountability
- Developing People
- Promoting Best Practices
- Delegating & Empowering
- Team Leadership
- Team Working

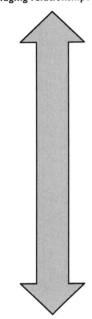

Emphasis on an *External Focus,* a *longer term perspective* and *on managing relationships*

Emphasis on an *Internal Focus,* a *shorter term perspective* and *operational considerations.*

*Figure A1.1*  Ranking of leadership competencies for the future[1]

## Note

1 Illustration reproduced with the kind permission of BSR. Originally published in: Hoffmann, A., Faruk, A. and Gitman, L. (2012). *Sustainability and Leadership Competencies for Business Leaders*. BSR. Retrieved from: www.bsr.org.

# Discovering your transferrable skills

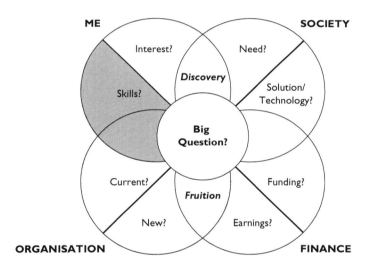

*This appendix expands the third 'leaf' in our Discovery process, 'My Skills' –
as described in Chapters 8 and 9 – and includes exercises, in addition to
the ones in Chapter 10 (numbered 18–24) to allow deeper thinking around
transferrable skills and competencies.*

*It is aimed at executives who have not had a real opportunity to look at
their careers before, outlining a stepwise approach.*

*If you are 'clear-ish' on the skills and competencies you wish to contribute,
pick and choose or create your own exercises on topics that interest you, and
then go to Exercises 23 and 24 to take an inventory of any tri-sector skills gaps.*

Being passionate about our Purpose but doing types of work, or using
skills, that we really don't enjoy, is not a good place to find ourselves when
we change careers. That can happen if we extrapolate from what our current
organisations want of our skills.

We therefore need to take a good look at what we enjoy doing *now*, discover hidden skills (that we take for granted) and understand what skills we need to develop to become effective tri-sector leaders.

Hence, transferrable skills for a Purpose-driven career are a mixture of 'hard' skills – what we know how to do – and our own qualities, values and aspirations – and what we would like to do.

We discerned earlier between skills and competencies as: skills being what you know how to do, and competencies how you do things. Below are exercises expressing both. If you get them a bit mixed up, it does not matter, but having two chances to think might unearth some gems.

We will use the same 'Dump–Sort–Contemplate–Choose' process we used in identifying our interests and societal need in Chapter 9.

### I Identifying hidden skills and abilities: what do you appreciate about me?

We all have blind spots, negative and positive. The negative blind spots are normally pointed out to us, but the positive blind spots rarely are. This exercise is aimed at identifying these positive blind spots.

If you did not do Exercise 1 when reading Chapter 9, I highly recommend you start here.

---

### Exercise I    What do you appreciate about me?

Ask five people who you trust and know reasonably well (not your closest long-standing friends, colleagues or family members) *three things* that they appreciate about you.

Don't specify or clarify anything, just listen and note down.

---

If you wish, you can also add further insight via character and values assessments. Two well-established assessments are the 'VIA Character Strengths Test'[1] and the 'Barrett Personal Values Assessment'.[2] Both are available for free online.

---

### Exercise 18    What is unique about me and what I bring?

With the information from the above exercises at hand:

- *Sort*: The information into themes.
- *Contemplate*: What patterns are coming out? Any surprises?

- *Dump*: In which areas of work could each of these skills and abilities be useful? In solving societal issues? Note them down.
- *Choose*: Which four or five areas intrigue you most at this stage?

Most of us have some real surprises when doing the exercises above. You will remember from Chapters 5 and 9 how my own life course completely changed when I discovered that I was a good coach. I had a total blind spot regarding these skills, as I took them for granted, something I 'just did'. I bet you will have some hidden jewels as well.

## 2 Deeply understanding what you are good at and enjoy doing

If this is the first time you are contemplating a career change, or you have never really looked closely at what you enjoy working with, what you are good at, your skills or competencies, the '20 Projects' exercise is revealing.

If you have already done some assessment of skills, jump to Exercise 20.

---

### Exercise 19   20 Projects: what I like and am good at

Take 20 A4 pages (physical or electronic) and divide them into quadrants.

- At the top of each sheet, write the name of a job position or significant project at work or externally, professional or volunteering, etc.
- Across the top of the top two quadrants, write the titles: 'What went well' and 'What did not go so well'.
- Across the bottom two quadrants, write the titles: 'What I enjoyed' and 'What I did not enjoy'.

Now fill in the quadrants for all your 20 Projects:

- *Sort*: Go through the 20 Projects and notice themes.
- *Contemplate*: What does this mean you are good at and enjoy? What are you not so good at and don't enjoy?
- *Choose*: What do you definitely *not* want in your next career? What are potential skills or ways of working you want to express in your next career?

---

The last point, what you do *not* want in your future career, is very important. It helps you stay clear of offers that look glamorous but would not bring contentment in your work.

As one executive expressed this:

> Thanks to having decided that I absolutely did not want any more weekly commuting by airplane to my work, I could say no – without any big soul-wrenching – to the first, very lucrative, job offer that came by shortly after my redundancy.

(NB: This executive can now walk to work . . . )

## 3 Making a skills inventory

Inventorying skills and expertise we have acquired over our career and looking at how much we can express the ones *we like to use* is also revealing. This is a time in our lives and careers when we should look at how we could use skills we enjoy using, not only the ones our employers find useful today.

---

### Exercise 20    The skills inventory

Note down the answers to the following questions:

- What particular *expertise* have you acquired during your life and career?

    o   Go through your CV and note down for each position what you learned/what expertise you acquired.
    o   Go through your 20 Projects and add additional insights.

- What are you told you are really good at doing?

    o   What have your performance appraisals shown over the past 10 years?
    o   Are there things you think they did not reflect?

- What do you also know you are good at doing?

    o   Add experiences from outside work.
    o   Add your insights from Exercise 1 – your hidden skills.

With this information in hand:

- *Sort*: Rank the skills listed above from top to bottom in terms of which skill you enjoy using the most.
- *Contemplate*: Look at the top five. In percentage terms, compared to how much you would like to express this skill, are you able to express these today, at work and externally?
- *Choose*: How much would you like to express them in your next career?

## 4 My competencies: the 'how and with what impact' we achieve things

As we discussed earlier, skills are what we know how to do, and competencies how we do things and achieve change.

By thinking about how we achieved our successes in our careers (or outside work in pro bono work, etc.), we can start to understand how we personally operate and affect change. This is important self-knowledge – when we know where we are strong and where we need help, we know when to seek assistance and also build better coalitions for change.

It is obvious that if we are all good at the same things, no project is successful. The same goes for leadership competencies; if we have a team of only visionaries – communicating compelling visions that get people enthused – there will be little concrete implementation . . .

---

### Exercise 21    How do I lead best?

Think about the major successes you achieved in your previous roles, internally and externally. Pick 5 to 10 that stand out.

- *How* were these achieved?
  - What steps did you undertake to reach your goals, and how did you implement these?
- *How* did you problem-solve and overcome challenges?
- Were these successes as part of a team?
  - If so, *how* did you get everyone on board, supporting and motivating them to share the common goal?
- *How far reaching was the impact* of what you achieved – from just you, your team, other teams in the organisation, the entire organisation, on your industry, on society?

With this information in hand:

- *Sort 1*: What are the themes coming out of how you do things?
- *Sort 2*: Rank them from strongest to weakest – in terms of your proficiency at each competency.
- *Contemplate 1*: What is the above telling you are your strongest leadership competencies?
- *Sort 3*: Now rank them on the impact achieved by using these competencies.
- *Contemplate 2*: Any new insight?
- *Choose*: Which five competencies of your most *effective* competencies – high proficiency and large-scale impact – would you like to use for helping solve societal issues? Any gaps?

If you have done all of the exercises above, you should now have four tentative lists of types of work, plus skills and competencies that you are good at and would like to use. It is now time to see how they match with the new leadership requirements, both the externally oriented leadership competencies and then the tri-sector skills.

## 5 Externally oriented leadership competencies

In Chapter 6, we spoke about the need for leaders to be more externally and stakeholder-oriented going forward. In Appendix 1, you can find a description of each of the top six competencies, plus political and policy orientation, as this competency has come to the fore recently.

---

### Exercise 22    My externally oriented leadership competencies

Looking at each of the seven competencies in Appendix 1 in turn:

- Rate yourself on each of these with low/medium/high for:

    o    Frequency: How often do you display this behaviour – never, often, always?
    o    Scope of impact: On yourself/your team, whole organisation, your industry and society?
    o    Nature of impact: 'None/neutral', 'improves internal processes', 'transforms business'.

- *Sort 1*: What are your *highly used* competencies?
- *Sort 2*: What are your *high-impact* competencies (scope and nature)?
- *Contemplate 1*: Are there particular strengths or gaps? Any surprises?
- *Contemplate 2*: How do these compare to your self-generated list (see Exercise 21)?
- *Choose 1*: Which competencies are strengths you would like to use in your next career? How could you do this in your current role?
- *Choose 2*: Which competencies do you wish to work on strengthening? How could you do this in your current role?

---

## 6 Tri-sector skills

Looking at tri-sector skills will be done in two steps. First, assessing our general strengths for these six skills, and then matching what we found above with one particular area.

First, let's refresh our minds with Nicholas Lovegrove and Matthew Thomas's definitions of tri-sector athlete skills.[3] In parenthesis is noted where we covered a particular topic:

1   *Balanced motivations.* Desires to create public value no matter where they work, combining their motivations to wield influence (often in government), have social impact (often in non-profits) and generate wealth (often in business). (Chapter 9 – Exercise 10)
2   *Transferrable skills.* A set of distinctive skills valued across sectors, such as quantitative analytics, strategic planning and stakeholder management. (Chapter 6)
3   *Contextual intelligence.* A deep empathy of the differences within and between sectors, especially those of language, culture and key performance indicators. (Chapter 6)
4   *Integrated networks.* A set of relationships across sectors to draw on when advancing their careers, building top teams, or convening decision-makers on a particular issue. (Chapter 9 – Section 8 and Exercise 12)
5   *Prepared mind.* A willingness to pursue an unconventional career that zigzags across sectors, and the financial readiness to take potential pay cuts from time to time. (Chapter 6 – Question 6.4)
6   *Intellectual thread.* Holistic subject matter expertise on a particular tri-sector issue by understanding it from the perspective of each sector. (Chapter 6 – Questions 6.1–6.3)

---

## Exercise 23   My tri-sector skills inventory

Look at the definitions of tri-sector skills above, and rate yourself honestly with low/medium/high on each category, reading the definitions carefully.

- *Contemplate*: What does the pattern of highs/mediums and lows indicate?
- *Choose*: Are there any areas that need attention? How could you start to develop this in your current role?

---

Now look back on your answers to Exercise 10 in Chapter 9.

### Exercise 24    Matching my motivations with my skills and strengths

Compare your answers from Exercises 1–5 with your answers to Exercise 10 in Chapter 9.

- *Contemplate*: Depending on what your motivations are, do your strong skills and competencies match your motivation?

    o   Pay particular attention to the scope and impact you seek and your ability to affect change with impact (see Exercise 5).

- *Choose*: If you have a good match, you can be reasonably confident that your ability to affect change at scale will work.

If your match is not so strong:

- How could you develop these skills?
- What help will you need to seek as you develop your Purpose?

## 7 We continue to develop insight as we go Discovering

Having an inventory and gap analysis of our strengths and improvement areas is just a beginning. As we go Discovering, we gradually learn what kind of skills will be specifically useful for our intended area of work, from the people we meet, from what we read, and from our new experiences.

Remember, as you go building your strategic network, ask people who are working in the area that you might want to work about what it is like to work there, and what skills and abilities are needed. Some basic questions to ask are:

- What do they do on a day-to-day basis?
- What are their major tasks and challenges?
- What are their joys and frustrations?
- What skills and competencies do they think are needed in the field?

This way, you will build a specific understanding of what it takes to be successful in this field, and if this is really what you want to contribute or not.

As we said in the opening, doing work we don't like to do any longer, because we are good at it, for our later careers with Purpose is not where we want to end up.

In this 'second half' of our lives, it is time to contribute what we are good at, and enjoy doing, for the greater good – in a way that makes us content.

## Notes

1 VIA Character Strengths Test: www.viacharacter.org/survey/account/register.
2 Barrett Personal Values Assessment: www.valuescentre.com/our-products/products-individuals/personal-values-assessment-pva.
3 Lovegrove, N. and Thomas, M. (13 February 2013). *Why the World Needs Tri-Sector Leaders*. HBR blog. Retrieved from: www.hbr.org.

# LinkedIn cheat sheet

*In this appendix, we look at how using LinkedIn strategically can help us achieve the career change we wish for.*

*When we go Discovering, our LinkedIn network is the key to a quick ramp-up of our networking activities. Below follows a short description of how LinkedIn can be used for this purpose after a bit of LinkedIn etiquette.*

As we have discussed throughout the book, building new, strategic and diverse networks is the key to any career change, and vital if we want to have impact on major world issues. We need to work across sectors, and therefore need to build trusted relationships, often far beyond our usual sphere of influence.

As we also mentioned, having a simple and clear profile on LinkedIn, including what you are interested in being contacted for, makes it possible for people to find you when they are searching for people to speak with. You can always choose to not reply to a request or In-mail (the LinkedIn email system), just like when requests arrive via your normal email.

You might have to pay for some of the search and email functionalities below, but if you are serious about building your network it is likely to be worth the cost for you. Explore the free service first and see how far you get.

## I LinkedIn etiquette

With everything you do on LinkedIn (like in life), always think of how you would like to be approached and how you would not like to be approached for creating a connection. The people you want to speak with probably feel the same way.

### Sending LinkedIn invites

Never send invites without a personal message. The only exception might be if it is one of your very old mates that don't care if they get a connection request without a word of greeting or explanation from you.

## *LinkedIn messages*

Write short, clear, well laid out, polite and professional messages, stating clearly what you are asking for. Remember that most people now read LinkedIn messages and invites on smartphones.

Spend considerable time on crafting a basic (and spell-checked!) message that can be adapted for various situations or from which you can reuse well-crafted phrases. Giving an opt out, using phrases such as 'if amenable to you', 'if OK with you' and 'if convenient for you', shows respect and makes us feel less pressurised in taking a call or a meeting, and therefore more likely to actually agree.

Most executives when starting Discovery are reticent to send messages to people they don't know well. In my experience, very few people mind receiving a short, clear, respectful and well-written message. Would you?

Conversely, think of how you yourself would react to a message – before you send it. If you would not mind receiving it, it will probably be fine.

Finally, avoid chasing people more than twice in a short period of time. They will remember. After a maximum of three messages in total, spaced out over a few weeks, it is clear that this person is not able or willing to speak with you *at this point in time*. A few months from now, the situation might be different, and you can try again, or try to get introduced by a common friend or business contact, i.e. a warm(ish) introduction.

## *Who to accept invites from*

You will quickly develop a sense for whom you should and should not accept into your network, but it is a wise precaution to only accept invites from people you know or at least have spoken to.

This is important for two reasons. First, why do you want people you don't know in your network if they don't seem to have anything in common with you? Second, there are also fraudulent profiles and scammers on LinkedIn. By being in your network, people are automatically credentialised to others in your network (i.e. other people are more likely to accept dealing with someone you have endorsed by including them in your network). Don't be paranoid, just realistic, like in normal life.

Therefore, always ask to speak with people you don't know before accepting them, if you think there might be mutual benefit in knowing each other. This is a somewhat time-consuming exercise, but very worth the time – these connections are about building relationships for future problem-solving together – not creating masses of 'dead' contacts.

You can 'un-accept' people if you realise you made a mistake. They will not be notified. It is good to make a 'spring clean' in your network periodically. If you wonder why on earth you accepted the invite, it is probably time to delete the connection.

## 2 Strategic LinkedIn networking: first-level connections

As we discussed in Chapter 9, our first task in building our networks is to contact alumni from previous employers and educational institutions we attended.

We are looking for people who have moved on to do something different and/or an area that interests, us whether full-time or extracurricularly. Through them, we can discover how they achieved their career change and obtain further contacts. We should also try to connect with a few people we know are uber-networkers – who have wide-reaching networks connecting networks.

These groupings are:

- previous colleagues we worked closely with;
- previous colleagues we briefly worked with or know in passing;
- previous employees who were there at the same time that we don't know;
- previous employees that worked there before or after us;
- alumni of our educational institutions that we worked closely with;
- alumni we briefly worked with or know in passing;
- alumni who were there at the same time that we don't know; and
- alumni that studied somewhere before or after us.

You can search on companies, educational institutions or any other search word you wish to find useful people.

## 3 Strategic LinkedIn networking: second-level connections

Once we have started to (even loosely) identify topics, sectors and organisations that we are interested in, LinkedIn comes into its own.

If you diligently link with your previous colleagues and alumni, and with the people they introduce you to, you will find that your network grows very quickly.

Once your network grows above about 250 connections, the system starts to identify people who you have connections in common with, so-called *second-level connections*. These are the 'weak links', a 'friend of a friend', mentioned earlier, in a twenty-first-century guise, that are the most powerful conduits to new opportunities.

You can also search for these deliberately – this is where the magic is. Let's say you are looking for contacts to discuss water technologies as an area and you have researched the names of companies in the sector. All you need to do is put these company names into the search engine, one by one, tick the first- and second-level connection boxes, and see who turns up . . . you will be amazed.

Once you have identified people you would like to speak with, it is easy to send a well-crafted and personally relevant email via LinkedIn to these identified second-level contacts, or directly to them if you can figure out their email, referring to the fact that you have so-and-so in common and that they can check you out with that person if they wish. The other person, being in both your networks, is in fact credentialing you – and the person you are contacting is quite likely to reply and help. This is why it is so important to be vigilant about who you let into your network, as they can do the same with you.

It is particularly easy to write to someone with whom you have several contacts in common. As you start to focus on particular interest areas, and extend your network there, you will find that this happens more and more often. You are becoming a 'someone' in their space.

An illustration: I got to speak to a famous sustainability personality that I had never been able to speak to in person at conferences when I discovered that we had 203 contacts in common on LinkedIn, and in-mailed him. He could not believe why we had never met.

Already when you have three to five connections in common, you are moving up in the 'priority ranking' of who is worth potentially spending time with. We are keener to give the little time we have to people with whom we have common interests and common contacts.

This is why paying for being able to in-mail people without sending invites is handy; they might be happy to speak with you, and then connect, but accepting a 'blind' invite is different.

## 4 Strategic LinkedIn networking: third-level connections

The LinkedIn third-level connections are like 'a friend of a friend of a friend', and you approach these in the same way as you would one of them.

Obviously, there is no direct very warm link (we both know X), that you can credentialise yourself with, but the fact that you even show up in each other's third-level network shows that you are moving in intersecting networks. This becomes very useful once you have identified the new areas you are interested in and the people you would like to learn to know.

This is where the 'problem-solving' aspect of networking we spoke about in Chapter 9 comes to the fore. If you are both interested in solving the same kinds of problems, the contact is natural.

It is important to have very well-worded messages in this instance, setting out why you want to speak with the person and what problem you are trying to solve. The problem at hand might be career change:

> I am thinking of what I want to do next and am contemplating work in the area XXX. As you have done a similar switch, I wonder if you would be willing to share some of your experience over a coffee?

It does not have to be much more complicated than that.

Further down the line, you might want insights into a specific field, organisation or activities, and messages might read something such as:

> I am working on developing a new financing mechanism for community-owned micro-grids in XXX, together with XXX Enterprise. We are trying to understand YYY, and wondered if you, with your global experience in this field, would be open to a short call. We would greatly appreciate any thoughts or input you might have on our learning to date.

When you are writing to someone you don't know, and have no connections in common with, it is useful to include links to your website (if you have one), blogs, articles or studies you have published, whether on LinkedIn, other people's websites, magazines, newspapers, etc. This way, people can better check if you are for real.

Including your Twitter ID at the bottom of your email also gives people an opportunity to see what topics you care about.

# Index